THE LAST DAYS OF DYLAN THOMAS

THE LAST DAYS OF DYLAN THOMAS

Rob Gittins

Macdonald

A Macdonald Book

Copyright © Rob Gittins 1986

First published in Great Britain in 1986
by Macdonald & Co (Publishers) Ltd
London & Sydney

British Library Cataloguing in Publication Data

Gittins, Rob
    The last days of Dylan Thomas.
    1. Thomas, Dylan—Biography   2. Poets, Welsh—
    20th century—Biography
    I. Title
    821'.912   PR6039.H52Z/

ISBN 0-356-10995-X

Photoset in North Wales by
Derek Doyle & Associates, Mold, Clwyd
Printed in Great Britain by
Redwood Burn Ltd
Bound at The Dorstel Press

Macdonald & Co (Publishers) Ltd
Maxwell House
74 Worship Street
London EC2A 2EN

A BPCC plc Company

Contents

1.	Prologue	7
2.	Time Enough to Rot	15
3.	The Far-Ago Land	34
4.	When Your Furious Motion	51
5.	The Hand That Signed The Paper ...	67
6.	Deaths and Entrances	92
7.	Within His Head Revolved a Little World ...	114
8.	Before We Mothernaked Fall ...	144
9.	Do Not Go Gentle ...	164
10.	Return Journey	194
11.	After the Funeral	210

Chapter One
Prologue

In the late summer of 1953, Dylan Thomas was in the troughs of a deep depression. Returning from America in that June he found himself back in a familiar rut: oppressed by financial troubles, besieged in his personal relationship with his wife Caitlin and struggling with a work that was becoming more sporadic and ever more painful to produce. His solution was characteristic – flight: back to America, his fourth such trip in just three years. America seemed to provide the respite Dylan needed; from penury, from the grinding and endless friction with Caitlin, from the increasingly oppressive demands of family and from that other great ogre in Dylan's life, the British Inland Revenue. By this time indeed, escape had become a familiar theme for Dylan. His poetry had come increasingly to celebrate an escape into his childhood past. John Malcolm Brinnin, Dylan's close friend in the US, recalls that Dylan always talked of writing a play called 'The Escape Artist'. Like one of his heroes, the great escape artist Houdini, Dylan Thomas took pride in being able to extricate himself from any situation in which he was involved. There is a sense in which the whole tragedy of Dylan's death was defined by this belief.

By the early 1950s Dylan Thomas' problems were various and contradictory. He had established himself as the leading poetic voice of his generation, as famed professional Welshman, and as notorious drunk and lecher. He had also settled in Laugharne. Laugharne in the west of Wales had been Dylan's permanent home since 1949 when the actress Margaret Taylor bought him his famous Boat House, his 'seashaken house on the breakneck of rocks', though he had lived in the area 'on and off' for fourteen years. Dylan and his new wife Caitlin had first moved into a tiny fisherman's cottage in the town's Gosport Street in 1938.

Laugharne was, and remains, a quirky idiosyncratic small village remote from the rest of Wales and governed, as it has been for hundreds of years, by its own charter. It still retains its own definite and occasionally hostile character. The village has a history that can be traced back to the middle of the twelfth century when its castle was built by the great Welsh prince Rhys ap Gruffydd. Eight hundred years later the novelist Richard Hughes came to live in the Georgian mansion that bordered the ruins of Laugharne Castle and it was Hughes who introduced Dylan to the life of the town and who handled his early domestic arrangements. Within a few months of their arrival in 1938, Hughes had arranged for Dylan and Caitlin to move from Gosport Street to a larger house behind the castle called 'Sea View'.

Dylan thus became the centre of a small coterie of artistic exiles and Laugharne somewhat reluctantly grew accustomed to the sight of artistic oddities prowling its narrow streets and drinking in the town's Brown's Hotel. Dylan for his part was to embrace the social life of his adopted Laugharne and absorb its characters in an artistic osmosis that, fifteen years later, would produce one of his greatest works, 'Under Milk Wood'. Laugharne was Dylan's retreat and his trap, his place of rest and his gloomy and god-forsaken Welsh bog. Laugharne was a contradiction that Dylan Thomas was unable to resolve. But it was only one among many. By 1953, many other areas of the poet's life were beginning to fall apart.

Dylan's poetic output had almost completely dried up. The year before, his publishers, J.M. Dent, aware that nothing substantial had appeared from Dylan since 1946, had brought out his 'Collected Poems, 1934-1952' in an attempt to reawaken public interest in Dylan's now desperately sporadic work. But this had only depressed Dylan, whose confidence was now in tatters. Perhaps it seemed like a memorial. In a letter to his Italian friend Marguerite Caetini he talked of giving up writing altogether, though he noted wryly that he would probably end up writing about his desire to give up writing. Nevertheless the malaise seemed deep. In a letter of apology concerning the late delivery of a promised book Dylan wrote of his inability to write anything but a 'tangled sentimental poem as preface to a collection of poems written years before'. When a local Welsh reporter interviewed Dylan he referred to Arnold Toynbee's description of him as 'the greatest living poet'. Dylan remarked that Toynbee must have been talking of someone else. Close friends have noted that Dylan, in the last eighteen months of his life, seemed to be in a state of great dread of losing his ability to write any poetry at all.

Dylan's family life did not lessen the strain engendered by this real or imagined poetic sterility. Problems loomed all round. His sister Nancy had been diagnosed as suffering from cancer the previous summer and she had undergone hospitalisation and surgery. Dylan's father had also fallen terminally ill. He had been suffering from throat cancer for some years but in the late summer of 1952 the condition became critical. There is a powerful sense in which the whole of Dylan's life was almost an unconscious tribute to his father and the last days of the old man's life were particularly agonising for his only son. The father's sight and senses failed him and Dylan felt his humiliation keenly. There is indeed a hint that at the very end Dylan's father reverted to a childlike state. In one of his last lucid moments he is said to have remarked, 'It's turned full circle now.' Dylan's father died on the 16 December, 1952.

At the same time Dylan's financial troubles were becoming oppressive. The roots of these difficulties lay in Dylan's most successful and remunerative working period in the late 1940s. The British film industry boomed in the few years after the Second World War, peaking in 1946/7 with thirty million people attending the cinema each *week*. A quota system designed to conserve foreign exchange restricted the import of foreign films and Dylan found ready and easy employment in the booming home film industry. He collaborated on two scripts for the British National Company and in 1948 was taken under the wing of Sydney Box of Gainsborough Pictures to write three film scripts. Those three films, 'Rebecca's Daughters', 'The Beach of Falesa' and 'Me and My Bike', were never made but Dylan was paid handsomely for his work. Perhaps it would have been better had he not been.

Principally due to his film earnings Dylan's declared income for 1947-48 was £2482 with £612 deducted for 'business expenses'. By 1949 the tax on the residuel – at least £500 – was due and Dylan had made no provision for such payment. At the same time his current earnings had diminished and Dylan had to find this tax debt out of his now greatly reduced income.

His first American trip should have solved this problem and it was indeed ostensibly lucrative – Dylan earned £2800 from that first tour. But once again he left himself with nothing to pay the British income tax due on this sum. The only money that remained from the trip was a few hundred pounds that John Malcolm Brinnin secretly posted to Caitlin Thomas, left behind in Laugharne.

Thus in addition to its attempt to collect tax on Dylan's 'good year' of 1948, the British Inland Revenue would soon try to collect yet more tax revenue on his new American earnings; a demand that was initially set at £1607. The next year the British National Insurance authorities also took an interest in Dylan's affairs and, by the middle of 1952, were threatening to prosecute him for unpaid contributions. These totalled £50 12/6d.

It was at this desperate stage that Dylan's agent David Higham took direct responsibility for Dylan's financial affairs, deducting a 'tax fund' for his revenue liability before passing on fees and royalties to his client. With careful husbandry and a proper utilisation of the American money there is no doubt that Dylan's financial problems could have been overcome. The money *was* coming in. Dylan had written to Stephen Spender in December of 1952 asking if he could set up a fund for him similar to the one he had attempted to arrange for Dylan in his earlier, more genuinely impecunious days. But most people Spender contacted replied that Dylan's income was now larger than their own.

The fact was that Dylan seemed curiously unable or unwilling to help himself. The effects of this reluctance were aggravated by the poet's lifestyle, a lifestyle that indicated either a gross irresponsibility concerning, or a remarkable indifference to, financial matters. Faced with financial troubles Dylan's immediate response was to borrow from any and all acquaintances. His appropriation of other people's assets had even led him, on one celebrated occasion, to steal a host's clothes.

Just why Dylan should have refused to help himself is unclear.

Perhaps Dylan's private conviction, his deeply-held myth of himself as the supreme escape artist, had taken too deep a hold on his imagination. His financial difficulties became just another test for Dylan, an obstacle he never doubted he could surmount.

Another problem on the eve of that last American trip was Dylan's health. In America itself his physical difficulties would come to overshadow all others, but in Britain they seemed merely a disparate collection of symptoms and ailments that were certainly incapacitating, but didn't in themselves hint at the disaster to come in New York. He was definitely asthmatic and this produced the breathlessness his mother was to note in Laugharne. The winter months spent in the damp west of Wales aggravated his chest complaints and brought on flu and bronchitis, though in a letter to Oscar Williams in October of 1952 Dylan erroneously called it 'pneumonia'. He also claimed to have been suffering from pleurisy.

Dylan of course frequently boasted of a poor constitution and a recurring range of illnesses, claims treated with scepticism by his long-suffering friends. According to the Reverend Leon Atkins in Swansea, Dylan claimed to be suffering from tuberculosis when only seventeen. Caitlin had long since tired of these claims: 'Playacting', she would snort even, on one occasion, when presented with an arm that was undoubtedly broken. But there is evidence now of a genuine and serious disability afflicting the poet on the eve of that last trip: Dylan was beginning to experience black-outs. One was said to have occurred in the bar of Brown's Hotel in Laugharne, yet another in the cinema in nearby Carmarthen. The truth of these incidents was initially difficult to assess, although the BBC producer Phillip Burton has said that he actually witnessed a Dylan black-out in his own London flat immediately prior to Dylan's departure. None of the friends Dylan would meet in the US knew of this new and worrying development and by the time they became aware of this condition, Dylan would be beyond all help.

Dylan's other problem in 1953 was his marriage. He had married Caitlin Thomas in 1937 and had moved to Laugharne the next year. The couple then lived in a succession of borrowed houses all over England and Wales until 1949 when they finally returned to Laugharne. Village life suited Dylan. Less so Caitlin: the undeniably parochial character of Laugharne and the subservient role of women there repelled her. The monotony and impecuniousness of her daily life grated endlessly on her nerves. But Caitlin was caught in a trap. She was well aware that Dylan needed domestic monotony to produce his finest work, yet was resentful of the demands that requirement placed upon her.

The passing years had aggravated this bitterness and frustration. Finances had always been stretched, but in the more carefree 1930s life with a poverty-stricken poet in one rented house after another had been an adventure. Indeed Caitlin's temperament and outlook were in many ways wilder than Dylan's, who never quite managed to shake off the middle-class conservatism of his suburban Swansea home in Cwmdonkin Drive. But the 1940s, war, and three children had their effect on even the aristocratically uncaring Caitlin who did not have Dylan's comforting faith in his ability to escape from his own self-made disasters. Increasingly she chafed at her role as the subordinate woman in male-dominated Laugharne, and resented the humiliation of indebtedness to the neighbours she despised and to the local shopkeepers who had extended credit to the Thomas family.

In the 1930s Caitlin could comfort herself with the thought that domestic drudgery was at least creating the conditions that would allow Dylan to produce his finest work. Almost all Dylan's significant writing was done when he was safely ensconced in his small back room in his native and familiar Wales. But as America beckoned, Caitlin found herself in an increasingly invidious position; a position that ultimately came to embitter her. Dylan was leaving his wife and his family behind and was embracing his new – and to Caitlin, much-hated – role of public performer. He was losing touch with the settled existence that encouraged the work in which Caitlin fiercely believed. More, his family left behind in boring old Laugharne were receiving little compensation for Dylan's increasing absences. Not much money was finding its way back from the gallivanting poet and Caitlin was left alone in an environment she hated, to face debt, boredom and the pains and tribulations of bringing a growing family to maturity.

Added to that, Caitlin was now deeply suspicious of Dylan's activities in the United States. She disliked his new role as public clown but the real root of her unhappiness lay in Dylan's familiar role as notorious womaniser, now extended beyond the Atlantic. The ideal of the romantic marriage was mocked by Caitlin in public but revered in private. She spoke many times of her desire that Dylan should not 'betray' her. She couldn't bear the 'physical act' of his infidelity. America, of course, provided many more opportunities for his continued infidelity and more scope for his pursuit of the 'physical act'.

On Dylan's second American trip Caitlin accompanied him and observed at first hand how his audience idolised her husband, and was made all too aware of the ready availability of the young girls that formed the large nucleus of his admirers. This phenomenon did not go unnoticed elsewhere. Elizabeth Hardwick has said that Dylan aroused 'the most sacrificial longings in American women. He had lost his looks, he was disorganised to a degree beyond belief, he had a wife and children in genuine need and yet young ladies felt they had to fall in love with him.' Not surprisingly, Caitlin saw it less charitably. These 'young ladies' were 'candidly if not prepossessingly spread-eagled, from the first tomtomed rumour of a famous name. They conducted their courting with the ferocity and tenacity of caged Amazons and nothing less than the evaporation of their prey would make them let them go.'

Dylan's proposals for a fourth American tour understandably made his wife deeply unhappy. All the poet wanted in the US, Caitlin averred, was to embrace 'flattery, idleness and infidelity'.

All this led to a grossly deteriorating atmosphere between Caitlin and Dylan which the couple's close friends could not fail to notice. Dylan's Swansea friend Vernon Watkins, had earlier tried to rationalise these rows as all part of some misjudged act. In the early years of their marriage, he told the photographer Rollie McKenna, Dylan and Caitlin would often go to a pub for an afternoon's drinking. If they found the atmosphere dull, they would liven up the place by staging a quarrel. Their voices became louder, the accusations flew, and others would join in. The atmosphere had thus noticeably 'improved'. This, according to Watkins, would rekindle all their passionate attachment. But over the years even Watkins had to admit that this game became more destructive. Reconciliation became less easy and 'once uttered, insults were not as quickly forgiven'. These rows often escalated now into physical violence with Caitlin the frequent victor in these exchanges. Margaret Taylor was told by Caitlin that after one of their rows she hadn't spoken to Dylan for a month. Perhaps she had more to fuel her anger than Dylan. 'I think I was the violent one,' she has said, and Dylan recognised this. In a letter to his Swansea friend Dan Jones, Dylan wrote, 'Isn't life awful? Last week I hit Caitlin with a plate of beetroot and I'm still bleeding.'

Vernon Watkins' wife, Gwen, observed their domestic situation with more insight than her husband. 'Caitlin', she has written, 'seemed ... permanently embittered by her life and although she made me uneasy and often indignant because of her behaviour in public I was firmly on her side ... her life seemed to me intolerable.'

America added a specific dissatisfaction to the couple's general unhappiness. Caitlin had even less influence than before over Dylan's affairs when they were conducted three thousand miles away. After his first American trip one of his new lovers followed Dylan back home to Britain and Caitlin discovered her letters. 'Mad with rage', Caitlin had brought the affair to an end and Dylan lay low for a few days, staging a timely illness that kept him out of harm's way. But on the eve of his fourth trip, Caitlin suspected something again. Dylan was never so indiscreet as to mention a name. But that there was a name Caitlin well knew. Dylan was itching to get back to New York for a variety of reasons, all of which he spelt out to his wife in Laugharne in that summer of 1953 and all these reasons were unimpeachable. But a more personal motive was dominating him the whole of that summer – the prospect of meeting once again his new lover in New York. She was Elizabeth (Liz) Reitell, the assistant at the New York Poetry Center and producer of his new dramatic work 'Under Milk Wood'. With this new affair, as Caitlin suspected unhappily, America had assumed a new importance and Dylan's philandering had taken a more serious turn.

Chapter Two
Time Enough to Rot

Dylan Thomas had flown home from his third and penultimate American tour on the 3 June 1953. London was in the middle of Coronation fever. All around were 'miles of cock-deep orange peel, nibbled sandwiches, broken bottles, discarded vests, vomit and condoms, lollipops, senile fish, blood, lips, old towels, teeth, turds, soiled blowing newspapers by the unread mountain'. Pausing only for a welcoming party, Dylan headed for Laugharne.

Dylan arrived back to little welcome from the suspicious Caitlin and little sympathy for his most recent injury. Dylan had fallen down a flight of stairs in America and had broken his arm. A photo-article by the journalist Mimi Josephson, one of Dylan's first engagements after his return, shows him with a plaster cast, a cigarette jutting from his lower lip, uneasily back in his workhouse in his village. Perhaps in response to the strained atmosphere, Dylan immediately wrote to his new lover in the US, Liz Reitell, though he addressed the letter from the Savage Club in London. The tone of the letter makes it clear that Dylan's thoughts were still thousands of miles away. 'I miss you terribly, terribly much,' the letter opens. Dylan might be home, but it was failing to contain him.

June dragged by with little attempted and less achieved. Dylan worked desultorily on new passages of 'Under Milk Wood'. He also wrote letters, one to John Malcolm Brinnin, and spoke of how much he missed America. He wrote of his determination to get back across to the States in the autumn and mentioned a literary conference in Pittsburgh to which he had been invited. All there was in Laugharne, he told Brinnin, was 'torpor', 'rain' and 'Ivy's dungeon'.

Dylan escaped for a while in July when in the company of

15

Caitlin and his daughter Aeronwy he went to North Wales to write for the BBC about the International Eisteddfod at Llangollen. But his bearing and appearance were already cause for alarm. The producer in charge of the BBC's coverage, Aneirin Talfan Davies, noted that Dylan was 'in a bewildered haze for much of the time'. The poor relations between Dylan and his wife were also noticeable. Vernon Watkins witnessed the tension between the couple in Laugharne that same month when he visited Dylan in the company of the French translator, Francis Dufau-Labeyrie.

Francis Dufau-Labeyrie had translated 'Prospect of the Sea' and 'Portrait of the Artist As A Young Dog' in 1946 and 1948 to universal acclaim, but despite sending Dylan copies of the text had received no response. The visit to Wales in July 1953 was thus something in the nature of an overdue reunion. After drinks in Brown's Hotel, the party retired to the Boat House. Dylan at the request of his dinner audience began to read some of his poetry. But a major disagreement over a minor issue suddenly blew up between Dylan and Caitlin. Their differences over the pronunciation of the word 'tear' in 'Over Sir John's Hill' led to a terrifying and unexpected explosion. Dylan and Caitlin screamed their own version of the word back and forth between each other until Watkins feared a genuine physical exchange. Neither guest intervened and the savage dispute eventually subsided into a sullen and resentful silence. Dylan's children had long since disappeared from the scene of an all-too-familiar domestic dispute. Watkins and Francis Dufau-Labeyrie went out to walk along the bay, with Watkins in particular deeply upset.

Watkins returned from his walk to find Dylan in his workshed, and for the remainder of the visit the threesome talked solely about poetry. Dylan spoke of his continuing dissatisfaction with 'Under Milk Wood'. The stage performances, he told Watkins, were reasonably good but the printed text still required attention. No one referred to Dylan's difficulties with Caitlin.

The next month Dylan recorded a television programme in Swansea, again with Aneirin Telfan Davies. Dylan was reading a story about a charabanc outing ('Our Day Out'). As so often, the script was actually completed at the broadcast itself, which

merely confirmed the poor relations already existing between
the higher echelons of the BBC and Dylan. The BBC objected
to the poet constantly referring to the text throughout his
televised reading. Dylan, they alleged, had prepared the
broadcast poorly. The criticism struck home, coming as it did
in the wake of Dylan's other insecurities over his wasting
talents. Back in Laugharne he wrote to Daniel Jones and to
Marguerite Caetini on the theme of his 'artistic inadequacy'.

Dylan was never short of complaints, but beneath the
tortuous scribbling, the contorted rhythms and the convoluted
expressions, he did indeed seem tortured and he was speaking
ever more insistently of escape, and of flight from Laugharne.
He told Dan Jones, 'I chew my nails down to my shoulders,
pick three-legged horses with beautiful names, take my feet for
grey walks, moulder in Brown's, go to bed as though to an
office and read with envy of old lonely women who swig
disinfectant by the pint, think about money, dismiss it as dirt,
think about dirt.' To Marguerite Caetini, Dylan was even more
vocal in his contorted grief. 'Why do I coil myself always into
these imbecile grief knots, sew myself blindfolded and
handcuffed into a sad sack, weigh it with guilt and pigiron and
then pitch me out to sea, so that time and again I must scrabble
out and unravel in a panic, bobbing and blowing bubbles like a
puny, wheezy Houdini ...'

One week later John Malcolm Brinnin arrived in Laugharne.
Brinnin and the photographer Rollie McKenna had been
commissioned to write an article on Dylan for the magazine
'Mademoiselle'. Its managing editor, Cyrilly Abels, had seen
the premiere performance of 'Under Milk Wood' in New York
earlier that May and had immediately bought the serial rights
for publication. Brinnin and McKenna had been asked to
prepare an accompanying article on Dylan's daily life in
Laugharne. Rollie McKenna had in fact been in Laugharne ten
days before and in Brown's Hotel with Caitlin had watched
Dylan's television performance. She had decided to postpone
the interview with Dylan until Brinnin's arrival in Wales. Even
on the first, brief visit, she noted that Dylan was 'bloated, his
expression worried, haunted'. Dylan was also suffering from a
deep cut over his eye, freshly scabbed. Later in New York,
Dylan would tell the actor Roy Poole that the injury had been

caused when Caitlin hit him with a coffee pot. Dylan's domestic difficulties were becoming ever more visible.

John Malcolm Brinnin met Rollie McKenna in London and together they travelled to Laugharne. They arrived on the 5 September and joined Dylan in Brown's Hotel. Brinnin himself witnessed the continuing tension between Dylan and Caitlin later that night at dinner when an underdone duckling produced another strained exchange between the couple. When the evening broke up, the excuse of a recent local murder provided Dylan with the opportunity to walk Rollie and Brinnin home to his mother's house in Laugharne's King Street where Rollie was to stay. Dylan walked back with Brinnin alone and the deeper cause of the evening's tension was revealed. Their conversation was dominated by Liz Reitell.

Dylan took the opportunity to check up on all details of Miss Reitell's movements since he had been away. Dylan also told Brinnin that Caitlin had somehow got hold of her name and was continually watchful, suspicious that he was receiving letters from her. Caitlin's suspicions were well-founded, but all communications were now being routed through Dylan's club in London. Brinnin answered what questions he could and listened to Dylan's complaints about Caitlin and his laments for the absent Liz Reitell.

But on that short moonlit walk from Laugharne along the lane by the sea to the Boat House, Dylan also spoke of his own fears of poetic sterility. Aside from 'Under Milk Wood' the only work he had begun, he told Brinnin, was a companion piece to his posthumous hymn to his father, 'Do Not Go Gentle Into That Good Night'. As Dylan and Brinnin stumbled along in the dark, the poet recited an extract from the piece:

Too proud to die, broken and blind he died
The darkest way, and did not turn away
A cold, kind man brave in his buried pride
On that darkest day. Oh, forever may

He live lightly at last, on the last, crossed
Hill, under the grass, in love and there grow
Young among the long flocks, and never lie, lost
Or still all the slow days of his death ...

When the two men returned to the Boat House, Brinnin retired immediately to Dylan's eldest son's bedroom to sleep. He had one overriding impression from the day: Dylan was unhappy and blocked in Laugharne, and Dylan desperately wanted to get away.

The next morning the issue of Dylan's future plans was raised briefly over breakfast but the only decisive point that emerged was that most of Dylan's earlier projects, including the visit to the literary conference in Pittsburgh, had fallen through. The rest of the morning was spent with Rollie McKenna, who directed Dylan around his old haunts in Laugharne while Brinnin compiled notes for his accompanying magazine article. The American trip was not discussed again until lunchtime. Then the Dylan party returned to the Boat House and Dylan, aware that the time was now or never, embroiled Brinnin and Caitlin in a debate on the proposed fourth tour, while Rollie McKenna, all the time determinedly diplomatic, took pictures of the anguished group.

Dylan, pacing up and down the Boat House's narrow balcony, rehearsed his motives for undertaking yet another trip. The primary motivation was the prospect raised earlier that year of a collaboration on a new opera between himself and the composer Igor Stravinsky. Dylan was to provide the libretto for the work, which was to concern the rebirth of the world, no less; the re-discovery of the earth following an atomic accident. The only survivors were to be an old man and his children. The children would then be transported away by visitors from another planet and before they went the old man would have to describe the wonder and beauty of the vanished world to the visitors. This would involve a 'recreation of language without abstractions or conceits', and indeed Dylan had already promised Stravinsky that he would avoid all 'poetic indulgences'. The original idea for a collaboration had been proposed by Boston University, but their promise of a commission had fallen through and Stravinsky was casting round for financial input from elsewhere. But the invitation for Dylan to stay with Stravinsky in Hollywood still stood, even though the expected cash advance would not now be forthcoming. This also meant that the anticipated free passage to California for Dylan and Caitlin had evaporated too. If

Dylan was to go he would thus have to go alone.

Caitlin, already distrustful of Dylan's real motives for undertaking the trip, was doubly dismayed at the thought of a long spell alone in wintry Laugharne. Further, as John Brinnin has recalled, she simply did not believe the painfully plausible scenario that Dylan sketched of a few engagements, a month with Stravinsky and then home with a bagful of money. What followed that afternoon was an elaborate charade in which Dylan sought to debate a decision he had in fact already made: that he would indeed get to America that year if he had to plunge into the sea at his Boat House and swim.

Dylan had an uphill struggle. Brinnin was also opposed to the idea of a fourth trip, though for more immediately practical reasons than Caitlin. For Brinnin, Dylan's genius was growing inward, was 'atrophying', and Brinnin saw a fourth American tour as only accelerating that process. America, Brinnin felt keenly, could now add nothing to Dylan's poetic reputation save its 'lesser side'. The 'big thing', Brinnin has said, 'was that (Dylan) was losing connection with his work, at least that particular work that speaks his genius. He was exploring his talent and his talent was for sale and I've always made that distinction. Dylan had great talent but he also had genius which don't always go together and so much of what he did in the years I knew him were the exercise of talent for which he was rewarded. But his genius ... was going into a slow congealment'. Brinnin arrived in Laugharne with this opinion firmly fixed, and Dylan's poor physical appearance confirmed him in his view that Dylan should not undertake another trip that year, perhaps not for another five years. Of course Brinnin still believed that which Dylan, deep down, did not: that the poet could remain in Wales and could produce again the quality of work that had proclaimed his genius throughout the world. Brinnin did not fully understand the varied and complicated factors that were turning the Welsh poet's thoughts ever more insistently towards 'escape'.

The setback over the collaboration might have dealt a blow to his plans but Dylan had other cards to play. A lecture bureau in America had offered him a transcontinental US tour at fees hugely in excess of those he could command on Brinnin's purely academic circuit. Dylan raised this prospect, playing on

Caitlin's ever-present concern over their precarious financial state. The proposal had arrived by letter that summer and while the audiences lacked inducement – being mainly professional organisations and women's clubs – the suggested fees demanded that the scheme be taken seriously. Dylan could have earned something in the region of three thousand dollars per lecture. The charade continued. Dylan raised another prospect, this time in London: an offer to script a film version of Homer's 'Odyssey'. This offer would come to nought, as Dylan knew, and the offer was raised only to be dismissed. The choice, Dylan seemed to be saying, was simple: London with unrealised offers; or America with the prospect of plenty. More anguished debate followed.

As the afternoon progressed, Brinnin became aware of the underlying determination deep inside Dylan to engineer another trip to the US despite the reservations of his immediate company. Even the existence of a new missile range on the nearby Pendine Sands, punctuating the afternoon with resounding rumbles and shaking the cliff-side house, provided Dylan with another excuse to get away from Laugharne. Caitlin remained obdurate, but as the afternoon progressed Brinnin became increasingly unable to withstand Dylan's persuasion and began – at first unconsciously but then more deliberately – to propose specific practical arrangements, should Dylan really be set on the trip.

Perhaps Dylan knew that Brinnin was forever susceptible to his appeals for help, and perhaps the afternoon's charade was enacted as to much to enlist his support as to placate Caitlin. Dylan presented to Brinnin that vulnerable and helpless side of his public persona that Brinnin had always been unable to resist and which he had assisted so often in the past. Brinnin simply could not cope with Dylan in personal terms. Dylan evoked emotions in the Director of New York's Poetry Center that he could neither understand nor rationalise and which made him peculiarly vulnerable to Dylan's influence. Faced now with this characteristic private dilemma Brinnin retreated into his public role as tour organiser and Dylan helpmate, and away from his private and more puzzling aspect as Dylan friend, confidant and helpless follower. In so doing, as he himself has acknowledged, he shares some responsibility for abetting Dylan in his 'final escape'. But it is difficult in truth to see how Brinnin could have acted differently and whether in any event it would have had much effect. Brinnin's half-articulated and complicated personal feelings for Dylan rendered him helpless where Dylan was concerned. In any case, with or without Brinnin's help, Dylan would have gone to the USA.

It was not a happy afternoon. Rollie McKenna's photographs, which all now survive, show a subdued and self-absorbed group.

With the plans not finalised, the group decided on a tour of the surrounding countryside to collect more photographs for the 'Mademoiselle' article. Perhaps depressed by the afternoon's debate, Caitlin decided not to go and Dylan's mother made up the party, which was to visit Dylan's childhood haunts at Llangain, Llanybri and Llanstephan, with Dylan's mother – Florence Thomas – as enthusiastic guide.

'Fern Hill', Dylan's childhood holiday farm, was the first port of call, though Brinnin noted that Dylan became 'nostalgic and unhappily thoughtful' at the disparity between the present house and his childhood recollections. A family visit followed to nearby relations with Brinnin and Rollie McKenna utterly bewildered by the strange Anglo-Welsh conversation. The party also took in a visit to Llanybri churchyard to visit the graves of Mrs Thomas' ancestors, and the seaside village of Llanstephan with its ruined hilltop castle and did not return to Laugharne till later that evening. Away from domestic strain and dispute, Brinnin saw that Dylan seemed more settled. He had drunk only one glass of beer all day. Rollie McKenna also noted that Dylan seemed 'peaceful and not interested in drinking'. Away from Laugharne the gloom brought on by the earlier discussion was dispelled.

Brinnin and Rollie McKenna stayed one further day in Laugharne. Brinnin spent some of the time in attending to financial accounts relating to Dylan's previous tour, and in trying to compile a documentary profile of Laugharne to balance and complement the text on Dylan. Lunch provided another opportunity for yet more discussion of the travel plans but Caitlin's attitude hadn't shifted one jot and Brinnin realised that little would be formally decided that day. After family photographs of Dylan, the children, Caitlin and Dylan's mother, the two American visitors set off for London.

Three days later, on the very eve of his departure for the US, Brinnin was paged in his London hotel. Dylan told him that the film deal in London – as expected – had fallen through. He would thus definitely be coming to America that October. He confirmed the range and purpose of the trip: performances of 'Under Milk Wood' at the Poetry Center, a few choice poetry readings and then a month with Stravinsky in California. At this stage Caitlin was still included in the travel plans. Dylan, it seemed, had almost engineered his escape. John Brinnin was sent home to arrange the final details.

In Laugharne, throughout the rest of September, Dylan worked on the new draft of 'Under Milk Wood' for America, and on his new novel 'Adventures in the Skin Trade'. He also gave a solo reading of 'Under Milk Wood' to the Tenby Arts Club in early October. In America, meanwhile, John Brinnin was arranging the full performances of the much-revised play at the Poetry Center and had fixed two firm dates, October 24 and 25. The first was to be the opening event of the Poetry Center season. Dylan also wrote two radio talks that were due to be recorded prior to his departure: 'A Visit to America' and 'Laugharne'. The latter was a lighthearted evocation of his adopted town and an affectionate look at its characters. Dylan recorded both programmes in Swansea on the 5 October and then met Vernon Watkins, the last time the two friends would see each other.

The meeting was easy and gave no hint as to prospective disaster. To Watkins, Dylan described the libretto of the opera he was to write with Stravinsky and talked about his father. He told Watkins that he had held his father's hand as he died. Dylan also quoted the first few lines of his unfinished 'Elegy' for his father, a work that Watkins himself was ultimately to complete. After joking with the older poet about the offer of an honorary degree from the University College of Wales at Aberystwyth (though the academic who made that offer, Goronwy Rees, recalls Dylan being 'openly delighted') Dylan left Swansea for Laugharne.

A few short weeks later, Watkins was to write of his own feelings for Dylan, setting his account in the context of that last meeting in Swansea. 'The man who, just before leaving for America for the last time, recited to me the lines of his unfinished Elegy for his father,' Watkins wrote, 'and the man who eighteen years earlier in his house above Swansea Bay, opened a file and read his poetry to me for the first time are inextricably bound in a personality from which time has fallen. The slight figure of a boy of twenty who read the first poems and the full figure of the mature but equally shy poet who recited the beginning of the Elegy, speak to me with a single voice.'

The travel arrangements relating to Dylan and Caitlin's passage to America had struck problems, however. John Malcolm Brinnin, charged with making those arrangements from the States, had found that October was, as it remains, the high season for westward crossings and that it was impossible to find sea-going accommodation for Dylan and Caitlin in mid-October. As finances were strained, Brinnin cabled Dylan and asked him to consider flying over alone, with Caitlin following by sea. A couple of days later Brinnin received a terse telegram from Dylan informing him that the poet would be travelling by air and would indeed be arriving alone. The message was ambiguous in its brevity. Whether Dylan was making his sole passage at Brinnin's suggestion or for some other reason, it was impossible to tell.

Dylan's last day in Laugharne was October 8, 1953. That day he also first made the acquaintance of the Welsh painter, Ceri Richards, who has subsequently illustrated several of Dylan's poems. The artist Fred Janes, a long-time friend of Dylan, introduced the two and it seems to have been an entirely happy and successful meeting. The two men that Constantine FitzGibbon has described as 'the greatest modern Welsh poet' and 'the man who may be Wales' greatest painter' liked each other on sight. But even then, the signs of domestic disruption were painfully in evidence. As the day wore on, Caitlin picked a quarrel with the ever-irascible Dylan and Janes and Richards hurriedly departed.

That evening Dylan and Caitlin travelled to the cinema at Carmarthen where, according to his mother, Dylan suffered a black-out. Dylan's family doctor, who was sitting in front of the Thomases, did not actually witness this, though he was at once approached by Caitlin, clearly concerned about her husband's health. The doctor promised an immediate examination at his nearby surgery in St Clears, but when the film ended the couple had disappeared. Dylan thus underwent no medical examination prior to his last American trip.

The next morning Dylan left Laugharne for the last time. His farewell's were characterised by a curious performance in which he returned to kiss his mother three times. What effect hindsight had here is difficult to assess, but she later claimed that Dylan, in those last few days in Laugharne, had a premonition of his death. Caitlin was travelling to London with the poet and the couple intended to take a short break in the capital before Dylan flew to the States. But as events turned out this journey was broken just a few miles from Laugharne, in Swansea, where Dylan had expressed a specific desire to meet his childhood friend Dan Jones.

Jones had attempted to avoid this meeting as he was working in his professional capacity as composer to meet an 'impossible deadline'. Dylan ignored this reluctance. He arrived in a taxi at the Jones' home dragging an equally reluctant Caitlin in his wake and forced the conscience-stricken Dan Jones out of his study and into a three-day drinking session.

As Dylan broke his journey in Swansea, the first hint came that now his objective was achieved – the fourth trip to the States – Dylan was having doubts about its wisdom and even its purpose. Dylan should have travelled on to London almost immediately and from there to New York, but he delayed in Swansea. He seemed to cling to his time with his childhood friend in his childhood town, reading to Jones extracts from the new revised version of 'Under Milk Wood' and listening in return to his friend's recently completed third symphony. (Dan Jones' next symphony would be written as a tribute to the deceased Dylan). Dylan also told Dan Jones that he intended turning from his rather personal type of poetry to 'a more public form of expression and to large-scale dramatic works'.

All the time Dylan's journey was becoming ever more delayed and Dan Jones' deadline was becoming ever more 'impossible'. Dan Jones was aware that, for whatever reason, Dylan did not want to leave Swansea and for a couple of days he did not press him to do so. But on the third day of the unplanned stop, Dylan's travel arrangements were in serious jeopardy as was Jones' commission. By some 'grim effort of will' Jones managed to get Dylan's packed suitcases as far as another childhood haunt: the book-filled emporium of 'Ralph the Books'. Here Dylan cashed a post-dated cheque and told Ralph that he would return by Christmas with a packet of money. A last pub-crawl took place and then a final desperate charade in which Dylan seemed determined to ignore the ticking pub clock and to miss yet another London-bound train. For her part Caitlin had little interest in insisting on her husband's departure and it was thus left to Dan Jones. Jones 'propelled Dylan to the station', he has recalled, and bundled him onto a train. 'As the train moved off I started, first walking, then running to keep up with it. Dylan stood at the open window waving one hand slightly with exaggerated weakness and smiling an odd little smile.' Dylan thus took his leave of his oldest friend. 'It was, in a sense', Jones has written, 'the last time I ever saw his face.'

In London the Thomases stayed with Harry and Cordelia Locke in Hammersmith, Caitlin's birthplace. Cordelia Locke was a friend of Caitlin's and had become reacquainted with Dylan and Caitlin in their South Leigh days in Oxfordshire in the 1940s. But the atmosphere between Dylan and Caitlin was now continually strained and tense. Caitlin's previous opposition to the trip was now buttressed by the prospect of Dylan embarking on it alone. Caitlin was well aware that Dylan was flying to meet his lover and Dylan's recognition of this caused him considerable guilt and some remorse. Caitlin was also well aware that her husband was in no fit state of health to undergo the rigours of yet another tour. Her impotence in the face of his determination created an atmosphere of mutual unhappiness in the Locke's Hammersmith home, with Dylan's guilt over the real motives behind the trip exacerbating the general unease.

The time that followed – the week before Dylan flew to the US – he later described as the 'worst week of my entire life'. Throughout this time Dylan was still working on the text of 'Under Milk Wood' and was now indeed under severe pressure from the BBC for the delivery of the script. Douglas Cleverdon, producer of literary programmes at the BBC, had actually commissioned the script from Dylan in 1950. The original broadcast was scheduled for the middle of 1951, but as with so many of Dylan's commissioned works, once the initial fee was paid the project fell from personal favour. By 1953 Cleverdon had waited three years for a final version.

Cleverdon was destined to wait a little longer. He had arranged to meet Dylan and his agent, David Higham, in Simpson's on the Strand on Monday October 12. Of course Dylan had delayed his journey, in Swansea, and did not turn up for the proposed dinner date. Instead he promised to arrive at Broadcasting House that Thursday (15 October) with the finished script. Dylan kept this appointment but he did not bring the finished script: that still required revision. He promised yet again to deliver the script within the next couple of days before he flew to the States.

It was while leaving Broadcasting House and a deeply dissatisfied Douglas Cleverdon that Dylan met again his future biographer Constantine FitzGibbon. This was to be the last meeting between the two friends. Dylan suggested – characteristically – that they go for a drink but then added, uncharacteristically, that they choose somewhere anonymous, where he was not known. Dylan led the way to a tavern in which he could reasonably hope not to run across any of his many and varied drinking companions in London. Dylan was now subdued, according to FitzGibbon. His emotions were somersaulting and his outlook was confused. He said that he had no wish to travel again to America, that he was so very, very tired. FitzGibbon also sensed an ambivalence in Dylan's attitude towards the Stravinsky project. Dylan was clearly excited at the idea of working with Stravinsky, yet equally clearly was terrified that his own contribution would be deficient in some way or even lacking completely. FitzGibbon of course had caught the poet at a vulnerable time. He had just visited Douglas Cleverdon with yet another excuse concerning the non-delivery of a script and had once again been brought face to face with his clear inability to deliver a completed script on time. Dylan stressed to FitzGibbon as he had earlier stressed to Caitlin that he would be completing the project in a relatively short space of time – as if he hoped that a strict and self-imposed schedule would somehow unlock a door, provide the key to his completion of the challenging work. It was crystal clear to FitzGibbon that on the very eve of that last American trip, Dylan was being continually assailed by the most basic doubts about his continuing abilities.

But FitzGibbon did not get the impression that Dylan was at all suicidal in his attitude. The poet may have been talking about death but 'he had been doing that in one way or another for thirty years'. Nevertheless his depression was genuine and deep-rooted. During the course of that last week Dylan also had a similarly anguished conversation with the film writer, Clifford Dyment. He told Dyment that he was in 'an awful state of debt and near-despair'. Dylan could not 'help himself ... I don't answer the door or the phone and I'm drowned in undone work and writs.'

Towards the end of his drink with FitzGibbon, Dylan's desires somersaulted once more and he suggested that they both move on to another pub, where he would now be known and where they would be among other friends. Perhaps Dylan had become bored. Or more likely, perhaps he had scared himself. They left the pub and within a short time were in another. Dylan soon became swallowed up in the usual crowd and slipped easily into his more usual persona of 'roaring Welsh boy' let loose in the big town.

On what *should* have been Dylan's last day in London – October 13 – Dylan visited the BBC producer Phillip Burton for a 'leave-taking drink'. Burton was the prime force behind the acting talents of Richard Burton from whom the actor derived his stage name. He had also produced Dylan's 'Return Journey' for its radio broadcast.

Dylan had come direct from a lunch with Louis MacNeice but the lunch date with an old friend does not seem noticeably to have raised Dylan's spirits. Phillip Burton was later to tell John Brinnin that Dylan was in 'an uncommonly unhappy and meditative mood'. Dylan accepted just one drink from Burton and soon plunged into yet another litany of fear and doubts, principally centred around his 'failing abilities'.

To Burton, the poet averred that his lyric-writing days were over, just as he had told Dan Jones a few days earlier that he intended now concentrating on drama. Burton formed the clear impression that Dylan believed that 'the part of his work that spoke his genius' had deserted him for ever. He still believed

28

that he was able to continue 'his own brand' of writing for the stage and radio, and indeed Dylan outlined to Burton a new play he hoped to write. The draft title of this new work was to be 'Two Streets' and it concerned the fortunes of two children – a boy and a girl – born in Swansea within a few streets of each other. These two children are unknown to each other at birth but their lives are linked: they share a midwife who attended both births. The play in fact would begin with screams – the screams of women in labour and the screams of the new-born children. Their lives would take place isolated from each other at differing ends of the stage. They would both live uneventfully, waiting for some 'fulfillment of their great capacity for life'. While locked in their different routines they pass close to each other hundreds of times but they never actually meet. At the very end of the play they do actually meet in a dance hall and are finally, belatedly, united at the centre of the stage. It was to be 'the love story of two people who were never to be lovers'.

When the conversation turned to the prospective collaboration with Stravinsky, Burton discovered the same insecurities as FitzGibbon and found that fear replaced the brief animation that Dylan had displayed as he described his new idea. Dylan confessed concern over his ability to complete the project, blaming his poor health as another burden which militated against a concentrated and professional completion of his various commissions.

It could have been an excuse and it is likely that Burton first viewed Dylan's pleadings as a convenient dodge. But Burton had an eloquent demonstration of the poet's changed and deteriorating physical state that very afternoon. Dylan asked Burton if he could have 'a bit of a lie down'. Burton showed him to his own bedroom and arranged to call Dylan within the hour. He set the alarm to wake Dylan who, after all, still had to deliver the final draft of 'Under Milk Wood' before he finally flew to the States the next day. Burton had sympathy for a fellow-producer trying to elicit a commissioned script. An hour later Burton heard the alarm sound and waited for Dylan's appearance. Another half-hour went by. Burton still waited. Still there was no sign or even sound of Dylan. Finally Burton entered the bedroom to find Dylan less asleep than in some apparent state of unconsciousness. He was breathing heavily, in laboured gasps. Burton was alarmed and attempted to rouse him, but without success. A thoroughly distressed Burton was about to phone for a doctor when Dylan suddenly sat up, wide awake. 'How long did that one last?' he demanded. To his worried companion he revealed that the 'black-out' was the second one that day. At lunch with Louis MacNiece he had suffered the first black-out and 'the poor fellow thought he had a corpse on his hands'. This is the first independent confirmation of Dylan's claims of 'black-outs' and it was a story Dylan's American friend, John Malcolm Brinnin, did not hear until 1978.

Dylan did recover sufficiently to make a characteristic phone call later that afternoon. Dylan may still have not finally determined the form and scope of his new play 'Two Streets' but that did not stop him telephoning Burton's actor protege, Richard Burton, to offer him the rights to the play. Burton had refused two days earlier to lend Dylan two hundred and fifty pounds for the 'education of my children' and he refused this fresh offer too. The incident is trivial perhaps, but demonstrates two things: that Dylan could recover from his bouts of unconsciousness almost immediately and suffer no apparent ill-effects; and that, even in the wake of deteriorating health and in the face of his continuing fears over his poetic abilities, Dylan was still attempting to feed his largest and most time-consuming need – more money.

Dylan left Burton's flat in the late afternoon to make the final arrangements for his trip, but a mix-up was now to delay him. Unaware that Dylan was to spend that week in London, Brinnin had arranged for Dylan's plane ticket to be delivered to Laugharne. Dylan returned to Hammersmith ready to depart to the US at the same time as his plane ticket was being delivered to the Boat House in Wales. The next morning Liz Reitell was to wait at New York's Idlewild airport for Dylan, but when she checked the passenger list Dylan's name did not appear. She waited three days for news from Dylan and this delay was to add another and unexpected element to the general strain when Dylan finally arrived in New York.

This delay had one positive effect, however, as Dylan was finally able to deliver the finished script of 'Under Milk Wood' to Douglas Cleverdon at the BBC on October 15, the day after his intended departure. Once again, save for this last twist of fate, Dylan would have failed to fulfil a long-standing commission and indeed, without this fortuitous delay, would never have formally delivered it. This delivery came as a signal relief to Douglas Cleverdon who had no wish to join the long line of disgruntled BBC producers who had failed to extract commissioned work from the errant Welsh poet. Aware of Dylan's impending departure, Cleverdon immediately arranged for the script to be typed by his secretary Elizabeth Fox, and returned the original script to Dylan on Saturday 17 October. The missing plane ticket had at last arrived in London and Dylan now cabled John Brinnin in the States. The cable read 'Pickett (sic) arrived couple days too late. Now catching plane 7.30 Monday 19th, desperately sorry. Dylan'.

Nothing had yet been done to arrange for Caitlin's later passage to join Dylan in the US and the situation between the couple may indeed now have deteriorated to the point that Caitlin had abandoned all such travel plans. Certainly Dylan was forced away from Hammersmith again and again in order to escape the constantly embittered atmosphere. Some time during this last weekend Dylan's major benefactor Margaret Taylor had joined the Dylan party and she could only have aggravated the generally poor relations between Dylan and Caitlin, since she brought with her reminders of past associations at a time when Caitlin was dwelling more and more on the existence of a current affair. Her presence was not at all what Caitlin wished for, two days before Dylan's departure to the land of opportunity. Dylan spent this weekend away from Hammersmith, drinking in a succession of Soho pubs.

Here yet another potentially catastrophic occurrence took place. During the course of one of these last drinking sessions Dylan lost the original hand-written manuscript of 'Under Milk Wood' which had been returned to him by Douglas Cleverdon only two days previously. Cleverdon was contacted and managed to rush duplicated copies of the typewritten script to Dylan just before he boarded the plane. It was thus not the original copy of 'Under Milk Wood' that Dylan took with him to the US. Cleverdon immediately embarked on a frantic search for the missing and priceless original copy, doubtless spurred on by a remark somewhat typical of Dylan that if he found the manuscript he could keep it. Cleverdon eventually traced the missing script to a Soho pub, the Helvetia in Old Compton Street. Years later, in 1961, Cleverdon sold the manuscript to the Times Book Company for £2000 and the script later changed hands for several times that price.

Dylan's last day in London was thus Monday 19 October. Cleverdon with the duplicated typewritten copies of 'Under Milk Wood', joined the farewell party at the Victoria Air Terminal that was to mark Dylan's departure. Dylan's plane was due to leave at 7.30 that night and a mixed group duly assembled; Douglas Cleverdon, Margaret Taylor, Caitlin and Harry and Cordelia Locke. The mood was unquestionably sober and depressed, doubtless influenced by Caitlin's implacable and brooding disapproval of the trip they had gathered to celebrate. Later Caitlin was said to have been suffering 'premonitions of disaster', though it is likely that this again was hindsight. Dylan was sober. The party limped on for an hour or so in the cheerless air terminal bar as the night claimed London. The guests frantically tried to rescue the occasion. This was the last of many such parties in England and Wales and these were only the latest in a long line of such guests at many various Dylan drinking parties. But the fact of its being the last such gathering has now lent every detail of that occasion a significance it may or may not have possessed.

This is especially true for the last act of that London evening. When the airport bus arrived to take the travellers to the terminal, Caitlin did not accompany Dylan to the bus and only Harry Locke walked with the poet from the bar. Whether this was Caitlin's final sign of disapproval is not now known. Leaving Caitlin and the others drinking in the bar, Harry Locke loaded Dylan's cases into the bus and stood while Dylan boarded. The poet was wrapped against the autumn cold in a camel-hair scarf and a huge heavy overcoat. He made his way to the back of the almost empty bus and turned to face Harry Locke on the deserted concourse as the bus moved away. As Harry Locke waved, Dylan answered with a thumbs-down signal through the back window.

Perhaps Dylan was referring to the presence of Caitlin,

whom Harry Locke was just about to rejoin. But future events were to give an entirely new and different significance to that bald and simple gesture. Dylan's return to kiss his mother three times in Laugharne, his gnawing self-doubt in London, Caitlin's 'premonitions of disaster' and the last glimpse of Dylan by one of his closest friends, have all built a persuasive though not completely convincing picture: that on the very eve of his fourth American trip Dylan was beginning to have ever more basic doubts about his ability to complete it.

Chapter Three

The Far-Ago Land

Liz Reitell was awaiting Dylan's arrival in America as Caitlin and the rest of Dylan's drinking companions continued to mark his departure in the Victoria Air Terminal in London, a session that went on for some considerable time. Inflight, high over the Atlantic, Dylan was having adventures of his own. The American-bound plane touched down at Shannon Airport to pick up Irish travellers. Among these travellers was an Irish priest homeward bound to New York after a visit to his spiritual homeland. He was already roaring drunk on embarkation and continued to drink as the plane headed towards the States. The drink turned the priest garrulous and obstreperous and the bar was eventually closed to him. This enforced abstinence brought on an attack of delirium tremens and the priest became increasingly abusive until, according to Dylan, he was finally bound and shut in one of the airplane toilets, having 'literally gone mad'. The priest was taken off the plane at Newfoundland in the company of an airline doctor.

A caveat has to be added to this story. Dylan always regaled friends with tales of those he travelled with, and if he is to be believed, then all these planes were continually filled with all sorts of freakish people. But this time perhaps the truth or otherwise of the story is secondary to the existence of the story itself. If the story was true, perhaps Dylan felt it presaged his own future. The sight of the drunken priest touched some deep chord. If the story was untrue, a Dylan fiction, it gave a clear indication of the lines on which his thoughts were running. In any event it is a curiously apposite story for Dylan to relate at the start of that last tragic trip. Liz Reitell, waiting in New York, recalls Dylan telling the story the minute he disembarked from the plane. He was 'amused and shaken', made 'grim

34

comedy of the whole incident'. But Liz Reitell, picking up Dylan's mood, immediately began to 'talk serious instead of fun'.

Liz Reitell was born on September 11, 1920. At the time of her first meeting with Dylan she was thus thirty-three to Dylan's thirty-eight. She had met Dylan through her role as Assistant Director of New York's Poetry Center, a post offered to her by John Brinnin who had known Liz as a student at the exclusive and liberal Bennington College some fourteen years previously. Liz Reitell graduated from Bennington in 1941 with a degree in Theatre Design, after an education that had included private schools in Pittsburgh, Harrisburg, Washington DC and New York City. Her varied career since graduation had included stints as a freelance painter and dancer and even a spell in army service in 1943 as an officer in the Women's Army Corps. Indeed in her new role at New York's Poetry Center she retained a certain military efficiency in her dealings with the artists and poets who passed through it. This efficient bearing was to provoke an instant antipathy between Dylan and herself at their first meeting earlier that year.

At that time John Brinnin, while Director of the Poetry Center, actually lived in Boston and also taught at the University of Connecticut. Thus much of the day-to-day running of the Center in New York was delegated to Liz Reitell, and many of the arrangements for the varied performanes fell within her purview. As Brinnin had hired Liz Reitell in late 1952, the arrangements for 'Under Milk Wood' were among the first she had undertaken and Dylan's notorious unreliability was thus one of her earliest discoveries in her new job.

In October 1952, the Poetry Center issued its annual programme, advertising the coming season. The first performance of 'Under Milk Wood' was scheduled for the following May. At the time John Brinnin believed that the six months between October '52 and March '53 would give Dylan ample opportunity to deliver a rehearsal script to the States. But that winter proved Brinnin wrong.

Brinnin despatched a series of letters to Dylan's home in Laugharne. At first they contained polite enquiries as to the progress of the work, but towards the end more frenzied messages demanded to know when the Center could expect the 'Under Milk Wood' script. Brinnin, all too aware that Dylan's intentions did not always match their end result, had instructed Liz Reitell to make the arrangements for the forthcoming performance but his confidence that the performance would actually go ahead became increasingly undermined as the new year progressed. Douglas Cleverdon would have sympathised.

By March 1953, Miss Reitell had selected the cast of actors ready to play the new Dylan work and rehearsal time had been allotted. In addition, the more formal side of the arrangements had been completed, with hundreds of tickets already sold for the play's premiere performance, now less than two months away. Eventually, under severe pressure from his increasingly agitated assistant, Brinnin telephoned Dylan in Laugharne and despite an appalling phone link did manage to confirm that Dylan would be coming and that the play would go ahead. A few days later a detailed letter arrived from Dylan proffering all sorts of excuses for his dilatory behaviour. They included the usual mixture of money troubles and domestic difficulties as well as the less well-worn Dylan heartaches centring around the recent death of his father. The manuscript of 'Under Milk Wood', Dylan said, would not be ready until the week of his sailing and Dylan further hedged his bets by expressing doubts about the very intention of performing a Welsh play with an American cast. Dylan suggested that he might himself make 'an hour's entertainment' out of the piece. The Welsh escapologist was already preparing his retreat in the event of his failure to fulfil yet another commission. It all tended to confirm Brinnin's worst fears, which would be further confirmed when Dylan alighted from the transatlantic liner a month later in New York's dockland. The play was far from finished and a great deal of work was still required to lick it into dramatic shape.

To Liz Reitell, the new girl in the job, the delay was excruciating. The only brief that Liz had managed to glean, second-hand through John Brinnin, was that there were to be male and female roles, that Dylan himself would play the lead voice, and that there would be about six actors required in all. To the self-confessed super-efficient Miss Reitell, such a sketchy scenario two months in advance of such a prestigious production was 'driving her crazy'. Dylan was thus already an object of considerable annoyance before the two characters had even met.

Their first meeting confirmed the long-distance impression. Dylan had arrived for his third American trip on the 21 April 1953, aboard the SS *United States*. Dylan disembarked, uncharacteristically sober, to be met by John Brinnin, and he immediately checked in at the Chelsea Hotel. The Chelsea had already become established as Dylan's second home in New York. The poet was booked into a large and airy room, 'exceptionally well-appointed' as Brinnin described it. Dylan then set out with Brinnin to the bars on Seventh Avenue, working up from the Chelsea to 34th Street and from there down to Greenwich Village. They reached Dylan's favourite bar in New York, the White Horse Tavern in the Village, by mid-afternoon.

The setting and decor of the White Horse was appealingly familiar to Dylan. The bar most specifically recalled Swansea in its interior decoration and in its dockside setting; frequented by dockworkers and dwarfed by the masts and funnels rising a few blocks away over the Hudson River. His American friends were certainly aware of Dylan's preference for that particular type of bar. 'Dylan', so Liz Reitell has recalled, 'loved dark, dock bars ... he liked waterfronts and here was a bar close to the waterfront with dark wood, low lights. It had just the right atmosphere; it was homing to him.'

The company was renowned for matching that atmosphere. On this occasion, Brinnin has recalled, when Dylan entered, the whole bar 'turned to greet him'. The tavern's host, Ernie – New York's equivalent of Ebie Williams in Dylan's Brown's Hotel in Laugharne – sent whisky to the poet's table. It was mid-afternoon. Dylan was in a dark low-lit dockside bar and he did indeed feel 'at home'. Brinnin had questioned Dylan on the script of 'Under Milk Wood' when the poet first disembarked, but 'unwilling to cast a shadow over his self-confidence', had pressed Dylan no further when he admitted that the play was still not ready. Later, in the White Horse, Brinnin felt himself similarly unable to raise with Dylan the matter of urgent appointments and details pertaining to the forthcoming lecture tour. Brinnin thus again suffered a curious and uncharacteristic paralysis of will when faced with Dylan. Brinnin, it really did seem, was just too much in awe of the figure he regarded as 'the most important poetic voice of his generation' for his and for Dylan's own good.

Brinnin's weakness here seems to have been the indulgence of over-affection. Dylan was to find Brinnin's new assistant a very different proposition.

Around six p.m. Dylan and Brinnin left the White Horse and travelled uptown to the prestigious Algonquin hotel on 43rd Street. Dylan wished to renew his acquaintance with the journalist Howard Moss, a close friend from previous trips. The atmosphere of excellent high spirits persisted, particularly as Brinnin failed to press Dylan on the more practical aspects of his trip. Dylan was also heartened by the general good-humour and affection displayed toward him. He was beginning to enjoy the stir his presence created.

But after a few minutes in the Algonquin, the Dylan party were joined by Liz Reitell. If Dylan was enjoying his rising status as a public figure he was unlikely to find that status accorded much weight by Miss Reitell. Tall, cool, with an attractiveness that was more handsome than feminine, she was someone who only tolerated poets and suffered fools not at all. As John Brinnin has recalled, by the time of Dylan's arrival, Liz had suffered through a long introductory season at the Poetry Center and had lost all awe of world-famous visiting artists and poets. She was neither shocked nor intimidated by the reports of Dylan's 'reputation'. She was not concerned by the rumours of his 'bad behaviour': 'I'm rather a professional at that myself.'

Brinnin telephoned Liz Reitell from the Algonquin Hotel and suggested that she come across to meet Dylan. Perhaps Brinnin was aware that Liz could do what he apparently could not, and that she would not be slow to introduce a much-needed discordant note into the good-humoured gathering and to wrench Dylan's mind back onto the more important matter of the trip's actual *work*. Certainly in his telephone conversation Brinnin suggested that she and Dylan talk about the 'Under Milk Wood' script. Whether it was ever actually spelled out that Liz was to play the part of Dylan's conscience is not clear, but she performed the role as if she had rehearsed for a month.

It was not a first meeting that promised well and it did not begin promisingly. Liz was annoyed by Dylan before she had met him. Dylan was painfully aware that she was yet another authority figure to whom he had made promises and for whom he had failed to deliver. In Laugharne he could hide the letters from the BBC and pretend they had never arrived. In New York, he could not hide from Liz Reitell. Her initial physical impression of Dylan did nothing to improve her general irritation. He was a 'rumpled, short fellow, a bit too fat'. Her eyes looked coldly into Dylan's. She came straight to the point. 'Where's that script?'

Liz Reitell recalls being 'very much on my job at that point'. The script of 'Under Milk Wood' was not produced, and Dylan simply ducked his head. The atmosphere became even chillier. Dylan tried to distract attention by a stream of frantic stories and anecdotes, but Liz knew that Dylan was dodging the issue and she showed it.

Soon the discordant note in the assembled company forced a change in Dylan's demeanour. It had already been a long day's drinking and the poet was tired. The genteel elegance of the Algonquin Hotel suited Dylan less than the informal atmosphere of the Greenwich Village bars. The silent, hawkish presence of Liz Reitell was now also a visible reminder of his tardiness in fulfilling his commission and of the work that lay ahead. Perhaps Dylan was already beginning to feel the cold breath of the sterility he feared. With the atmosphere several degrees cooler, a quite trivial incident involving a spilt Martini and a disapproving look from a passing waiter spurred Dylan to move on from the Algonquin and ultimately to finish the evening drinking alone.

Nevertheless Liz Reitell seemed to have had an effect on Dylan. Brinnin returned to his teaching engagements after this meeting and Dylan joined him in his Boston apartment a few days later, using Brinnin's home as the base for his various speaking engagements outside New York. This apartment was a peaceful retreat on the prestigious Memorial Drive looking out over the Charles River Basin and towards the golden dome of Boston's State House. When Brinnin returned in the evening of Dylan's first day in Boston, he found Dylan surrounded by scraps of the unfinished text of 'Under Milk Wood', and as

Dylan talked it became clear that he was finally recognising the approach of the performance as a distinct reality for which he would need to deliver a completed script. Dylan hadn't felt such pressure in Laugharne or even in the first few hours of his arrival in the US. Perhaps it was simply the shortage of time that made the approaching engagement suddenly real. Or perhaps it was the fact that, till then, all Dylan's experiences had been filtered through the mollifying agency of John Brinnin; Brinnin who found it impossible to blame or harangue Dylan for almost anything, Brinnin who lived constantly with the 'primal innocence at the core of (Dylan) that caused judgement to be obliterated, accusation to dissolve in mid-air'. But Liz Reitell was a jarring factor, an uneasy and (from that first meeting) a constant reminder.

Liz Reitell in New York was now constantly on the phone urging completion of the script. Dylan was reminded that the cast was eagerly awaiting delivery, the producer was keeping anticipation at fever-pitch. The pressure was intense and deliberately maintained. On one occasion Liz even suggested that she accompany Dylan on his various speaking engagements and that they could then work all night if necessary on the revisions to the play.

The escapologist was thus being denied his escape. It was now clear that the 'Under Milk Wood' committment would have to be fulfilled and that there was now a highly determined production secretary in New York who would make sure of it. John Brinnin's writing table was soon ruined by beer stains and ash burns as Dylan struggled manfully with his script.

Dylan's personal relationship with Liz Reitell was slow to improve. Liz was still the harridan screeching for her play and Dylan the hunted, rumpled figure trying to dodge her cold stare. But despite this, change was on the way, and that change manifested itself at the very first and highly traumatic rehearsal of 'Under Milk Wood'. The first to realise it was Liz Reitell herself.

There was a definite element of insecurity on Liz Reitell's part, quite apart from her worries over the script. She was painfully aware that the cast she had assembled for that first performance was hardly up to Broadway standard; they were then largely amateur actors and office workers culled from the

Poetry Center staff.[1] The Poetry Center was not a wealthy institution and could not afford to employ professional actors and actresses, even for such a visiting celebrity as Dylan Thomas and for such a prestigious production as 'Under Milk Wood'. The union scale of pay for actors rendered professionals out of the question, and so a curious system came into being in which unemployed actors and actresses were hired as temporary help in the theatre – running the switchboard, helping out backstage – and when the occasion arose the helpers took part in the various dramatic productions. The net effect was that there was a stockpile of talent readily available on the Poetry Center premises and a decision was made early on to exploit it instead of employing 'outside' personnel. These necessarily young and inexperienced actors were peculiarly susceptible to world-famous visiting poets and soon fell under the spell of Dylan's undoubted and powerful charm. Dylan's directing technique increased their admiration and affection. He made them all feel, Liz Reitell has said, as if it were a *mutual* project, ever encouraging them to make suggestions and always considerate of their lack of experience.

His careful and patient handling of their largely untried acting skills won them over. Soon their admiration had turned into a much more robust expression of undying affection, at least on the part of one of the female cast members. At a party given after the first performance Dylan sat on the floor with Nancy Wickwire. Nancy was clearly overcome with adoration of the Welsh poet and she looked up at him and said 'Dylan, Dylan Thomas, I'm in love with your soul.' Dylan replied, 'Oh damn, I thought it was my body you were after'.

Thirty years later none of the surviving cast members had lost their youthful hero-worship of Dylan or their regard and admiration for his 'work of genius', 'Under Milk Wood'. Neither had Liz Reitell. The cast may have decided that they were all in love with Dylan by the time that first rehearsal was over. They did not know then, and nor did Dylan, that Liz Reitell had begun to experience exactly that same emotion at exactly the same time, and to experience it keenly.

[1] Dylan's fellow actors for this first production were Dion Allen, Nancy Wickwire, Sada Thompson, Roy Poole and Allen Collins.

This 'new' Dylan was only the first factor working to bring Dylan and Liz closer together. The second was the quite extraordinary experience involved in the first performance of the play itself. Liz Reitell's obsessive concern for the 'Under Milk Wood' script had certainly worked on Dylan, but it was still some way from completion on the very eve of the first night curtain. Dylan was working on the script right up to the last possible minute and was still scribbling additions and emendations on the train bringing him to New York for the actual performance. Thirty years later Brinnin claimed that he never had a doubt that the play would go on. 'There was enough to make an evening,' he has said, but whether there was enough to make a satisfactory evening, one that would live up to the audience's high expectations, was unclear. 'The thing people forget,' Brinnin has said, 'is that Dylan was a perfectionist ... three hundred and fifty or four hundred versions of one modest-sized poem, and 'Under Milk Wood' went through that kind of scrutiny over and over again ... there was that kind of perfectionism and there were the demands of an audience which had bought its tickets eight months previously, waiting for the curtain to go up ... and the two came rather closely together.'

They did indeed.

Despite the confidence he claims thirty years after the event John Brinnin had still prepared two speeches for that first night: an introductory speech welcoming the audience to the first night of the play; and a cancellation speech lamenting its non-appearance. The actors had only seen the full 'Under Milk Wood' script on the very *morning* of its first performance and, at that stage, Dylan had still not written the final ending. Throughout the whole course of that agonised day, Brinnin juggled the two speeches while Dylan dithered over the final shape of the play. He continually scribbled corrections and additions to the text throughout the afternoon rehearsal session.

At approximately 5 o'clock that evening the cast broke for a dinner rest. The performance was scheduled for 8.40 p.m. and a final run-through was arranged for 7.30 p.m. While the rest of the cast took their break, Dylan and Liz retired to Rollie McKenna's nearby apartment on 88th Street where Dylan worked on the last-minute changes to the script. Two typists from the Poetry Center office were in attendance and they typed the new sections of script after they had been made legible by Liz Reitell.

One hour into this frantic re-write, a major crisis blew up. Dylan announced that he simply could not go on. Brinnin began to juggle with his cancellation speech once more. A third of the play – including the all-important final scenes – still required attention. Liz Reitell told Brinnin that the evening's performance would have to be cancelled.

Dylan overheard their discussion and immediately decided that such a prospect was unthinkable and that the performance *must* go ahead. An ending of the type he originally envisaged would take far too long to complete and in any case, Dylan was not in the frame of mind to accomplish such a last-minute feat. Instead he decided to substitute a makeshift ending and, now in grim and sober mood, buckled down to fashioning the play into some form that would make for an intelligible evening's entertainment.

The final run-through approached. Even then the final scenes were not ready. Brinnin was still trying to decide between his two draft speeches, unsure, despite Dylan's determination, whether they could really proceed. The run-through ended unsatisfactorily at 8.10 p.m. and Dylan went away to scribble yet more last-minute changes. The curtain was due to rise in less than thirty minutes.

In the event the remaining fragments of that evening's version of 'Under Milk Wood' were not handed to the cast until the last few minutes before the curtain rose. They rehearsed totally new speeches as they were applying make-up preparatory to going on stage.

The nightmare intensified. The very last lines of dialogue – including the very end of the play – were not handed to the actors until they had actually taken their places on the stage.

The ordeal of the first performance still lay ahead, of course, and this first performance threw up a fresh crisis of its own. The audience numbered in the hundreds and many had purchased tickets months in advance. The sense of occasion was strong and the general air of anticipation was enormous. This was to have a near-disastrous effect on the reception of the play.

As the play opened John Brinnin and Liz Reitell positioned themselves at the rear of the auditorium. The rather sombre opening of 'Under Milk Wood' encouraged a predisposition in the audience to accord the play a very serious reception. Brinnin indeed felt that the audience had met 'in a kind of reverential conclave' and that the members of the audience were in 'a druidical grove listening for the voice of the bard'.

The bawdy lines early in the play did provoke the odd explosion of suppressed laughter but this was quickly silenced. The audience clearly felt that such merriment mistook the play's more serious intent. The opening speches thus passed in an agony for Dylan, for his fellow actors on stage and for John Brinnin and Liz suffering in the very midst of the unresponsive audience. It was not until ten minutes into the play that one member of the audience had the nerve actually to laugh outright. More joined in and soon there was a general awareness that they were watching a comic piece. After this uneasy start the performance truly flew and the whole auditorium responded fully to this portrait of a small Welsh village and forgot their earlier feeling that they were participating in some kind of religious ceremony.

The play ended in darkness, as the lights faded on the stage, and for a moment the hall was silent. Then the applause burst through the silence as though through a physical barrier. In all, Dylan and the cast took fifteen curtain calls, the last for the Welsh poet alone.

Thankfully the entire performance was preserved on tape. Just before the play began, one of the actors, Al Collins, placed a small home recorder with a single microphone at the front of the stage. That recording was never intended for commercial purposes, as it was planned that Dylan would record a more polished and final version of the play on his next trip. But Dylan died before that could be done and Al Collins' makeshift recording is all that now remains of 'Under Milk Wood' with its author participating. A large, gentle and sincere man, Al Collins believed he had divine guidance. 'God,' he said, 'must have touched me on the shoulder.'

Through the applause, Dylan can still be heard thanking the cast. 'Thank you, thank you,' he is repeating.

The experience was one to provoke extreme emotions, and it

did. Within days of that first performance Dylan and Liz Reitell were established as lovers. The relationship from that point on developed naturally in a courtship that, though initially cautious, became increasingly intense. Dylan and Liz worked together in a professional capacity, had the occasional drink together in New York bars, then began to take extended rambles through the labyrinth of Greenwich Village streets. To Liz, this deepening of her relationship with Dylan confounded her expectations. Dylan was not the man she had believed him to be. She began to recognise what she regarded as Dylan's extreme sensitivity, the 'thinness of his skin' and she began to feel an avowedly protective responsibility for him, which then translated into love.

For his part Dylan had found another protector who could shield him from the demands of the outside world; a role that placed Liz in the curious and highly contradictory position of protecting Dylan from the kind of pressure that she herself originally represented. She remained clear-sighted enough to realise that the relationship at the start was advantageous to Dylan in a way that was not usual in most romances, and that there was a sense in which Dylan used her. Dylan would take her along to functions and gatherings 'for a sort of buffer. He was frightened of being alone, I think. Not in the day when he was working, but when the shadows came he would want to be with somebody.'

This need to be with somebody would remain even in the 'roaring times'; 'When Dylan was roaring, into one of his roaring drinking times, he was anybody's, anybody who wanted him and would ply him with enough drinks and with interest to amuse him enough for a moment. He belonged to this person, he was swept along with the tide in that way ... we would go to a party and he wouldn't pay any attention to me. He would be in the middle of being the party boy, which he was and nobody could be more absolutely fascinating. But if, for example, I would leave him to go home then the next morning when he called me ... he would make it clear that I abandoned him.'

Significantly, then, from the very beginning of the relationship, Dylan's vulnerable side was constantly to the fore and Liz was forced to assume a protective role. From the very first, Liz felt responsible for Dylan, precisely because of the poet's lack of personal responsibility. Dylan's actions continually invited others to worry about him and many in the past had flocked to do just that both in Britain and in America. Liz Reitell now gladly joined that long and occasionally auspicious line.

The advantages for Dylan then, were clear. On Liz Reitell's part the rewards are less easy to explain. Certainly a protective feeling towards Dylan was implicit in their professional relationship and that protective feeling could easily convert into love. They had both suffered through the sometimes frustrating, sometimes infuriating experience of bringing 'Under Milk Wood' to fruition and there was an element of relief and catharsis attendant on that event which would work to unite those involved. There may well have been a touch of professional admiration on Liz's part at witnessing the Welsh magician stage yet another daring rescue of his material and his reputation. Finally there was the experience of encountering a totally different Dylan at the rehearsals of his play, a Dylan who overturned her prejudices and her initial impressions. Dylan, sensing Liz's changed attitude, may have confirmed the process by deliberately approaching her, recognising the new possibilities. Dylan knew that Liz Reitell was, like his wife Caitlin, a strong woman. For whatever complicated reason, Liz Reitell came to be Dylan's Caitlin-in-exile in the U.S.A.

This new relationship brought about a definite change in Dylan and the ever-watchful John Brinnin first registered this change a few days later. The cast had noticed nothing at this point, and indeed Roy Poole recalls that none of them recognised a new intimacy between Dylan and Liz until well into the trip and after several rehearsals and performances. 'We were all such innocents in those days,' he has recalled.

John Brinnin was less so. Dylan came to stay with Brinnin again six days after the first performance of 'Under Milk Wood'. The two friends embarked on a sightseeing tour of the area, killing time between engagements. Dylan 'seemed more relaxed and happy than at any time I could remember,' Brinnin has recalled, 'and proof of this was his showing only the mildest inclination for drink.' He was settled and happy, quiet. He talked of work almost exclusively and of his future projects and as they drove Dylan outlined to Brinnin the 'Two Streets' idea he was to outline to Phillip Burton a few months later in London; his 'love story of two people who were never to be lovers'. It was a propitious moment for Brinnin to deepen the conversation and to probe the origins of the new settled persona the poet was presenting to the world. Brinnin already had a shrewd suspicion that it was related to Liz Reitell.

Both Liz and Dylan had confided in Brinnin their initial dislike of the other but subsequent conversations in snatched phone calls from New York, had made it clear that 'their mutual dislike had either been tempered or forgotten'. On Brinnin now raising the subject of Liz, Dylan plunged in warmly. Liz was 'the most wonderful woman (Dylan) had met in America'. She had 'completely taken charge of him'. She was marvellous, all hostility had been totally forgotten, she was his new 'protector' – it is significant that even in that first conversation Dylan referred to her protective function. Brinnin felt immediately that this new relationship was the key to Dylan's changed state of mind.

To Brinnin that realisation was double-edged. Regard for Dylan had led Brinnin into a state of total distraction as his sense of responsibility clashed with Dylan's own lack of responsibility and with Dylan's occasional cruelty. He was immediately concerned about the cost of this new relationship to Liz Reitell and also may have suspected that in withdrawing from his own role as Dylan's protector – which he undoubtedly had – he may have been partly responsible for this new situation. His contact with Dylan had plucked Brinnin out of his 'usual orbit of sanity into a maelstrom of doubts and anxieties in the calm centre of which, blowing his bubbles, floated our beloved poet'. Brinnin now saw Dylan dragging Liz along that same road and this perception brought a contradictory reaction: pleasure, at the effect the relationship was having on Dylan, and at the 'new' Dylan who was so clearly in evidence; and fears for his assistant who had now relieved his burden in more ways than one.

Nevertheless, from then on all Brinnin could do was observe. For better or for worse the affairs and fortunes of his assistant were to be bound up with the affairs and fortunes of his most important friend.

This then was the relationship to which Dylan returned on

his fourth and last American trip on the 19 October 1953, and that relationship had remained unchanged. But the Dylan that returned was most definitely not unchanged.

Liz had borne the four-month separation from Dylan with a certain degree of equanimity, taking comfort in the strictly temporary nature of the poet's absence. At the airport waiting to meet him again she had felt an 'enormous, accelerating excitement'. But that sensation was shortlived.

The very first moment of their meeting alerted her. 'There was a strange moment when I did see him,' Liz has recalled, 'because he looked so ill. He looked so different. He was not that robust person whom I had said goodbye to in June.' Dylan in that first instant 'looked frail, pale and shaky. He looked delicate and he looked sad too, tormented, quite tormented.'

As Dylan approached Liz on the airport concourse the confusion continued. He made no joyous greeting but merely told her that he must have a drink, and headed straight for the airport bar. He was only prevented from beginning this fourth American trip as he had ended so many others by a strike of airport staff. Liz emphasised the unacceptability of crossing a union picket line, and the couple set off for Manhattan and the Chelsea Hotel.

Part of the reason for Dylan's dispirited appearance was made clear during this taxi-ride into Manhattan. He told Liz of the horrors he had endured with Caitlin in that last week in the Lockes' home in Hammersmith. He had also been shaken by the inflight incident with the priest. The taxi-ride was solemn and preoccupied, where Liz had expected a more typical lover's reunion. Dylan just wanted to get straight to the Chelsea. But there more problems awaited him. The Chelsea Hotel was familiar territory for Dylan. Liz has noted that for Dylan the hotel was 'like coming home in a sense. The Chelsea is a place that puts its arms around you the minute you walk into the lobby and Dylan felt this.' But the delay in Dylan's travel plans had forced the management – five Hungarian gentlemen, elderly and renownedly caring – to cancel Dylan's reservation. His original large bright room facing onto 23rd Street was now substituted by a 'smallish back room'. To Dylan, the change of room was unacceptable. The poet wanted a room 'just like the one he'd had before', Liz recalled, and he was not placated by the promise of a transfer to a larger room a few days hence.

For a man notoriously indifferent to his surroundings, the incident of the room played obsessively on Dylan's mind. But it is likely in retrospect that the cause of his unease and disappointment was less the desire for a large room than the desperate need to recapture something of the conditions of his previous trip. Dylan was forever a man who attempted to re-experience past pleasures and delights in order to deal with a turbulent present. Perhaps in those few short and troubled months in Britain, that previous American trip had assumed the status of some much happier time free from domestic and immediate financial troubles.

It was all a bad start to a doomed trip and although Liz Reitell insists that she felt no premonition of approaching disaster, the omens were all around. The room soon became peopled with Dylan's own imagined horors: on the second night he told Liz that he had just seen 'the most gigantic cockroach in the world – with teeth'. To Liz, 'the wrong kind of room set the tone for his second visit in a way – it wasn't right ... and somehow the room was like one of the straws that broke the camel's back. It kept cropping up, this damn thing about the room.'

Thwarted in his search for a drink in Idlewild and disappointed in the Chelsea, Dylan headed off with Liz for a drink in the Silver Rail on Seventh Avenue. It was all a bleak and depressing reunion for Liz, very different from the meeting she had anticipated for four months in lonely New York, waiting for her lover's return.

Thankfully, the only engagement that Dylan had planned for that first night proved a beneficial affair. Later that evening Dylan was to attend a reunion rehearsal of 'Under Milk Wood' with the original cast, prior to the play's next performance on the following Saturday, 24 October. Here, and at last, Dylan began to recover; though it would have been remarkable had he not. From the time of their first meeting with Dylan, relations between the poet and his first cast seemed to have to have been on some exalted plane on which mere mortals meet their idol. Roy Poole and Al Collins would return to their families each night speaking of their experience of working with a 'genius'. Dylan did not object one little bit to this idolisation and he now basked and began to relax in the rapturous welcome accorded to him as he walked in for that first rehearsal of his fateful fourth trip. The depressed poet soon began to revive in the midst of the uncritical acclaim he so rarely found at home with Caitlin in Wales.

This atmosphere of general well-being even lessened Dylan's anger at the discovery of difficulties with the 'Under Milk Wood' text, brought with him so hurriedly from London. This text, hurriedly typed by Douglas Cleverdon's secretary, was found to be littered with typographical errors, and worse, errors of omission. Dylan's almost illegible handwriting and dense linguistic style had clearly mystified the poor typist and Dylan's first task at that reunion rehearsal was to edit each page of manuscript, rectifying the mistakes and substituting the correct expressions. He also added the passages that had been omitted and set to work to remove others that had since fallen from grace. In the easy atmosphere of that first rehearsal, all this was of no moment. Earlier it would have proved overpoweringly frustrating. A welcoming phone call from John Brinnin, still in Boston, accentuated Dylan's feeling of general well-being.

After that rehearsal Dylan announced that he wanted a drink and he, Liz and a young poet friend (probably David Lougee), travelled across Manhattan to the White Horse in the Village. The atmosphere was once again relaxed and easy. Dylan's drinking was not excessive and was for social purposes only. Dylan and Liz drank till two that morning and then retired to Dylan's small room in the Chelsea. The lovers' reunion had been rescued, it seemed, but only just.

Liz lay with Dylan in the Chelsea that first night and pondered the new and changed lover that had returned. Dylan seemed dispirited and depressed, lacklustre and curiously distrustful. It could have been the trip, the effects of the last wearing week in London, anything. But even as Liz the lover reassured herself as to the temporary nature of Dylan's depression, Liz the professional refused to be completely assured. There was more to Dylan's condition than she herself could immediately fathom. From the time of their first reunion, there is a sense in which Liz was just hanging on behind Dylan for the ride.

Chapter Four

When Your Furious Motion

Looking back on her lover's first few days in New York, Liz Reitell was to realise that these set the tone for the whole trip to come; reassuring periods of calm and stability would overbalance suddenly and without warning into tempestuous derangement.

When Dylan arose the next day Liz decided on a morning walk around Greenwich Village. Dylan, Liz had decided, was just too much of a public personality for his own good. Even in the very short time he had been in New York, she had already fielded several approaches to the poet. 'Even in his hotel room', Liz has recalled, 'the phone rang constantly and people would immediately cluster around in a bar if they recognised him.' So Liz proposed that she and Dylan go out together for a simple walk. These walks would become a constant feature of their time together. They were 'where we could be away from anyone else ... we were able to respond to things outside of ourselves and that brought a sort of freshness to being with him.'

But it is likely that, even then, these walks were as much for Liz's benefit as for Dylan's. Liz was already attempting to build her own protective cocoon and to preserve the fragile illusion in which she truly believed: that Dylan would be fine if only she were allowed to protect him from a world trying – knowingly or unknowingly – to hurt him.

It has to be said, of course, that there was an element of self-protection in Liz's desire to shield Dylan from the threatening world. Her time with Dylan was necessarily short and implicitly precious and so long as there was nothing to threaten Dylan, there was nothing to threaten their relationship as lovers. In those early days of that last trip, Liz desperately wanted to preserve herself and Dylan as an entity and this desire led her to exclude those who might contrive to take Dylan from her. It was only later she was to realise fully that Dylan's demons were not from without but from within.

It was only later, too, that Liz realised that the supposedly therapeutic walks on which she escorted Dylan also played a part in accentuating the poet's general and already pronounced instability. She had hoped to exclude Dylan from a hostile and threatening world but her method was misconceived on two counts. First, the world that Liz sought to exclude was often the very world that Dylan so eagerly embraced. Secondly, those walks actually immersed Dylan in the atmosphere she intended to avoid. John Brinnin has said that 'the tawdry commercial streets on the edge of Greenwich Village contrasted with the green-hedged lanes of Laugharne tell that part of Dylan's story which he himself was unable to resolve'. Dylan's personality was composed of tensions that stretched back to his childhood, that derived from his early life in industrialised Swansea bounded on all sides by the splendours of rural Wales, from the cloying and loving attention of his mother contrasted with the stern reserve of his father; tensions that manifested themselves in the dual character of the 'roaring boy' and the quiet and settled family man. Both sides of that personality had been in evidence that summer in Laugharne and in London and it was indeed a duality that Dylan had never been able to resolve. New York spoke more to the roaring boy than was good for Dylan. America did not kill Dylan, as some alleged after his death, but it did tempt the roaring boy; it did speak to that part of the poet that threatened his stability, detested though that stability may have been in dull and dreary Laugharne. Liz Reitell may have been an 'island in the swirling maelstrom of troubles', but the maelstrom itself held a strong fascination for Dylan, a fascination that on occasions would turn into an obsession. That maelstrom was in evidence all around him on the streets of New York and while Liz believed that she was isolating him, she was merely parading before him objects which so attracted him.

Another of Dylan's preoccupations was to surface which should also have alerted Liz to the disaster to follow if only there had been time to assess its significance. As the couple walked on that first morning from 23rd Street towards

Greenwich Village, Dylan spotted a billboard advertising a new film, 'Houdini', prompting the first serious conversation of that last trip. Dylan told Liz that Houdini fascinated him. The conversation was unusually intense and Liz gained the clear impression that the poet 'associated with Houdini in some deep psychic way'. As they walked Dylan told her that the worst horror in the world was to be hopelessly trapped. They walked on, and Dylan continued to dwell on Houdini and the horror of 'traps'. He told Liz that he wanted to write on just that subject. The new edge to the poet's voice prompted Liz to ask if the subject were autobiographical. Dylan merely smiled wryly.

Thus there were continual hints of instability, and it was not long before those hints became flat statements. At lunch at a seafood restaurant the next day the other side of Dylan's now volatile character asserted itself eloquently. For no apparent reason the food that was placed before him suddenly threw Dylan into a towering rage. It was 'inedible' and Dylan refused to eat even a mouthful. It was not his reaction to the food but its intensity and disproportion that alarmed Liz. This kind of tantrum was not characteristic of Dylan in Liz's somewhat limited experience and probably upset her more than it would have those Dylan friends of longer standing who had become inured to such outbursts. Liz attempted to pacify Dylan but the poet would not be calmed and he soon lapsed into a bout of furious sulking. The lunch disintegrated into a highly uneasy and embarrassed affair. The disparity between the occasion and its effect was so acute that Liz was robbed of words and unsure how to act. There were clearly depths here that she was unable to fathom. She could only propose that they return to the Chelsea. The couple duly made their way back to Dylan's hotel where the poet was to work on the draft text of 'Under Milk Wood'. Dylan was still 'in a rage'.

Liz was shaken. But now she had to leave. She made Dylan promise that he would spend the rest of the afternoon working on his play, and then she left him alone in the Chelsea while she travelled uptown to the Poetry Center office. Later on she would not leave him while he was in his unpredictable moods despite the undeniable pressures on her. Liz could not easily assume the role of full-time nurse, caring exclusively for Dylan. It was one of the ironies of the poet's dilemma that he required a capable woman to cope with him, but that such a woman would be unlikely to have the unlimited time necessary to devote to that task. Liz still had duties of her own to attend to at the Kaufmann Auditorium.

But with his shaky nervous condition pressing ever more insistently upon him, Dylan was in no mood for work. And he had a thousand distractions with which to indulge himself. Dylan was of course a celebrity, far more of a personage in Manhattan than he was back in Britain, and he enjoyed the very company that most specifically threatened him. Dylan 'enjoyed the swarms of admirers', Liz has recalled, 'he enjoyed the enormous opportunities for all kinds of partying ... he liked the more relaxed, more liberal personal lifestyle.' Dylan loved 'crowds, crowds of students, crowds of hangers-on at the White Horse, he needed them, he wanted them, he enjoyed it ... he wanted to put himself in those crowded places and have that kind of experience.' Liz must have suspected as she hurried uptown to the Poetry Center, that some group or other, some companion or other, would soon be knocking on Dylan's door and that the ever-susceptible poet would be totally unable to resist.

Dylan worked for a short time in the Chelsea but it was not long before he was duly interrupted. In this case the interruption came from a deputation of organisers of a group called Cinema 16. This group was arranging a symposium at which it was intended that Dylan would speak. Whether they telephoned and were invited to drop round, or whether more innocently Dylan had been ambushed by them in the Chelsea Hotel is not now known. They arrived within a few minutes of Liz Reitell's departure and brought with them several bottles of whisky and beer to help finalise the arrangements.

A short while later an eminent literary critic dropped by at the Chelsea to talk with Dylan and he too was sucked into the already-riotous party. This critic seems to have been a rare exception, an academic that Dylan actually admired. He usually found them threatening. At a party in Boston on one of Dylan's previous trips, he had met another eminent American literary critic and the occasion had not been a happy one. The critic had immediately plunged into a long question in which Dylan was compared to other poetic notables and was then asked to comment on his place in the realm of English literature. Dylan had simply shuffled his feet, looked at the floor, and had said nothing. Brinnin has recalled that when Dylan met the scholar I.A. Richards, his personality changed completely. 'In the company of such men he gave the appearance of being amiable and intellectually at ease. Actually he was never quite himself.'

The roots of Dylan's reserve here can be traced back to his intellectually acidic father. At school Dylan was an academic failure. His father had concluded wryly that Dylan 'was not teachable'. Brinnin has remarked that, in later life, Dylan's attitude towards clever academics seems to derive from a desire to prepare a face, to find a public language that would not betray him, to prove, usually by voluble distraction, that he was not only the confounding poet of dubious reputation but, a scholar among scholars, a man of critical faculty even if he chose never to exercise it. Liz Reitell has noted too that Dylan hated the 'precious affectations of the literary lion followers ... the academic types who were enormously precious about their work and their own understanding of things literary, (who could) therefore speak to Dylan the way the commoner couldn't.'

But on this occasion the critic seemed less the threatening academic than the friend and Dylan relaxed in the new company and started drinking seriously and heavily. Partly as a result of his having refused lunch earlier in the day, Dylan very quickly became almost totally stupefied with drink. The party rolled on for another hour or more until Liz Reitell, her role as Dylan guardian still fresh in her mind, telephoned from her office at the Poetry Center. When he answered Dylan's voice was hardly recognisable and he could barely construct a coherent sentence. Totally alarmed, Liz abandoned her duties and hurried downtown to the Chelsea. By the time Liz had travelled the considerable distance between her office and Dylan's hotel, the poet had drunk more of the proffered refreshments and Liz found him incapable. His conversation was no longer even connecting with his company. Liz immediately asked the visitors to leave and, faced with the redoubtable Miss Reitell, none of Dylan's afternoon drinking partners refused. Liz then ushered Dylan into bed and stayed with him for the next two hours, having learnt the first painful lesson of the consequences of her absence: the new Dylan could not be trusted by himself.

But once again Dylan's powers of recovery, those powers that even his closest friends found so remarkable, asserted themselves. After a couple of hours of besotted sleep, the poet awoke comparatively sober and alert. Liz had already organised the worksheets of 'Under Milk Wood' and Dylan was thus able to attend to the day's major task. He dictated new speeches to Liz, composed on the spot but with a quality unchanged from those speeches he had previously agonised over for months in his cliffside shack in Wales.

Another rehearsal of 'Under Milk Wood' had been planned for that very evening in the Poetry Center. Liz had been supervising its arrangements when she was called away to the Chelsea. Now, recovered and repentant, Dylan insisted that he could attend. Liz had private fears about his health and ability to withstand the rigours of a rehearsal in the face of this first fall from grace. These fears were soon confirmed. By the time the couple arrived at the Poetry Center Dylan had again collapsed as the residual effects of the afternoon's drinking session claimed him. Waves of nausea swept over the hapless poet. Dylan was obviously now too ill to participate in any effective way in the rehearsal and was persuaded to rest in the Poetry Center's Green Room while Liz took his place on stage. Dylan was still not left alone. Liz arranged that he was joined by Herb Hannum, a New York architect and friend of Liz's, whom Dylan had met the previous year. The two men had struck up an instant and genuine friendship. (Liz and Herb were also to discover a deep regard for each other during these difficult weeks in New York and this affection was later to deepen after Dylan's death. The couple married in 1958.) Herb Hannum now became Dylan's confidant and physical protector for the duration of that night and the next day.

Dylan's physical condition was now worryingly erratic. He was alternately firing up to very high temperatures and then lapsing into freezing cold. Hannum covered him with overcoats borrowed from friends and Poetry Center staff, but even then Dylan claimed that he was frozen. Hannum decided, probably in consultation with Liz, that food was the answer, and he left

Dylan alone for a few minutes while he went to buy provisions from a nearby delicatessen – some clams, chowder, crackers and coffee. He also bought brandy and hot water bottles.

Hannum noted that Dylan accepted these ministrations 'like a baby', but no-one who had known Dylan for any length of time would have been surprised by that. Throughout his married life Caitlin had often commented, amazed, on her husband's propensity to slip back into a childhood persona and to allow himself to be pampered and cossetted with bed-time treats. As a grown man, he still asked his mother to remove the tops from his morning boiled eggs. Had it not been for the rehearsal taking place a few feet away on the Poetry Center stage, it is likely that Dylan would have continued to accept gratefully Hannum's care and would have lapsed back fully into his childlike role, substituting Hannum on that occasion for Liz Reitell.

But the rehearsal was working on Dylan's mind. 'Under Milk Wood' was still not in its finished form, as he had testified to Vernon Watkins earlier that summer in Laugharne. Worried and fretting about the progress of the rehearsal, Dylan could not sleep deeply as he needed, but merely dozed, jerking into consciousness every few seconds and making plaintive enquiries about the events on stage.

At the first rehearsal break, the couple were joined by Liz Reitell. Liz had called back simply to type new sections of script but the sight of the 'Under Milk Wood' producer galvanised Dylan into making an effort at recovery. He declared that he wanted to attend the rehearsal that was to resume in just a few minutes. When Liz attempted to dissuade him, Dylan insisted and neither Liz nor Herb Hannum were able to reverse that decision. Just twenty minutes of rehearsal time were now left. Dylan made his slow and laboured way from the Green Room to the stage and managed to get through the rehearsal, buoyed again by the welcome from the actors and their encouragement. The full cast of 'Under Milk Wood' thus finally experimented with the new sections of script. But when the rehearsal was over, and Dylan returned to the Green Room, he became ill and nauseated once more. He retched on the floor of the Green Room. He lost his balance and retched again violently. Hannum helped the gasping Dylan to his feet and leant him against a wall.

Liz and Herb Hannum were now totally alarmed. Dylan may

have appeared depressed in his first few days in the US, but now he seemed dangerously frail too. Worse, it was clear that Dylan's illness was not just physical and did not simply arise from his afternoon drinking session. As Hannum gently laid the poet down on the Green Room couch, Dylan grabbed his coat lapel and whispered to him urgently, 'I've seen the gates of hell tonight.' Dylan's physical ills, it seemed, were derived from some deeper and previously unsuspected mental anguish.

This fact has led many among Dylan's friends to insist that the poet, in the last few weeks of his life, was beginning to anticipate its end. Dylan's actions, which so often seemed to court disaster, have lent force to that view. But Dylan's own testimony contradicts that easy impression. It is true that to Herb Hannum that night he said, 'Oh, but I do want to go on – for another ten years anyway. But not as a bloody invalid – not as a bloody invalid.' But Liz Reitell has insisted on Dylan's determination to keep going. 'In his anguish,' Liz has said, 'he did say that he wanted to die, he wanted to go to the Garden of Eden.' But the more sober Dylan, 'in the more serious of our moments together,' said that he 'didn't want to die, that he did, he *did* want to go on'. In his grief-stricken and most anguished moments, overcome by inner doubts and beset by his financial and personal difficulties, Dylan gave every indication of embracing his own personal disaster. Together with the actions which occasionally and deliberately embraced the most painful and potentially dangerous options available to him that indication was confirmed and the picture accords neatly with its end result: Dylan's headlong descent into desperate living leading to desperation and death. But the situation, Liz Reitell insists, was not that simple and the progression of events is not so persuasively sequential. Dylan did not want to die. Despite the fact that he felt like death and spoke of death so much of the time, that he 'was too sick too much of the time', as he told Herb Hannum, Dylan never believed deep down, nor did he desire in his heart of hearts, that it would all end in death.

Dylan knew the key to his recovery. He was aware of what would lift him out his self-imposed mire. In the Green Room that night, Dylan lay back on the sofa after being carefully placed there by Herb Hannum. He closed his eyes for a few seconds and then opened them again, apparently calmer and more settled. Then he told Hannum, 'Tonight, in my home, the men have their arms around one another and are singing.' Dylan knew he should have opted for safety. He knew that Caitlin was right. He should have stayed in Wales, that year and the previous years, where he produced his best work and where he could sink, comforted and cossetted, into his much-needed domestic monotony. America by itself did not kill Dylan but Wales, on its own, could have kept him alive.

Throughout the whole of this last period in New York, in fact, Dylan talked a great deal about Laugharne, about his home, his family and his children. In a sense, there is no clearer barometer to his erratic emotional state and confused desires. In Laugharne, earlier that same summer, he held America and Liz Reitell to himself as a kind of talisman against the horrors that were threatening daily to envelope him. In America later that same year he reiterated his faith in Laugharne and his family, having found that his problems could not be solved by the simple substitution of his country, his family or his lover. His troubles, Dylan was beginning to realise, were more deep-seated than that and would be far more difficult to solve.

Perhaps that realisation began to dawn that very night, though Dylan had probably carried it with him for months. Certainly Liz Reitell and Herb Hannum, their anticipated night out with Dylan in tatters, were painfully aware that the poet had plumbed new depths. Liz realised that all she had previously suspected of Dylan's depressed condition was confirmed. There was really only one course of action left. Liz and Hannum transported Dylan from the Poetry Center downtown to the Chelsea and both waited with him until he finally drifted off into a troubled sleep.

Liz and Hannum talked at Dylan's bedside as the poet slept. The conversation was inevitably about Dylan. Hannum in particular was shaken by the deterioration. Gone was the healthily and bouncily irrepressible figure he had known earlier that spring.

Both Liz and Hannum were now exhausted with the effects of caring for their charge and Hannum left the Chelsea though not before making arrangements to call back the next day. Liz had to attend to duties at the Poetry Center the next morning and it is likely that she asked the willing Hannum to attend to Dylan in her absence. Liz then stayed on in Dylan's room but there was no new alarm, and the rest of the night was passed in relatively untroubled sleep.

The next morning, Dylan was still sleeping when Liz awoke. She did not wake the poet but left him slumbering as she made her way to the Poetry Center via her apartment on Charles Street. Liz was confident of Hannum's arrival within a few minutes of her departure and indeed Hannum called at the Chelsea just a short time later. Dylan was just beginning to awake, and Hannum, reconciled to his new role as nurse and helpmate, immediately escorted Dylan out of the Chelsea and into the nearby Chop House for breakfast. Dylan accompanied him meekly, like a lamb. Neither Liz nor Herb wished a repeat of the previous day, when Dylan's refusal to eat had set up a disastrous afternoon and wretched evening.

But Hannum was also determined on one other course of action. Even after a night to absorb its effect, Hannum was still deeply concerned by the physical and mental anguish he had witnessed and was determined to probe its causes and attend to its cure. Hannum was thus witness to one of the most remarkable outpourings of that whole last trip, in which Dylan for the first time made a seemingly genuine effort to articulate his insecurities and fears.

Over an extended breakfast session Dylan sat opposite Hannum and gazed at the bustling 23rd Street with unseeing and unfocused eyes. He told Hannum that he had 'never been this sick before, never this much before'. The previous night had clearly acted powerfully on Dylan's mind. 'After last night,' he continued, 'and now this morning, I've come to the melancholy conclusion that my health is totally gone. I can't drink at all. I always could before, but now most of the time I can't even swallow beer without being sick. I told myself that if I'd only lay off whisky and stick to beer I'd be all right, but I never do. I guess I just forgot to eat and sleep for too long. I'll have to give up something.'

Hannum, alert to any hints of a deeper disaster, immediately seized on the last remark and asked, 'What do you mean, Dylan? Do you mean life?'

Dylan was by this time stone cold sober and he paused while

he considered. His answer when it came was chillingly uncertain. 'No,' Dylan replied, but then added, 'I don't know, I want to go on, but I don't know if I can. I don't feel able any more. Without my health, I'm frightened. I can't explain it. It's something I don't know about. I never felt this way before and it scares me. When I was waiting for the plane this time in London I found I was drinking in a mad hurry ... like a fool. Good God, one whisky after another and there was no hurry at all ... I had all the time in the world to wait, but I was drinking as though there wasn't much time left for me ... to drink or to wait.'

Whether this story of obsessive drinking was factually accurate is difficult to assess – certainly none of the poet's drinking companions at the Victoria Air Terminal in London have remarked on Dylan drinking as maniacally as he later recalled. It is possible, of course, that he may have been drinking alone before he actually embarked but again, and as with the story of the priest, the fact of this story may be secondary to its existence. Fiction and fact were beginning to coalesce and the distinction between them was now subordinate to their effect. It was enough at this stage that Dylan felt both to be real.

'I was shocked' he continued. 'I felt as though something in me wanted to explode, it was just as though I were going to burst. I got on the plane and watched my watch, got drunk and stayed frightened all the way here ... really only a little booze on the plane but mostly frightened and sick with the thought of death. I felt as sick as death all the way over.'

Dylan paused and his physical ills and difficulties pressed upon his mind.

'I know I've had a lot of things wrong with my body lately,' he told Hannum, 'especially the last year or so. Since I was thirty-five I've felt myself getting harder to heal. I've been warned by doctors about me but I could never really believe them ... that I was ever seriously sick or in any real danger. I didn't know how to believe it ... or maybe I did believe it but I couldn't accept it. I think I just felt I might be getting older, faster than I expected to, older than I should be at my age. But now I don't know. Maybe I've always been frightened but didn't know it until I couldn't drink when I wanted to.'

Hannum listened to Dylan's outpourings as the traffic roared past on 23rd Street. Back in Wales Dan Jones had read, with something of the same concern, the same outpourings in the anguished letters Dylan wrote to him prior to his last departure. In Italy Marguerite Caetini had similarly noted with concern the extent of Dylan's volubly expressed inner anguish and doubt.

To Herb Hannum, listening to Dylan in the Chelsea Chop House, a crisis seemed close at hand. He had only known his Welsh friend a comparatively short time. He had not witnessed any of Dylan's health difficulties in the past. On his last trip in the early spring, Dylan had been confident, lucid, buoyed by the new affair with Liz Reitell. The contrast now was particularly acute and Dylan's talk of death was particularly alarming. Hannum was beginning to feel, as Liz was also coming to fear, that Dylan was 'carrying the knowledge of his own approaching death ... that this second trip became a framework of illness and he was ... a moving being within that framework'.

But Hannum believed that Dylan's symptoms were less physically based than mentally derived. At the close of Dylan's long and anguished monologue, Hannum suggested cautiously that Dylan consult a psychiatrist. The idea immediately intrigued Dylan. Psychiatrists were unheard-of in Laugharne and would be a rarity today. Dylan would have welcomed close professional concentration on the intricate workings of his mental life. He'd never had a professional audience for his anguished deliberations about himself. However, Dylan initially resisted the idea while he considered it. Hannum mistook his hesitation for reluctance. The suggestion was changed to that of a physician, the doctor that Dylan had met on the previous trip, Doctor Milton Feltenstein.

Doctor Feltenstein had treated Dylan after one of the poet's accidents. In the last few days of that last trip Dylan had attended a performance of Arthur Miller's 'The Crucible'. Leaving a pre-theatre dinner party Dylan had fallen down a flight of stairs. Ensconced in the auditorium later, his arm began to ache and then to throb wildly and painfully. Dylan, never one to endure pain lightly, began to complain loudly, to the point that he was asked to leave the theatre. A hurried inspection by Liz Reitell confirmed that Dylan's arm was broken.

Liz had by now installed herself as Dylan's nurse in addition to her other roles and in that capacity arranged for Dylan immediately to see her own family physician, Dr Feltenstein. The subsequent and speedy appointment actually proved a more salutory experience than Dylan could have anticipated, as the doctor took the opportunity to warn Dylan severely about his general health. He spoke particularly witheringly about the damage being done to Dylan's system by his prolonged bouts of drinking. Dylan was now suffering from gout, from alcoholic gastritis and from a broken arm and the combined effects placed him in a mood unusually receptive to the doctor's admonitions. Dylan promised Doctor Feltenstein that he would stop drinking, and then confounded the sceptics by actually giving up drink for whole periods at a time before he left for the UK.

Four months later, Dylan resisted the idea of this new visit, though not through any antipathy to Dr Feltenstein himself. Liz Reitell recalls that Dylan liked and admired Feltenstein and indeed in one of his transatlantic letters that summer, Dylan had asked Liz to give his regards to Dr Feltenstein, he of the 'witty ways and winking needle'. Feltenstein, in his stern counselling of Dylan, would have also presented himself as a 'nurse and manager' figure and was therefore even more attractive to Dylan, forever searching for a mother's care.

But then Liz joined the party. She had found a note from Dylan in the Chelsea asking her to join them. Herb Hannum immediately sought to enlist her help in convincing Dylan to consult a doctor.

Liz and Herb may have discussed this idea the previous night. Indeed, the conversation may have been pre-arranged. In any event Liz embraced the notion enthusiastically, as if she had been thinking along precisely the same lines. Perhaps already she was feeling the need to share the burden of Dylan's illness and a physician seemed the obvious answer. Liz and Herb became ever more insistent, and Dylan eventually gave in to the combined pressure and agreed to see Dr Feltenstein once again. Liz left to make a phone call to the doctor's surgery and was rewarded with an immediate appointment. Before Dylan had time to change his mind he was hurried from the breakfast table at the Chelsea and out into the 23rd Street rush.

Liz's call had alerted Feltenstein to the fact that his advice, delivered so forcefully on Dylan's previous trip, had not been heeded by his patient. But Feltenstein was not to give up quite so easily. He had been Liz's family physician for years and there is no question that the personal interest Liz was so clearly taking in her charge had added an edge to the doctor's admonitory advice. It was evident to Feltenstein, within a few minutes of meeting Dylan once again, that the path that in the Spring he had warned Dylan was foolish, was fast becoming overtly dangerous. Dylan now had both immediate and more long-term problems to which the doctor had to attend. In the immediate future, the poet faced the prospect of more performances of 'Under Milk Wood'; in the long term he had to change his entire life style. Feltenstein, while more concerned with the long-term difficulties, was also vitally aware that his patient had commitments to fulfil and this was not just a recognition of contractual obligations. Feltenstein already knew that the fragility of Dylan's health was at least partly psychologically based. Whether Dylan ever fully articulated the doubts and insecurities he had expressed so forcefully in London is unclear but it is likely that Liz Reitell would have made clear to Feltenstein that Dylan was in the midst of some deep crisis of confidence over his work and his continuing abilities. Any fresh evidence, or insistence on the doctor's part, that Dylan could not meet his commitments was thus the last thing that Dylan wanted to hear and probably the least helpful course of action. So Feltenstein decided on a more short-term programme of help.

Dylan had ignored his previous instructions. Feltenstein now re-emphasised his earlier warnings. But his immediate help was more practical. Before Dylan left the surgery he was injected with ACTH, a cortisone-based drug that was fashionable in the early 1950s, designed to give its recipients a boost. This was intended to help Dylan through the next few days.

This consultation and treatment occupied the whole of the early afternoon and Dylan and Liz left the doctor's surgery with words of warning still ringing in their ears. Feltenstein was not about to under-sell his instruction. As they walked away, negotiating the Manhattan late lunchers, Liz desperately tried to probe further into the current Dylan malaise, to discover precisely the nature of the poet's inner anguish. But now Dylan was less ready to talk about the problems than the symptoms. Perhaps he had talked enough, and perhaps the doctor's warnings had scared him. All he would tell Liz was that 'I have such a feeling of dread. A terrible pressure – as if there were an iron band around my skull.'

But Liz felt that the Doctor might have missed a vital component in Dylan's illness. Dylan's actions in the first few days of that trip had confirmed her in her earlier suspicion that drink was a potent factor in Dylan's current instability. As far as she was concerned, one of the truths of Dylan's condition was absolutely clear: Dylan was a classic alcoholic. He was a 'clinical case of alcoholism'. This view clashes with that held by several of Dylan's other friends, most particularly Vernon Watkins who didn't believe that Dylan's drinking was any more than occasionally excessive. But then the loyal Vernon Watkins always believed the very best of his talented Swansea friend. Liz Reitell's opinion was shared by Dr James Smith who was called in to examine Dylan in the last stages of his later illness. Dr Smith headed the alcoholism unit at Manhattan's Bellevue Hospital institution and Dylan appeared to Dr Smith to be a classic alcoholic. In Dr Smith's view this was actually linked to Dylan's nationality. Liz Reitell has recalled a 'quiet talk' she conducted later with the doctor. 'I asked him,' she has said, 'what do you think is behind this illness of Dylan's? He said, some people call it Celtic blood guilt, the something that drives the Celts to destroy themselves so frequently … as though feeling guilty, as though guilt were built right into the blood.' The concept of 'Celtic guilt' has now taken hold in today's more fashionable Welsh circles.

Dylan also drank for less nebulous reasons too, according to Liz. He drank because he was 'alone'. 'A night darkness', she has said, 'was something that Dylan could write about … more poignantly than anyone could. He felt it and I think that alcohol was an escape from that.' Dylan, according to his new New York lover, used drink to escape that 'terrible aloneness he felt in the world. His loneliness, it was with him all the time.' Liz cited as evidence of this essential loneliness those sections of

'Under Milk Wood' where Rosie Probert and Captain Cat are singing of their journey into the darkness forever. Those passages of the play that spoke of loneliness, Liz felt, were autobiographically based.

John Brinnin has not accepted this view of Dylan completely. It is true that he too saw the key to Dylan's volatility as lying in his daily consumption of alcohol. 'The happiest times,' Brinnin has said, 'were days in the astonishing times when (Dylan) would have one drink or none all day long.' But the existence of those days makes Brinnin unhappy with the simple view of Dylan as a classic alcoholic. 'On the days when Dylan was not drinking, I'd be the one that would have the drinks and Dylan, for some reason, would not. Whatever definition of alcoholism he fits, this is a rare thing. I've known alcoholics and they don't let a day pass by without a drink and he would do that very happily.' In Brinnin's view, Dylan's drinking was not evidence of alcoholism but 'a kind of adrenalin that would take over when the occasion demanded it.'

But as Dylan and Liz strolled up Third Avenue after the consultation, the injection of ACTH was beginning to take effect and all concern over Dylan's health began to be dispelled. Dylan began to feel more physically buoyant than he had felt for days. The sense of physical well-being worked on his mental state and Dylan began to feel more 'resilient' in every respect, free, as John Brinnin has put it, of 'self-concern'. Dylan even began to take a new interest in his immediate surroundings and as they were passing an Army and Navy Stores, Dylan went in to buy some handkerchiefs and some American workingmen's shirts. The previous spring Dylan had taken several such items back to Wales.

The collective spirits were beginning to be restored. Dylan and Liz left the store in a more settled and happier frame of mind to travel uptown to attend the final rehearsal of 'Under Milk Wood'.

At the same time John Brinnin was travelling from his home in Boston to meet Dylan for the first time on this last trip.

Chapter Five

The Hand That Signed The Paper ...

John Malcolm Brinnin was the single most important factor in
Dylan Thomas' arrival on the American scene, the key figure in
ensuring that Dylan truly reached the wide and general
audience Brinnin believed to be the poet's true constituency,
and the driving force in the attempt to regularise Dylan's
financial affairs.

Brinnin held an important position in Dylan's life and one of
the tragedies of their relationship was that Dylan found it far
too easy to manipulate Brinnin and had no compunction about
so doing; in the process ignoring him and his proffered advice.
In the end Brinnin meant less to Dylan than Dylan meant to
Brinnin. This net effect was compounded by an awe on
Brinnin's part, both personal and public. Brinnin loved the
man and he loved his work and this further handicapped his
attempts to exercise any real influence over Dylan's actions.

John Brinnin is a mass of complexes and has provoked
contradictory responses amongst those who encountered him.
Caitlin Thomas (who was later to find comfort in his arms and
to physically attack him) was particularly forthright as
concerns John Brinnin. 'To me,' she has written, 'he is a
creature certainly not from this world and not formed of mortal
clay but from some prehistoric planet undiscovered by men,
and of translucent liquor, solidified into moon-opaque,
cloud-gargoyled shape.' According to Caitlin, Brinnin
inhabited an 'air-conditioned stratosphere of his own ... no
doubt, as he intimated, he seethed underneath and his private
life was fraught with excruciating, unprintable dramas: but
externally he was smooth, affable, wonderfully polite in warm,
caressing tones sunken with understanding; and so visibly
sensitive that he made me feel like a rhinoceros rooting in an

exquisite bed of flowers.' It is clear that Caitlin was never going to forgive John Brinnin for his studied and determined impartiality at the time Dylan was deliberating his last American trip.

John Brinnin came from an academic background and was still teaching at the University of Connecticut while he held the post of Director of New York's Poetry Center. Prior to Brinnin's appointment the Poetry Center's seasons of poetry readings were small-scale affairs, attended by small audiences (twenty-five to thirty people in a two-thousand seater auditorium) and performed by largely unknown or unfashionable practitioners. Brinnin was invited to become Director of this institution on account of his own academic background and on the strength of his own growing reputation as a poet. He would be a good choice, it was felt, given his public persona and his private interests. When Brinnin was duly approached for the post his response was telling and characteristic. His first question was whether he could invite the British poet Dylan Thomas to come to read in the States.

To John Brinnin, Dylan's poetry was 'everything'. It was 'a new voice and an astonishing voice and simply brought a new generation into being'. He had been reading Dylan's work for some fifteen years before his fateful appointment at the Poetry Center and had written reviews of that work for the *New York Times*.

Brinnin was well aware that Dylan had been anxious to get across to the States for some years. Harvard University had hoped to bring the poet across the Atlantic to read, but at the last minute the plans had fallen through. In a letter written in 1945 to his unofficial literary agent in the US, Oscar Williams, Dylan wrote, 'I can read aloud through sonorous asthma with pomp; I can lecture on the trend of Y or X at the crossroads of Z; whither? with an assurance whose shiftiness can be seen only from the front row, I can script and write radio films (sic) of a sort; I can – and so on with the list that could be, and is, supplied by every person fit for nothing but his shameful ability to fit into the hack ends of commercial, intellectual or personal advertisement.'

Though Brinnin was not to know this at the time, Dylan knew Brinnin's reviews of his work and this was a crucial factor in the poet's ready acceptance of Brinnin's offer to appear at his Poetry Center.

The wary poet had also checked Brinnin with his own publisher, who had known the American from the age of fifteen. But the offer really was too good to refuse: five hundred dollars for the poetry reading, plus air fare, plus the prospect of more readings to come.

Dylan did not embrace the offer quite so eagerly as his impecunious circumstances might have pressed him to, however. To Dylan, it 'wasn't really worth his while' coming all the way over to the States just for a couple of readings at the Poetry Center, and he asked Brinnin if it would be possible to set up a more extended tour; perhaps of the whole United States.

Brinnin, already excited by the imminent and long-awaited prospect of Dylan's arrival in America, approached various lecture agents with the suggestion that they handle Dylan Thomas. 'That involved' Brinnin has said, 'going to agents who were set up to do these things, but his reputation preceded him. I was in this position – sort of death of a salesman – dragging from one to the other and they would sit back and smoke a cigarette or chew their gum and shake their heads. And this was rather a pathetic scene.'

Brinnin's sense of responsibility for Dylan seems to have been already highly developed before he even met him. To Brinnin, these early dealings with the New York lecture agents were actually painful. 'I was trying to get rid of the man before I ever saw him,' he felt. It seems remarkable now that Brinnin should feel so curiously protective about and guilty towards a man he had never met, but it was an attitude that set the tone of their whole later relationship. The tour was clearly not going to materialise through a conventional lecture agency and so Brinnin made Dylan an offer. 'When finally I'd exhausted every channel I said, well, if you will trust me to do it, I have academic connections and I'll see what I can do.' Brinnin duly wrote to everyone of his acquaintance in the large American academic community asking whether they would like to hear Dylan read in their respective institutions. The enthusiastic response was sufficient to encourage Brinnin to add one more role to the many he already embraced: that of lecture agent for the visiting Dylan Thomas. For his part, Dylan 'couldn't think of anything nicer'. It should be said that Dylan's recollections of this acceptance differs slightly in tone from Brinnin's, though the facts are unaltered. Subsequently Dylan wrote to his agent on 1 December 1949, 'John Malcolm Brinnin has written to me at length suggesting that he, as a well-known lecturer, literary journalist, etc, in the States, and Director of the Poetry Center ... should become my secretary and agent for my stay there ... He said that the lecture agencies which prefer novelists anyway, have nowhere near his own acquaintanceship with the institutions etc which like poets, and would take for their services anything up to forty percent. He, although he would do it for friendship as a fellow poet (dear God!) cannot afford to do so and would have to ask (a percentage) of what I make on my appearances as a reader and lecturer. I cabled back and agreed ... believing that Brinnin will do a really good job for me (I hear extremely well of him from Laughlin).'

It is unlikely that the determined, if then somewhat naive Mr Brinnin knew quite what he was letting himself in for. He was certainly not aware then, as he was to realise later, that the trips and the attendant pressures and problems were to 'stop his life'. Nevertheless, it was his heart's desire that he should bring Dylan Thomas to the US and this had been the major motivation for his assumption of the top post at New York's Poetry Center. As such, Brinnin was perhaps even more committed than Dylan to the American trips.

John Brinnin was avowedly 'not phased by the stories that I'd heard (about Dylan)', though of course it was principally in the US that Dylan's reputation for misdemeanours was forged. The less appealing side of Dylan's actions hadn't really impinged on the public imagination in the way it would with the opportunities for misbehaviour he discovered in America. All that Brinnin had heard by this stage was that 'Dylan was somewhat of a heavy drinker, and that he was a roustabout'.

Brinnin's first meeting with Dylan confirmed this long-distance impression. Alighting from his plane (yet again with another stream of stories concerning his fellow-travellers), Dylan had taken the hapless Brinnin on a tour of the New York bars, occasioned, so Brinnin believed, by the poet's first glimpse of overpowering Manhattan. Dylan escorted John Brinnin on a mad merry-go-round of bars and clubs and riotous parties throughout the duration of that first stay, and then left an exhausted Brinnin waving goodbye on the New York quayside. But Brinnin formed three major impressions of Dylan on this first trip and they remained consistent throughout the whole of their friendship. There was firstly concern over Dylan's health. Several times Dylan would break into long spells of coughing that racked the whole of his body, brought tears to his eyes and left him momentarily speechless. Dylan told Brinnin that it was 'cirrhosis of the liver'. 'These attacks,' Brinnin has written, 'were as a rule brief, did not seem to alarm him and he recovered always within a few minutes, seemingly undisturbed by a collapse that would have sent almost anyone else to bed.' Brinnin also witnessed Dylan's ability to trawl admirers everywhere he travelled and in every bar he visited and that too would remain a consistent experience. But one impression remained above all others. 'I knew that, above all,' Brinnin has said, 'I wanted to take care of him, against my will, to impose my notion of sanity on his, even, inadmissably, to protect him from himself. Just as certainly I knew that I wanted to get rid of him, to save myself from being party to his self-devouring miseries and to forestall any further waiting upon his inevitable collapses. Yet I could do neither. This weakness, this ability neither to reject or accept, neither wholly to go nor to stay, troubled the air through which I had to witness the phenomenon of Dylan Thomas'.

This was an uncertainty and a confusion that was again to remain consistent throughout the whole of Brinnin's dealings with Dylan. These dealings engaged Brinnin's personal feelings in a way he had not expected and with which he was unable to deal with his usual efficiency. Even as Dylan's very first trip drew to a close Brinnin records feeling 'desolate'. 'The meaning of Dylan's voyage,' Brinnin has said, 'was incalculable for those of us who had come to know him intimately.'

But by Dylan's fourth trip, Brinnin had decided to withdraw from his caring role and had relinquished the position to the eager and enthusiastic Liz Reitell. The confusion attendant on that close care had led Brinnin into a state approaching nervous collapse, and his equilibrium, he had belatedly decided,

71

was best served by keeping a distance from Dylan Thomas. Brinnin made a determined effort to withdraw and his determination was firm. As a consequence, the first personal contact between Brinnin and Dylan on this last American trip did not occur until a few days into the trip itself; until immediately after Dylan and Liz's fateful consultation with the Doctor Feltenstein. Up to that point Brinnin had received few reports from Liz about their common charge since Dylan's arrival in the US. There is no clearer demonstration of Brinnin's new resolve not to be sucked into the whirlpool of speculation and frenzied concern that surrounded the day to day activities of Dylan Thomas.

Dylan and Liz had travelled from Feltenstein's surgery, with Dylan reportedly 'feeling better'. Nevertheless, when Brinnin first saw him at rehearsal, Dylan was supervising the action from a seat in the front of the auditorium and was not directly participating in the action on stage.

The house lights were low, and in deference to the concentrated activities taking place on stage, Brinnin simply slipped quietly into the next seat to Dylan and, after a whispered greeting in the half-darkness, settled to watch the rehearsal scene. Though Dylan was the ostensible director, there is no record of the poet actually contributing any instruction to the actors on stage. Brinnin recalls that 'Dylan was sitting in the audience actually watching the others do it'. The scene lasted about ten minutes and then the house lights went up. Brinnin has documented his immediate reaction.

'I was so shocked by his appearance I could barely stop myself from gasping aloud. His face was lime-white, his lips loose and twisted, his eyes dulled and gelid and sunk in his head. He showed the countenance of a man who has been appalled by something beyond comprehension.' Thirty years later Brinnin's recollection was less graphic but no less forceful. 'The lights went up, I looked at him and something in me was chilled.' Despite Dylan's reported improved health, his physical appearance must still have demonstrated a marked deterioration for Brinnin to register such a dramatic change. He'd met Dylan himself in Wales after all, just a short time before. 'I'd seen him in (early) September, this was hardly a month away and the deterioration was shocking, just a drastic change in his

72

face. Maybe it wasn't so much physical as the spiritual thing I sighted or sensed. I don't know, but it was immediate.'

The sight of Dylan fallen so low did not encourage easy conversation and Brinnin made an excuse to leave the auditorium while he sought out Liz Reitell. Liz was now supervising the backstage arrangements while Dylan was concentrating on the final rehearsals.

'The Under Milk Wood' cast were also now acutely aware of the change in Dylan and aware that the poet was not the man they had met on his previous trip in the spring. Roy Poole has recalled that Dylan's illness was now a constant background to this last trip and was fast becoming the most important factor of their whole time with Dylan. The staff at the Poetry Center also recalled Dylan's poor physical appearance and his lack of effective control over his own play as it was assuming final shape. Now John Brinnin had also become forcibly acquainted with Dylan's new state of health.

Liz Reitell lost no time in giving Brinnin a resume of Dylan's agonised talk from the previous night and from that morning. She confessed that she had no idea what had really caused the drastic change in Dylan and she had no clue as to where it might lead. But she made one thing absolutely clear to Brinnin: her unease and concern was not the usual apprehension that involved all those who dealt with Dylan and which revolved around his erratic behaviour and actions. This was different and if Brinnin sought confirmation of that difference he had the silent testimony demonstrated in Liz's bearing, demeanour and expression which themselves showed clearly the strain of coping with the changed Dylan.

But all that was for later. For now, Dylan had agreed to meet Brinnin and Liz in an Irish bar after the rehearsal ended and Brinnin took his preoccupied leave of the rehearsal to attend to the office duties that had accumulated in his absence.

In the meantime, and while Brinnin worked, the rehearsal ground to a halt and Dylan sought out Liz backstage.

Brinnin completed his duties a short time later and made his way to the rendezvous for his first talk with Dylan of this fourth tour, eager to plumb for himself the depths of Dylan's deteriorating state. Dylan and Liz, though, did not turn up.

As it turned out, this non-appearance by Dylan and Liz was

73

all due to 'a confusion over time and place', but it was a particularly unfortunate and acute misunderstanding for both Brinnin and Dylan. There was a definite element of insecurity and sensitivity on both men's part. Allied to Brinnin's absence during the first few days of his trip, the mishap aggravated a dim but real feeling in Dylan that he was losing touch with his first friend in the US and that Brinnin was now perhaps seeking to disassociate himself from his troublesome friend. It plunged Dylan, ever sensitive to mood, into a deeper depression than may have been occasioned simply by his problematic health and made him positively antagonistic to the Director of the Poetry Center. For Brinnin's part, waiting alone in the Irish bar those two or three hours later, the absence of Dylan and Liz left him 'puzzled and downcast by this defection'. It hit Brinnin much harder than might have been expected, possibly because it touched a raw nerve. Brinnin was acutely aware that there was indeed a sense in which he had deliberately distanced himself from Dylan, particularly since his most recent arrival in the States. He suddenly became uneasily convinced that by his absence now, Dylan was paying him back. Once this feeling took hold, Brinnin began to 'tabulate little failures' in Dylan's treatment of him in the past. He began to review instances of omission on the poet's part. Dylan was at that moment doing exactly the same thing. The simple problem of a missed appointment was being magnified by the two close friends and briefly the whole relationship between Dylan and John Brinnin was seriously threatened. Brinnin waited for an increasingly gloomy time and then telephoned Dylan's hotel. Again there was no response. Brinnin then searched for Dylan and Liz in the other bars near the Poetry Center, but could not locate them.

Brinnin joined the audience that night in the Kaufmann Auditorium for the first performance of the new and now much-revised 'Under Milk Wood'. This was the first performance of the work on that fourth American tour. Brinnin was still oppressed by his disturbing afternoon and concerned by the lack of contact from Dylan and it seems that he could not shake it off. He was in a state of transition, deliberately moving away from Dylan in a process that was acutely painful to him. Like all states of uneasy transition, the experience was deeply unsettling. The 'disembodied' figure of Caitlin's categorisation was suffering torments of his own and for the present it wrecked his enjoyment and appreciation of the evening's performance. 'While it was a good one,' the gloomy Brinnin has recorded, 'I felt it did not quite succeed in striking the fire of those performances I had seen in May.' Of course, Brinnin was not in the more receptive frame of mind he had enjoyed in May. He was now, as he himself admits, acutely 'conscious of the whiteness of Dylan's face as it showed through all the lights focused on it'. The fact of Dylan's illness was clearly beginning to affect everyone associated with him and was starting to influence Brinnin's responses. That illness was soon to pervade everything. The first performance of the much-revised 'Under Milk Wood' ended with the audience ecstatic and on their feet and the stricken Director of the Poetry Center preoccupied with his own relationship with the agent of the common adulation.

Rollie McKenna had arranged a celebratory party for Dylan and the cast of 'Under Milk Wood' at her nearby apartment. When the cast arrived, she too was alarmed and disturbed by Dylan's appearance, and was struck, as John Brinnin was struck, by the contrast between the present Dylan and the Dylan she had met with Brinnin in Wales just a month previously. She was also immediately struck by the psychological change in Dylan as well as the more obvious physical deterioration. He was ill, so Rollie McKenna could quite clearly see, 'in body *and* in spirit'.

Dylan's general behaviour had now changed too. Where his behaviour in New York had earlier been openly riotous, he now seemed more muted. There was one sign of hope exhibited at this party if the Dylan-watchers were searching for one. Offered a drink as he walked through the door, Dylan refused and maintained that refusal throughout the evening. Dylan was taking Dr Feltenstein's advice to heart, and characteristically he was making no bones about the motives for his self-imposed abstinence. When questioned, he simply repeated the phrase he had first used to Herb Hannum in the Kaufmann Auditorium Green Room: 'I've just seen the gates of hell. That's all.' The words were delivered casually but with maximum effect. Even in the depths of his apparent misery, it seemed, Dylan was still judging precisely the public effects of his private misery.

Rollie McKenna's party limped on, its principal guest failing to perform his usual role of party clown, and ground to a halt earlier than might have been expected. By midnight only a small coterie of guests remained: Rollie McKenna, Liz Reitell, John Brinnin and Dylan. This group had still not talked freely and intimately and the unease from the afternoon's missed encounter hung like a shadow over the heads of the three friends. But then, as the party ground into forgettable oblivion, Dylan began to grow unaccountably expansive. Dylan's mood was usually contingent on a large gathering around him witnessing his riotous actions and his much-rehearsed imitation of the original 'roaring boy'. But this time the intimacy of the small uneasy group seemed to suit him. There is no record of Dylan beginning to drink, but he became boisterous and more talkative. He became, as Brinnin has said, 'more like his normal self'. The afternoon's debacle had still not been mentioned and its mystery remained unsolved, but Brinnin also began to relax a little. Dylan's reversion or partial reversion to type was beginning to reassure, with its assumption of normality. Brinnin would have been reassured further had he known that the distance he sensed between Dylan and himself was not a strictly personal perception and was not unique to himself alone.

For her part, Liz Reitell had suffered through a changed basis to their relationship and had suffered a changed Dylan. The poet, and the relationship, were not now the same. Now Liz was beginning to feel a new coldness in Dylan, over and above the difficulties occasioned by new depression and his concern about his health. This new reserve may have derived from his changed physical state but it was a reserve that Liz was having increasing difficulty in penetrating and which was causing her increasing distress.

It is difficult to pinpoint exactly when this change in Dylan first impressed itself upon his New York lover. Certainly she had become conscious of a depressive state from the time he disembarked at Idlewild, but over the next couple of days she became gradually aware that his responses towards her were not the more usual responses of a happy lover revelling in a new and satisfying relationship. There was a depressed coolness in the first few days of that trip that only confirmed Liz in her own unhappiness and in a growing feeling that there was a distance between herself and Dylan which was becoming increasingly difficult to bridge.

The seriousness of this insecurity in Liz is difficult to assess, but one factor emerges as absolutely clear. Liz and Brinnin's general well-being was becoming dangerously dependent on Dylan's, which added a factor of general instability into the general depression suffered by this trio of close friends.

For now, although Dylan seemed to have recovered, demonstrating Liz's observation that Dylan 'had a tremendous ability in the absolute worst of times to suddenly ... flip himself over as though he were a coin and suddenly be joyous and brisk and full of fun', although he had restored some semblance of party spirit, this new mood did not completely restore Dylan's closest friends and the evening ended only with a bald arrangement that they should all meet the next day at Brinnin's hotel.

If Brinnin had believed that this meeting was intended by Dylan to clear the air between them he was immediately disabused of this notion. Dylan told Brinnin that he wanted to discuss the monetary aspect of his trip and this introduction of Dylan's financial circumstances struck a jarring note that the meeting the next day was to confirm. It seemed to emphasise Brinnin's major role as provider and tour organiser and to limit his cherished personal role as Dylan's close friend. Brinnin duly left for his hotel for the second time that day, confused, hurt and not a little angry. Liz retired with Dylan to the Chelsea, still unable to penetrate Dylan's reserve and not fooled by his new bearing and demeanour at Rollie McKenna's party.

Events, of course, were crowding in on Dylan, which contributed to his air of preoccupation. The first performances of 'Under Milk Wood' had concentrated Dylan's mind on the now fast approaching and much-dreaded collaboration with Igor Stravinsky. Dylan's health, he had been told, was approaching crisis point and the precarious nature of his physical well-being had been forcibly spelled out. Further, he had still done nothing specific about his primary purpose in undertaking this fourth American trip, at least as expressed to

Caitlin – the attempt to regularise his financial affairs. It was about this last issue that Dylan engaged Brinnin the following day at his hotel.

By that time the process of respective disassociation had grown more acute, the various protaganists each having a troubled night in which to nurture their varying senses of abandonment and guilt. As Dylan and Liz arrived at Brinnin's hotel, the tone and atmosphere confirmed that feeling. Dylan and Brinnin greeted each other, so Brinnin recalled, 'like strangers'. Dylan immediately began to speak of money.

Brinnin was hardly listening, merely registering Dylan's presence while he tried to deal with his feelings. He was now experiencing acutely what many of Dylan's Welsh friends had come to feel – however reluctantly. There was a wilful and ruthless streak in Dylan that used relationships for his own personal advantage and abandoned those relationships when they were no longer of any actual worth. Vernon Watkins was to suffer this ruthless quality perhaps more than any other of Dylan's close friends, though loyally he would never admit it. Now John Brinnin began to feel it acutely, and it gave a totally different mood to a discussion that, in truth, both men had conducted dozens of times in the past.

Dylan opened the interview by demanding that he receive more money for the trip. Brinnin immediately felt as if he were the agent of Dylan's financial troubles rather than the prime force in their deflection. Now, as he smarted under a keen sense of rejection, it became suddenly plausible that he had ever been merely a procurer of financial advantage. Where before Brinnin had been delighted to assist in placing Dylan's affairs on a sound financial footing, now Dylan's concentration on finance alone hurt him deeply. 'The whole tone of our interview struck me,' said Brinnin, 'as being like that of a business conference between someone who wanted money and someone who supposedly could be made to supply it, if sufficient pressure were brought to bear.' Brinnin became ambushed by his insecurities into devaluing their whole past relationship.

Dylan's attitude was certainly unfortunate and he was undoubtedly displaying once again those numerous failures of feeling that had hurt so many of his close friends in the past. But even so, Brinnin's reaction here seems extreme. There must have been one other factor built into the general instability fully to plunge Brinnin into this overt depression; a factor that perhaps Brinnin himself only partly understood. It seems now that this further factor was provided by the presence of Liz Reitell.

In a real sense John Brinnin and Liz Reitell were competitors in the fight for Dylan's affections, and in an equally real sense, each was deeply unsure of that affection and of their own respective places in the scale of that affection. There may well have been a sense in which Brinnin, at the same time as he was withdrawing from Dylan, felt resentful at the assumption of his place in Dylan's life by his former assistant. Liz Reitell was unhappy herself with Dylan's reaction to that assumption. The complicated emotions existing in Brinnin's hotel room made the whole episode deeply unhappy, and the meeting soon lapsed into a semi-silence as Brinnin, 'overwhelmed by this impasse in which disappointment and anger were equally at work,' found himself 'barely able to speak'. Thirty years later Brinnin was to confess that it was at this meeting he first fully realised that he would never 'know really what Dylan means to me ... I'm not so self-deceived as not to know that he was a phenomenon that came within my purview that perhaps I didn't quite know how to deal with in personal terms ... Those were not normal years for me ... they were years of an engagement the depths of which perhaps I'll never understand.' Brinnin's devotion to Dylan never attained the status of a sexual relationship but it rivalled the intensity of such a relationship, leading Brinnin to approach Dylan – as Elizabeth Hardwick has noted – with the quality of a hallucination: 'as if I couldn't take my eyes off what had happened.'

The interview ended unsatisfactorily for all involved, with little accomplished and much damage done. The morning limped to a close and the time was fast approaching for the matinee performance of 'Under Milk Wood'. The threesome duly trooped out of Brinnin's hotel and headed in a taxi for the Kaufmann Auditorium. But while the sober and depressed mood continued to claim Brinnin and Liz, Dylan, as he had the previous night, suddenly and unaccountably recovered. Brinnin records that he was suddenly 'chipper and full of song as a lark'. The reasons for this shift in mood can only be a matter of speculation. Perhaps it was the eloquent demonstration he had just witnessed of the power he still exerted over his two major Stateside friends. Perhaps it was the fast-approaching performance of 'Under Milk Wood' that was galvanising him into a more positive frame of mind. Whatever the motive, it had little effect on Brinnin and Liz. Liz trailed behind Dylan into the auditorium to assume her place behind the scenes of the production while Brinnin decided that he could not face the performance. He made his way instead to the Rollie McKenna's apartment, as melancholy and lugubrious as it was possible to be.

A huge audience had gathered in the Kaufmann Auditorium for that matinee performance and the cast, probably buoyed by the 'new' Dylan, after the previous few days of the ill and tired Dylan, gave what has been described as the 'greatest performance of the play'. Dylan himself is on record as regarding this performance as the one he himself finally longed to hear. Among the numerous visitors backstage was the eminent choral director Robert Shaw who had reportedly been moved to tears by the performance. But throughout the whole of that electrifying experience John Brinnin had been morosely ensconced in the apartment of Rollie McKenna.

Rollie McKenna was a good companion for Brinnin that long afternoon. She was, and remained, at a slight distance from the emotions surrounding Dylan and seems never to have been sucked into the mad whirlpool that claimed many another of Dylan's friends. In the midst of the anguished deliberations in Laugharne earlier that same summer, Rollie detachedly photographed the debating group, each member lost in their own private indecision. The photographer was to complete her assignment in the most unpropitious of circumstances where another might have felt it to be an intrusion. This detachment and independence on Rollie's part provoked curious reactions. Brinnin himself has always seen Rollie McKenna as 'a balance of contraries'. This balance was composed of 'humane perception and aesthetic strictness' and of a 'conservative disposition entirely open to the boldest manifestations of eccentricity and latter-day bohemianism'. This 'conservative disposition' was particularly appreciated by Caitlin Thomas. 'There was his (Dylan's) friend Rollie, the least American in the vacuum-cleaner sucking sense, of anybody we met, she was the most refreshing after the douches of gush that were later released over Dylan's unbowed head'. Rollie's coolness became renowned. 'Even in the Dylan crisis,' Caitlin has written, 'when everybody seemed to be going mad in their various ways, or was it only me magnifying them, I never saw her ruffled once and it slightly annoyed me that nothing could make her show one sign of weakness. But I was not fool enough to think that she felt nothing; she simply believed in not showing her feelings and was one of those rare people who did, and how few they are, what she believed in.'

Her regard and affection for Dylan was genuine if clear-sighted. Brinnin has described her photographs of Dylan as less a 'reportial account' than a 'loving tribute', and Rollie McKenna's work was later to have a positive creative influence in stimulating Vernon Watkins to write his poem about Dylan, 'The Present'. But it was the memory of her 'cool, unpossessive company' that remained with Caitlin and which was the aspect of her character that John Brinnin embraced that long Sunday afternoon in New York.

Unknown to Brinnin, Rollie McKenna had already become a confidant of Liz and Dylan's and was able to bring a degree of comfort to the depressed Brinnin as a consequence. Brinnin had not arrived at Rollie's apartment with the specific intention of unburdening himself, but his obvious poor spirits could not be left alone by Rollie without betraying a lack of interest she most certainly did not feel. Under her prompting, Brinnin eventually told Rollie of the previous afternoon's events. Rollie was now to explain those events though not wholly to reassure the melancholy Brinnin.

Rollie told Brinnin that while he was making his unsuccessful attempts to locate the Welsh poet, Dylan and Liz had telephoned Rollie in an equally unsuccessful attempt to locate him. Rollie, in ignorance of Brinnin's whereabouts, had then been the recipient of a similarly anguished outpouring from Dylan and Liz who told Rollie that they believed Brinnin had been avoiding them. Dylan had been puzzled by Brinnin's absence during the first few days of the trip and was now equally puzzled by his apparent absence that afternoon.

This news assuaged Brinnin's feelings to an extent, but he

had really fallen too low to be rescued by this new knowledge. The personal relationship between himself and Dylan, he believed, had sunk too far. He told Rollie McKenna that he had already decided he would leave New York immediately and abandon his relationship with Dylan. This course of action Rollie immediately opposed. There followed a stern tussle of wills.

Brinnin, of course, did not really want to leave New York. He merely wanted confirmation that there was some point in remaining. Rollie was aware of that, but was aware too that the game was more than a charade and that there was a genuine anguish inside Brinnin that could magnify into a deep and lasting bitterness were matters not taken immediately in hand. The dispute duly dragged on until Rollie absolutely and resolutely insisted on that which Brinnin wished to hear in any event – that he must not leave the city without seeking out both Dylan and Liz and thrashing out the whole matter with them. Rollie now performed the same function for Brinnin as she was later to perform for Caitlin at the memorial service for her husband, when Caitlin saw Rollie 'standing upright and clean cut, courageous as a Viking on the outside of the crowd and I stumbled towards her.' Rollie similarly was Brinnin's island in his sea of troubles that afternoon and there is a real sense in which she truly rescued Brinnin's relationship with Dylan. In the light of future events it is fortuitous that she did. Had Brinnin left the city then, he would never have seen Dylan alive again, and the small errors of omission would have magnified into a glaring void that would never be resolved. As Liz Reitell wrote, thirty years later, 'Grief is tolerable, regret is not.'

Back in the Kaufmann Auditorium, the performance of 'Under Milk Wood' was now approaching its end and another party had been planned for the late afternoon. This time however the party was not the easy, light-hearted affair that Rollie McKenna had planned the previous evening but was instead another new trial and source of worry for Liz Reitell, constituting as it did another downward step. This party had been arranged by a Dylan acquaintance whose principal function in the past had been as procurer of various women for Dylan; sexual contacts for the poet's immediate gratification.

Prompted by his now-close association with Liz, Dylan had refused all such invitations since his return to the States, though this may have been due to the women on offer being, as Dylan perceived them, of rather 'inferior quality'. But the procurer had told Dylan that he had managed to get hold of a 'real prize' for that afternoon, a 'refugee countess'. A delighted Dylan immediately resolved to attend and he dragged a now thoroughly miserable Liz Reitell along with him to the party, where his host was to introduce the impressionable 'refugee countess' to the predatory poet. Liz had good grounds for believing that their relationship was deteriorating.

Liz witnessed this introduction and it did not help her general mood. She did not find Dylan's latest change of character particularly appealing either, as the poet suddenly abandoned his self-imposed abstinence and began gulping down tumbler after tumbler of Irish whisky. This change was not occasioned by the 'offering'. The refugee countess was not a particularly gripping proposition by all accounts. (According to Dylan later, her sense of 'cosmic despair' was the most attractive thing about her). Dylan's behaviour switched, it seemed, due to an instability and unpredictability that was fast becoming characteristic. Indeed, Dylan's behaviour degenerated now in a similar way to that of his Irish priest on the American-bound plane a few days previously; behaviour that had reportedly shaken Dylan deeply. Tumbler after tumbler of whisky began to disappear down the Welshman's throat as his behaviour became ever wilder and ever more obstreperous.

Liz, with Doctor Feltenstein's warnings to Dylan ringing in her ears, did not welcome the sight of Dylan disregarding the doctor's advice. She was hurt by the blatancy of Dylan's dalliance with the willing countess. Her discomfort was compounded when Dylan, now totally disregarding Liz's presence and feelings, escorted the new girlfriend up the stairs of the town house.

Downstairs Liz waited in a pit of misery as Dylan's absence grew longer and longer and its cause became ever clearer to everyone in that room. Dylan was gone for over an hour, and Liz felt the humiliation of her abandonment keenly. Brinnin's absence, too, did nothing to help Miss Reitell's keen sense of isolation from the two men she could reasonably have regarded as her two closest friends on earth.

John Brinnin was by now making his way to the party on Sutton Place, strengthened by his new resolve and stiffened by Rollie McKenna's insistence that he confront Dylan and Liz with his insecurities and fears. The attempts by Rollie to fire Brinnin to this action had clearly taken some considerable time, as by the time Brinnin arrived at the apartment, the party was in its final stages and only ten people were left in the lounge, eating a makeshift supper around a low lounge table. By this time, too, even Dylan had returned from his encounter with the countess, rejoining the partygoers and the thoroughly wretched Liz. The refugee countess had not yet reappeared, presumably having remained upstairs.

John Brinnin bounced into the party, as he records, with a 'feint at cheerfulness'. He first approached the disconsolate Liz, as Dylan was the centre of attention around the supper table, but he gleaned little from her save evidence of her own deep depression. That evidence of a wider depression further fuelled Brinnin's desire and need to thrash his immediate difficulties out with Dylan Thomas. He joined the supper party but there was clearly little opportunity to talk with Dylan on any serious level in that kind of company and Brinnin now had little inclination to dissemble. He felt in danger of losing the most important, puzzling and intriguing friend he would ever know, and that knowledge was oppressive and demanded resolution, immediate resolution. That the circumstances were difficult merely made Brinnin determined that the circumstances should be changed, not that he should abandon his resolution. Brinnin knew he was facing an uphill struggle. It was always difficult to engage Dylan on a meaningful personal level. Liz Reitell has testified that Dylan would talk easily about 'life and death' and 'the great questions' but 'it was difficult to engage him personally in questions that affected and involved him.' It was difficult, Liz has said, 'to be serious with Dylan, to have that kind of very very serious talk which was instructional to him ... in other words trying to get him to do something that he found ... impossible.' The immediate company complicated further that typical Dylan reluctance and Brinnin was now in no mood to box clever in the field of party politics. He left the supper table, approached Liz and asked that she and Dylan join him immediately, upstairs and away from the main body of the company.

Liz approached Dylan, who agreed. Thus for the second time that night Dylan ascended the stairs with a woman – this time Liz Reitell – for a showdown – this time with John Brinnin.

By now darkness was falling. The ships were docking on the Hudson River immediately outside the apartment window and neither Dylan, Liz nor Brinnin felt inclined to turn on the lights. Their meeting was thus in half-darkness, lit only by the light spilling in from the hall-way. Each member of the group seemed instinctively to know how to heighten the drama.

What followed was a curious amalgam of self-abasement, self-indulgence and genuine feeling. Brinnin has recorded the fact that he had already rehearsed his speech to Dylan and Liz during his taxi-ride to Sutton Place. In that half-lit room, however, his business-like resolve clashed with his deeply disturbed emotional state and this clash proved too much for the 'detached' Brinnin. With Liz and Dylan watching from the sofa opposite, Brinnin began his prepared speech and then found words inadequate to express his feelings, probably because he did not fully understand them himself. So Brinnin gave up the unequal struggle and simply began to weep.

Dylan did not share Brinnin's feelings as Brinnin himself well knew. The sight of Brinnin in distress would not in itself have been enough for Dylan also to give way. But the poet was already in a state of considerable confusion over the activities of the past few days and, it is likely, now suffering considerable guilt over his treatment of the faithful Miss Reitell. Brinnin's open display of private misery tapped into a chord of more general misery within Dylan and shortly he too began to weep. Liz clearly felt herself unable to remain unmoved in the face of such accumulated misery and the trio were soon weeping together in the dim, half-lit room. Both Brinnin and Liz had their own private and specific reasons for their misery. Dylan's misery was specific, but the exercise undoubtedly did the whole group a great deal of good. Brinnin and Liz found their sense of isolation and abandonment shared by Dylan and with that general discovery came the means to resolve it. It was now that Dylan spoke what Brinnin was to realise later were the last direct words that would pass between them. 'Holding my face in my hands as I attempted to regain composure, I felt strong arms about me. Standing behind me as he held me very firmly Dylan spoke the last words I was ever to hear him say directly to me "John, you know don't you? This is for ever".'

Brinnin took the meaning of these words in his own special way. His friendship with Dylan had been re-established, he believed, and from that point on nothing would be allowed to threaten it. Their new relationship was fixed 'for ever'. Dylan's words could, of course, be taken in a myriad different ways and they can appear frighteningly prophetic given the fact that they were uttered a few days before his collapse into death. But as with the last sight of Dylan at the Victoria Air Terminal, every statement and utterance made by Dylan from this point on would be charged with a special significance.

For the time being, the 'absurd and foolishly dramatic scene' (in Brinnin's own later, embarrassed words) had lifted the tight-lipped tension of the previous two days. The trio embraced and left the upstairs room to re-join the main body of guests in the lounge below. Brinnin and Liz sat together on a low couch. Dylan grabbed a fresh tumbler of whisky and joined the rest of the party-goers gathered around the fireplace at the other end of the room.

Thus Dylan became absorbed in the party once more. Brinnin and Liz in turn became absorbed in a discussion of their mutual and all-consuming interest; Dylan.

The previous scene in truth had satisfied and eased Brinnin more than Liz Reitell. Liz's confusion was more deeply rooted, and Dylan's unpredictable behaviour had hit her hard. One positive outcome of the previous scene – aside from reassuring Brinnin – was that it had permitted Liz and Brinnin to discuss Dylan freely and easily. For Brinnin there was now no point in pretending that his affection for Dylan was merely that of an interested tour organiser with a special interest in poetry. Brinnin and Liz were now bound together by their common recognition of a fellow-feeling towards and about Dylan. 'Now that the emotional pressures of the day had been lifted,' Brinnin has said, 'and their causes dispersed, we felt bound by an understanding perhaps possible only to those to whom Dylan had been a living delight and a living torment.' As Dylan began drinking again, just a few feet from them, Brinnin and

Liz dissected him and their respective feelings about him.

It was Liz's turn first. She was, so she informed Brinnin, ambushed by several features of her relationship with Dylan. There was Dylan's perceptiveness concerning herself which drew her to him and which led to a certain degree of dependence upon him as the custodian of special knowledge. Speaking thirty years later, she has said, 'I am a rather large person, I'm tall, I have large features, I'm a conspicuous kind of person, I have a very loud and carrying voice most of the time ... I'm noticed when I come into a room, showy, a rather showy person. Given this exterior personality, Dylan could see right beyond that and I think he's one of the few people who knew me, who really knew me, who knew my insides, who knew my real self and at some point, at the White Horse, I was carrying on loudly and (someone) said something about "Oh Liz, here you are yapping away barbarically as usual – cut it out now". And Dylan turned to this person and said, "No, this isn't that kind of person at all. Liz is very long and very gentle. Inside that showy exterior there is a very shy, gentle person". Dylan, I think, saw that in me almost immediately and some people never do and he saw it in me without my having to tell him.'

This perceptiveness pierced the susceptible Miss Reitell but was dangerous too as she was just beginning to appreciate. Partly because Dylan discerned in Liz that which others missed, she found him the 'most lovable human being' she had ever known. She also admired his genuine compassion and careful handling of the 'Under Milk Wood' cast, which only increased her affection for the puzzling Dylan. But Liz was becoming aware of another facet to Dylan's actions which sapped her emotions and which tested her resolve. Those actions bordered too dangerously on the self-destructive for Liz Reitell and tested her self-perceived role as Dylan's protector to the hilt. Dylan, she felt, in his first few days in New York, was testing her and her love for him, and she doubted that she could withstand that pressure.

Brinnin had his own theories as to the motives for Dylan's actions. Dylan, so Brinnin said, 'had an instinct for drawing to him those most capable of being annihilated by him', a judgement that would strike a chord in many of those who had known Dylan in America and in Britain. Certainly Dylan inspired deep loyalty and affection in those he used and abused and more than one friend of Dylan's had found himself trying to defend indefensible actions. Brinnin also told Liz that he believed Dylan had an instinct for identifying precisely those who were susceptible to that power and there is certainly a sense in which Dylan pursued Liz, who very quickly fell under Dylan's spell, while he did not even attempt to engage Rollie McKenna, who most certainly would not have found the poet so personally fascinating. Certainly, too, Dylan was well aware that he could manipulate those who deeply loved him, as his masterly manipulation of John Brinnin in Laugharne amply demonstrated.

Liz, independently of Brinnin's analysis, was fast coming to the same conclusions. Dylan, she was fast coming to believe, was a 'destroyer', and it is difficult not to sympathise with her. Dylan had already claimed all her working and many of her waking hours. The sole occasion on which she had left him on his own to attend to her own duties at the Poetry Center, she had found him later almost totaly stupified with drink. But in addition to these physical demands on her time, she was now feeling a specific mental pressure consequent on Dylan's wilder actions and this was proving more insidious and more deadly. Brinnin recognised this. The attentions that Dylan demanded 'whether these were conscious or unconscious had caused her to lose all sense of her own existence and to be attuned only to his'. Dylan's typically helpless pose had worked once again, and Liz had assumed responsibility for Dylan where he would apparently assume none for himself. It all placed Liz in an invidious position. She was an independent woman fulfilling a demanding job. Love affairs, even with major poets of unreliable reputation, should not lead to such a state of depressing personal torment.

Both Brinnin and Liz discovered that night that they were both thinking along exactly the same lines, that 'the consequences of our having known Dylan was a mutual revelation – our feelings were identical and the bewilderment we shared was of the same nature, and sprung from much the same experience'. In Brinnin's case, that discovery had led to a deliberate decision to withdraw. Liz, too, had to preserve her own sense of sanity. And she was fast coming to exactly the same decision.

Despite the comfort derived from the previous scene upstairs with John Brinnin, Dylan still posed too large and too overpowering a threat to Liz's personal well-being, too acute a concern. He was too little like the joyous companion he had been on his previous trip. Perhaps having made sure of her Dylan had little need to try to keep her, and any course of action was now possible. Having won her once, Dylan did not need constantly to repeat that exercise. Previously the tension that his lack of self-regard engendered had been bad enough but now Liz had to cope with the additional tension of his apparent lack of regard for her.

Liz felt at breaking point, and her conversation with Brinnin confirmed her in her feeling that this torment was not unique, nor was it peculiar. It was not evidence of any failing in her but was a more general and in a sense inevitable attitude spawned by contact with the poet. Her consequent resolution was communicated to Brinnin as they sat on the sofa that night. 'Tonight she was going to let him know that she could no longer be with him, and that she could no longer take care of him.'

All the time they talked, Dylan was picking up his earlier role as renowned party-goer. Unfortunately for Liz's sense of well-being, the refugee countess had now rejoined the party and Dylan had resumed his attentions once again, uncaring of Liz sitting a few feet away from him. He now began drinking again too, and tumbler after tumbler of whisky began disappearing down his throat once again. Dylan's behaviour became ever more drunken and ever wilder and he began to spill cigarettes and drink over himself, growing generally more stupified and more in love with his own drunken self. Brinnin and Liz, watched from the sofa in despair, and Liz found ready fuel for her new anguish and her fresh resolution.

For Brinnin, this fresh instance of Dylan's misbehaviour was particularly disturbing. He was becoming well aware of the widespread notion that Dylan presented only the performer to his American audiences and not the more serious poet, that he presented only the roaring boy and not the more committed artist. Now Dylan was confirming everything that was worst about his own reputation, inspiring the stories that were to spill out of a thousand mouths in the wake of Dylan's death. Brinnin was still acutely sensitive about this portrait of Dylan thirty years later. 'You get the impression now', he has said, 'that we lined up to watch this clown performing'. Dylan at his best was available to his American audience as well as Dylan at his worst. Yet the clown was still a powerful symbol and Dylan was that night confirming that symbol for all to see. That was painful to Brinnin and humiliating, Brinnin felt, for Dylan himself.

Both Brinnin and Liz felt that there was little point in remaining to witness Dylan's descent into his own stereotype. They both now decided to leave, the beneficial effects of the previous exchange cancelled completely by their talk about their common charge and by Dylan's fresh activities as the life and soul of the drunken party. Getting up from the sofa they both lingered in the hall for a few seconds, collecting their coats on their silent way out from the party.

As they made for the front door, Dylan suddenly appeared from behind them, aware that they were about to leave. He was, so Brinnin recalled, 'like a child who fears he has been deserted, his eyes wide and rueful'. The poet spoke only three words: 'Here I am.' He fell into step behind them as they left, presumably abandoning the refugee countess still sprawling on the floor behind him. It is significant that even here, when Brinnin's distaste for Dylan's actions was at its height, and the pain occasioned by those actions was at its most intense, he should still describe Dylan in terms most commonly reserved for recalcitrant children. The language speaks volumes for Brinnin's attitude towards Dylan.

But even here they were destined not to be alone. Whether attracted by Dylan's presence or simply because they wanted a ride, several of the party-goers decided that they would accompany Dylan. They crowded into a taxi with Brinnin, Dylan and Liz and stayed with them for the ride downtown. Brinnin was to catch a train to Boston from Grand Central Station. After a riotous and deeply unhappy taxi-ride, Brinnin was dropped off to make his solitary and thoughtful way home.

Dylan spent the rest of the short taxi-ride trying to persuade Liz Reitell to accompany them back to the White Horse for a nightcap, but Liz, sticking to her guns, refused. Dylan's parting words to Liz that night were, 'I used to have a friend that lived here.' The taxi pulled up outside Liz's flat. 'You still do,' she told him, and then left him in the taxi with the rest of the revellers. Perhaps Dylan took the parting words as a sign that her disapproval was only temporary. Dylan and the rest went on to the White Horse where they stayed, drinking, for most of the night. Then, as the party finally ended, with Liz Reitell alone in her apartment, Dylan went back to the Chelsea with another girl 'procured' for him by his party-fixer. The poet's energies were as sexually active as ever.

For his part, John Brinnin sat alone in his train compartment riding back to Boston. He had made his last personal contact with Dylan and had played his last role in the conscious life and affairs of his puzzling and contradictory friend. He had enjoyed and endured his first and last meeting with the Welsh poet on that final doomed trip. He had bid a farewell of sorts, it was true, but its inadequacy was to haunt him for ever. Later Brinnin was to take comfort from the realisation that this was a common and widespread regret. No-one, he was to discover, ever really says goodbye to Dylan.

Chapter Six
Deaths and Entrances

Liz Reitell was to discover that truth the very next day. For if Liz truly believed, as she hurried back to her Charles Street apartment, that she had rid herself of Dylan Thomas before he threatened her further, she was deluding herself. Dylan's hold on her was already too deep and too insidious for mere common sense or even strident self-preservation to stand in its way. After a miserable night from which she emerged determined that the events of the previous evening should not be forgotten, Liz discovered that her new resolve lasted just one morning.

Liz could not let even that first morning pass without contacting Dylan. She phoned the poet early on matters ostensibly connected with the production of 'Under Milk Wood'. But the fear that Dylan might have ended the evening suffering from some injury was uppermost in her mind. It seems that Liz was already unable, even when she was labouring under the greatest sense of betrayal and public humiliation, to rid herself of an obsessive concern for Dylan, as a mother might continually fret for a disobedient and forever truculent child. Nevertheless, her resolve did prevent her from actually travelling the short distance to Dylan's hotel, and her enquiry concerning some detail of the production satisfied, Liz went uptown to the Poetry Center office to re-acquaint herself with her much-neglected office duties.

Liz worked throughout the rest of the morning, but in truth little was achieved as, impotent in her self-imposed exile from Dylan, Liz worried constantly about his ability to manage without his keeper. This malaise continued until mid-afternoon when the continuing silence from Dylan and the limbo into which it had precipitated Liz was suddenly broken. Dylan called her, Dylan was indeed in trouble, Dylan had been drinking heavily and Dylan had decided that he now needed Liz 'terribly'.

Dylan had risen in the Chelsea with his girlfriend of the previous night but had rid himself of her in the course of the morning. Her name does not now survive and it is unlikely that it survived in the poet's recollections even the course of that one morning. Dylan immediately embarked on another drinking session, compounding its effects by refusing all food.

Curiously, Dylan now made his way uptown to the Algonquin Hotel, rather than staying in his more natural milieu in Greenwich Village and drinking in the White Horse. It is not clear now why Dylan should have strayed so far from his normal patch but by this stage it could have been part of a general dislocation on Dylan's part. For by now, the poet was clearly deeply deranged. Dylan had demonstrated a worrying unpredictability in his first few days in New York. Now, it seemed, he had lost his balance completely.

By the time Liz arrived, Dylan was already roaring drunk and thus must have been drinking from the time of her first phone call earlier that morning. Dylan had probably been drinking whisky since mid-morning. He had encountered an initial, token resistance on Liz's part that she join him but in the face of Dylan's entreaties, the long-suffering production secretary had agreed.

Liz discovered Dylan to be in the midst of some new drinking companions. The poet himself was downing one whisky after another, in quick succession, emptying his glass as soon as it was filled. He was fast becoming unhinged. Liz joined the group silently and observed Dylan's deterioration. Dylan hardly acknowledged her.

For some reason the conversation turned to war and Dylan suddenly plunged into a fantastical 'recollection' in which he spoke of his own experience of war, describing its horrors in ever more lurid detail. Dylan's manner soon became as violent as the horrors he described. Dylan, of course, had no direct experience of war and he had been refused entry to the army on medical grounds. He had spent the war years in London, writing propaganda scripts for film documentaries. Dylan's ever-fertile imagination was merely supplying its own imagined horrors.

There *is* a possible biographical source for these stories, as Paul Ferris has noted. In the war years Dylan and his family lived for a while in the seaside village of Newquay at a bungalow called Majoda. A Commando captain returned to the village from active service and discovered his wife on what he regarded as irritatingly close terms with the Thomases. This irritation was fuelled by what he felt was their condescending attitude towards himself.

One particular evening he believed that Dylan had ignored him in a Newquay pub, and another incident later that same night in which an inconclusive scuffle arose out of some unfortunate remarks, placed the soldier in a mood for vengeance. He had kept his weapons while on leave and had a considerable store of ammunition. At ten-thirty that night he decided to advance on Dylan and his companions in their rented bungalow. By now he was dangerously drunk.

The captain intended to shoot over the bungalow to frighten the Thomases but in his drunken state he misfired dangerously inaccurately. With Aeronwy, Dylan's daughter, and a friend's baby asleep in one of the bedrooms, Dylan found himself and his family under fire, bullets ripping through the asbestos walls of their rented home. It was a genuine miracle that no-one was killed. The captain then made a commando-like raid on the bungalow itself and burst through the front door with his stock of grenades now primed and ready. He loosed another magazine of shots into the ceiling and began raving at them. He called them all, improbably, 'egoists'. Dylan was reportedly the 'coolest of the lot'.

The Commando captain was eventually persuaded to abandon his attack and was later to be charged with attempted murder, though the charges were to be dismissed through lack of evidence.

Now, ten years later in New York, this incident appears to have been dredged from Dylan's memory and his deranged mental ravings had transferred the 'combat' in Newquay to a more traditional wartime incident in Turkey or the Middle East. Liz told Brinnin that Dylan's talk became 'disconnected, violent, maudlin and obscene'. The disturbance deep inside Dylan was becoming acute and Dylan's ravings were now beginning to attract the attention of other drinkers in the hotel bar. Liz attempted to restrain her ranting charge but without success. It was clear that there was to be no immediate end to this agonised and imagined outburst. Dylan now attracted the attention of the Algonquin waiters, recalling the first occasion on which Dylan and Liz met, when Dylan also incurred the disapproval of the Algonquin authorities with a spilled drink. Now a waiter was again despatched to Dylan's table in an attempt to quieten him.

The poet was by now 'helplessly gripped by his fantasy' and 'ranted on about blood and mutilation and burning and death'. In a last-ditch attempt to quieten him, Liz gripped his hand, tightly. Dylan immediately lost control and began to sob.

Liz's disapproval was easy for him to take. The simplest expression of kindness was not. John Brinnin has said that 'the briefest review of Dylan's emotional life would suggest that no man was ever more adept at killing what he loved, or suffered more in the consequence'. Back home in Laugharne, Dylan would frequently be assailed with guilt over his treatment of Caitlin and his family. Now, in the Algonquin Hotel, his guilt and inner torment revolved around his treatment of Liz Reitell, triggered by the simple act of Dylan's hand being held by the ever-supportive Liz. This new sobbing episode distressed the other drinkers just as much as the poet's earlier ravings, but this time Dylan's behaviour excited sympathy rather than the earlier disapproval and alarm. The waiter who had been sent to remove Dylan now told Liz, 'Take care of him. He is a good man.' The couple remained in the hotel for some time while Dylan made a recovery of a sort, and then indicated that he wished to leave the hotel bar.

Once outside the Algonquin, Dylan's behaviour became erratic again, perhaps triggered by the New York hustle. Dylan's actions were coming to assume, ever more insistently, the mantle of the deranged and disturbed. Liz was well aware that Dylan was not completely incapable with drink, yet he walked in a 'tottering lunging parody of drunkenness'. As people passed him in the street, Dylan made faces at them, goggling at them with 'gargoyle gestures' and swearing loudly all the time, unaware or uncaring of his public location. Dylan was beginning to be absorbed by and into the public persona of Dylan Thomas the renowned poet; the public persona he had first created in his early Swansea days and whose essential myth, carefully cultivated over the years, had preceded and confirmed him everywhere he travelled. Dylan was now beginning to lose himself in this myth, where before it had been a useful shield with which to deflect the curious and the inquisitive. The myth and the man were fast becoming synonymous. Perhaps Dylan was beginning to find it an easy answer to his new dilemma.

But even here Dylan could not sustain the role totally uncritically. Dylan's developed sensitivity soon clashed with his present boorish behaviour to produce one of those internal conflicts that always wracked the poet severely. The couple paused at an intersection on Broadway and this physical halt jolted Dylan into awareness. Dylan immediately became instead miserable and suddenly rational, aware of what he was doing and apparently overwhelmed by it. He turned to Liz as they waited on the New York pavement and said, 'You hate me, don't you?' His behaviour had burned deep into his consciousness and he attributed to Liz the only conclusion he expected she could reach. Liz's reply was characteristically pithy. 'No,' she told him, 'but it's not for your want of trying.' This remark calmed Dylan and his behaviour quietened, became less erratic, at least for a few hours. Perhaps Dylan recognised a characteristic trait: the attempt to hurt those for whom he felt deeply. Whatever chord it struck, the remark pulled him up short. For a brief period, there was a welcome respite.

But Dylan and Liz still had an immediate problem which was occupying Liz's thoughts all the time they walked from the Algonquin – how to spend the rest of the day. There was no performance of 'Under Milk Wood' scheduled for that day and no rehearsal which might break Dylan's present and self-destructive cycle of sleep and drink. But then, walking across the intersection at Broadway, Dylan suddenly spotted the movie houses on 42nd Street and immediately decided that he wanted to watch a film. Relieved that he did not want to drink, Liz accompanied him into one of the crowded cinemas, where they sat through a Micky Spillane gangster film and a Western. Dylan enjoyed both, so Liz recalled, 'hugely'. He relaxed, and became 'absorbed and delighted'.

But as Liz sat with Dylan in the dark theatre, it cannot have escaped her attention that once again she was absent from her duties at the Poetry Center and that she was with Dylan on the very same day she had resolved to stay away from him. Now she was trailing behind Dylan once more, firmly back where Dylan wanted her to the exclusion of all other demands on her time. Whether Dylan ever saw their relationship in quite those harsh terms is difficult to determine, but the fact remains that Liz had attempted to break with Dylan that very morning and one simple phone call had brought her back obediently into the fold. For Dylan, it was all as simple as that. For Liz, the day marked a turning point in her relationship with Dylan. Perhaps her own reactions and actions had surprised and scared her.

The entertainment ended and Liz found Dylan to be sober and more receptive to her advice. It was still only late afternoon and Dylan was at a loss what actually to do. His thoughts now turned once more to drink, but not to a roaring session, to a quiet and reflective drink that he and Liz could share together. Dylan's conscience was now indeed pricking him deeply and he wanted to make amends. He wanted to demonstrate to her that they could get back on the rails. His choice of venue was thus apt. He wanted, he said, to go to Goody's, one of the bars in the village that was not associated with any of the maniac times, but was a good and quiet place where the couple had spent many peaceful evenings together on the previous trip. After the excesses of that day and of the previous night, Dylan wanted to go there, he told Liz, 'in a spirit of reunion'. With hindsight, this may well have been Dylan's last genuine attempt to gain control over his own actions through a re-discovery of the essence of the relationship he had once shared with Liz.

But in Goody's, Dylan's anguish began to reassert itself once more. Dylan was now swinging from a settled calm to black despair. This drink in Goody's that was intended as a type of reunion became instead 'one of the most piercing, the most serious of our moments together'.

Liz was constantly discovering fresh layers to Dylan's internal torment where previously she might have believed she had plumbed the depths. Now it was the poet's developed and near-paranoid sensitivity that claimed her attention. 'Dylan's whole conscious time,' Liz has said, 'was like walking on your eyeballs. He had the thinnest skin I had ever seen.' This sensitivity directed Dylan's anguish inwards to a minute examination of his own emotional torment and led to another great outpouring on the poet's part.

Dylan spoke to Liz now of madness and of his own fears that he might be insane. Though she practised her now-characteristic role as Dylan-comforter, it has to be said that Dylan's fears were beginning to be shared by Liz. It would have been remarkable, in the light of Dylan's recent actions, had she not speculated on the poet's mental balance. Dylan's actions had scared even Dylan.

He told Liz that he feared there was 'something terribly wrong with my mind'. Significantly – after the previous evening's activities – he linked this mental instability with sex. Dylan asked her if she thought it might be some sexual imbalance. Dylan's sex life had always been active, of course, though not perhaps quite as active as he himself was wont to claim. In his early adulthood, Dylan had been ripe and open to any kind of sexual experience and this even extended on one occasion to a homosexual experience with the painter Max Chapman, though the scope of that encounter was strictly limited. Indeed, Chapman has specifically decried the sexual basis to their friendship. 'My own experience,' he has said, 'was really based on one boozy evening, the first when affectionate physical expression went beyond accepted bounds and physical contacts of a kind were reciprocated. All we ever did was feel under the table and some french kissing. You wouldn't say he was a queer, but he wasn't averse to being affectionate to his own sex if he found them in some way interesting.'

Dylan's early poems were replete with sexual energy of a type that spoke of his tender inexperience and it is quite possible that Dylan was still a virgin at the age of nineteen in morality-conscious Swansea. Later, of course, life was rich with sexual possibilities and there is a great deal of evidence that Dylan took advantage of them all, though as his wife was also taking advantage of those same possibilities that in itself is not so remarkable. But Caitlin was taking advantage of these sexual possibilities in an entirely different spirit to Dylan – almost in a spirit of revenge. Dylan hurt Caitlin through his sexual adventures and she set out to pay him back. Thus sex had become a battlefield between Dylan and his wife. It is possible that Dylan's philandering with his Sutton Place hostess the previous evening was an unconscious way of attacking Liz Reitell and John Brinnin for their apparent abandonment of him. The next day – as with so many 'next days' back in Britain – remorse was eating away at him.

Dylan's thoughts continued to run on this 'sexual imbalance'. Returning from a cigarette machine a little later, Dylan spoke of his disgust at a couple kissing in an adjoining booth. The Dylan who, just a few hours earlier, had been sprawling with a romantic hostess on a party floor in full view of the assembled company, now told Liz that he found such public expressions of private affection to be 'filthy'. Liz's breath was taken away, largely because of that very dislocation.

An amazed Liz told Dylan that he spoke like a 'Puritan' and this acted on Dylan quite remarkably. He was in any event in a highly introspective mood, bordering on a fascinated obsession with himself. 'Yes,' he told her, as if he had just grasped an immutable and highly charged truth. 'Yes. I *am* a Puritan.' But Liz was not interested in the poet's ostensibly significant statements about himself. She was far more interested in the deeper answers to Dylan's difficulties and in discovering the real causes of his current instability and irrationality. Liz had suffered the whole of the previous evening through an anguished conversation about Dylan with Brinnin and she was now desperate for some professional help. As she had earlier urged Dylan to consult a physician for his physical ills, so she now urged the poet to consult a psychiatrist to probe his mental anguish. Liz could no longer control her lover's behaviour, nor her own, and the instability that Dylan was exhibiting ever more insistently was communicating itself to her more forcibly all the time. She was beginning to find it impossible to deal with Dylan in any way that preserved her own psychological integrity, and perhaps now she wished to shift that burden from her shoulders alone. But her insistence was having an unfortunate effect. She was now backing Dylan into a corner when the poet would have preferred to speculate dreamily on his own internal complexities. Dylan agreed with everything that Liz said, but he agreed far too quickly and far too abruptly for this to carry any real conviction, or for Liz to be reassured that he actually intended to do anything about it. Before Liz could press him further, Dylan told her that he must leave the bar, that he could not stay there 'a minute longer'. It seems that he could not endure 'a minute longer' her assault on his reluctance to help himself.

The couple made their way out as the bar clock struck midnight. It was now 27 October, 1953, Dylan's thirty-ninth birthday, and perhaps therein lies one clue to his depressed and occasionally deranged behaviour of the whole of that last trip.

Dylan's thirty-ninth birthday was a particularly poignant occasion for the poet. Caitlin has always said that her husband wished to end his life before he was forty. This youthful bravado had now caught up with Dylan and that fateful birthday was now firmly in sight. Perhaps on the very eve of that age, Dylan had remembered his careless boast and had felt a chill wind blowing from the other side of middle-aged decline.

Dylan stepped out from Goody's and towards a waiting cab. As he climbed in, a young man approached as so many had approached Dylan in the past and asked if he were Dylan Thomas. The young man was a fan, and Dylan stared at him. Taking the silence for confirmation, the young man launched into an 'explosive paean of hero worship'. He ended the exposition by asking for Dylan's autograph. All the time he talked, the incident was working strangely on Dylan. Perhaps the boy's adulation was an uncomfortable reminder of his past poetic skills and a further reminder that perhaps now they had deserted him for ever, just when he was approaching one of his most prestigious assignments – the opera project with Stravinsky. Dylan listened to the boy's outpouring and then, leaning on the window, wrote 'Dylan Thomas. October 1 birthday'. As he gave the autograph and its message to the boy, Dylan told him that he was really only posing as Dylan Thomas. It was a typical throw-away Dylan remark, perhaps just a bit of fun. But this time Dylan meant it. By now his belief in himself – on a personal and professional level – was at an all-time low. Liz escorted Dylan back to the Chelsea – the events of the previous few days had warned her against taking absolutely anything for granted – and then left him in the hotel. Dylan promised to phone her the next morning.

The night passed without any contact from Dylan. The poet

was beginning to sink lower and the spirit to defy even his own best interests was beginning to desert him. For there was at the least a defiance in his earlier drinking sessions, in his wilful flouting of the medical advice offered by Dr Feltenstein and the advice offered by Liz Reitell and John Brinnin. When Liz telephoned Dylan at the Chelsea the next day, Dylan was safely there.

It was now Dylan's birthday morning and Liz returned to the Chelsea to share a quiet breakfast. Dylan was again a changed man, this time from the self-destructive fiend of the previous day or two, and no more acute indication of that change can be seen than in Liz's decision to spend the day working in the Poetry Center office, trusting Dylan to his own devices. He was still ill, it was true, but Liz was comforted by her past experience of Dylan's illnesses. 'No matter how ill, how desperately low he had been perhaps half an hour earlier,' she has said, 'he would do this flip side sort of thing. I wasn't burdened with thinking about it all the time because these were times of joy, times when Dylan seemed to be just fine. And that always made me hopeful ... would restore my hope that he was going to be OK. That he was going to be able to get out of this pit.' Liz probably checked on Dylan during the day, but Dylan seemed to have spent it quietly preparing for the birthday party that had been arranged for him that night.

This party was to be held at the apartment of Rose and David Slivka, two friends of the Thomases, though Rose was an especial friend of Caitlin. David Slivka was a sculptor and Rose was then a budding journalist and author and the couple had met Dylan on his first visit to the US. Characteristically, Dylan had propositioned Rose but she had resisted the invitation with humour and equanimity.

The relationship deepened during Dylan's second visit, with the introduction of Caitlin to Rose. Rose Slivka, perhaps in sympathetic identification herself, came to feel for Caitlin in her role of 'artist's wife'. The two women struck up an immediate friendship and they became devoted companions. Rose would be the one American to whom Caitlin would turn when the events of that very last trip took their fatal twist, and the sympathetic identification that Rose Slivka felt for Caitlin would acquire an added intensity during the manic events surrounding the last few hours of Dylan's life.

Caitlin had described Rose Slivka as 'my little valiant Rose, my special close friend'. She 'had the gift of the chameleon, she coloured herself from head to foot in my mood of daft distracted irresponsibility'. Her husband David was described as 'wise'. They were a good choice of host for Dylan's birthday celebration and they had indeed invited all Dylan's American friends, those friends that would celebrate the occasion with sensitivity and with genuine warmth rather than those who would embrace yet more indiscretions or lapses of behaviour on the part of their guest of honour.

Liz Reitell has stressed Dylan's eager anticipation of this event. 'All his closest friends in New York were invited and he looked forward to it enormously, so did I. This would be a marvellous occasion.' And even if the day had not started that well, 'there was always the possibility, the likelihood even, that he would suddenly bounce back, just rise out ... and have a good time.'

Liz joined Dylan at the White Horse at six. Howard Moss, Dylan's journalist friend from the *New Yorker* had arrived at the Chelsea too, around late afternoon, to buy his friend a birthday drink. This was Dylan's first drink of the day and when Liz arrived he was clearly sober. But he was also clearly ill. More friends joined the trio at the White Horse, many in eager anticipation of another roaring session with the original roaring birthday boy. But Dylan, with Liz watching carefully, did not respond. Howard Moss left the sober and quiet Dylan after a couple of drinks and Dylan and Liz left for the Slivkas' party. Dylan liked the Slivkas' apartment. Then, as now, it was in the heart of Greenwich Village – the area of New York that Dylan liked best – and it looked out over the Hudson River, once more taking Dylan back to his early Swansea days with its homely dockside setting. An elaborate dinner had been prepared by the ever-hospitable Slivkas and the guests invited to celebrate the occasion had already arrived. With Dylan struggling in the White Horse a few blocks away, the stage was set for the disaster that followed.

Dylan and Liz left the White Horse in the company of some of the invited friends who had gathered for the pre-party drink. But their arrival at the party, instead, as Liz hoped, of galvanising Dylan into action once more, now only deepened his wretchedness. He was · unaccountably nervous and ill-at-ease, though just why he should have been so nervous in the midst of well-known and well-liked company is now difficult to see, other than as yet another particular and irrational symptom of the general malaise affecting Dylan.

The poet did not enter into the general conversation, he did not drink any of the refreshments eagerly proffered and he did not partake of any of the dinner that had been laid out on the tables that lined the living room of the Slivkas' small apartment. Again the company only seemed to depress Dylan and it is impossible to speculate on what demons the gathering was summoning to Dylan's anguished mind. 'Dylan', as Liz said, 'could only stay at the party for a little over an hour. He just couldn't bear to stay.' Dylan suddenly announced to the concerned and somewhat devastated company that he had to leave and that he had to leave immediately. He could not now stomach the scenes and the friends with whom he had enjoyed amusement and easy distraction. He wished to be alone, he wished to be left to his own devices and be abandoned to his misery and his grief, unspecified though it was. He now seemed to wish to contemplate that inner mental state, undistracted by the friends who might attempt to deflect him.

When his hosts and the rest of the party guests realised that Dylan was indeed truly wretched and was truly unable to continue with his allotted role as party guest of honour, David Slivka offered to drive both Dylan and Liz back to the Chelsea, where Dylan could rest. Dylan and Liz duly climbed into the Slivkas' car and were soon speeding back uptown to 23rd Street while the somewhat deflated party continued to struggle in the wake of the principal guest's unexpected absence. And as Liz sat in David Slivka's car driving through the New York night, she was becoming uneasily aware that Dylan's illness had taken another downward turn. Deep down she had retained a great faith in Dylan's ability to rescue himself – presumably some of Dylan's innate belief in the artist as escapologist had worked its effect on her. But this time, for the first time, the escapologist had not struggled out of his trap. This time the trick had not worked. The implications for Liz, with the suffering poet complaining loudly and miserably beside her, were deeply worrying. Thirty years later she was to reflect that Dylan's birthday party 'marked the beginning of the last days in a formal sense'.

David Slivka dropped Dylan and Liz at the Chelsea and then drove back to try to rescue his party. Dylan made straight for his room without even a look at the hotel bar and fell immediately upon his bed. He began to complain loudly and obsessively. His obsession was his current malaise, whose causes now seemed myriad.

There seemed first to be his age. Dylan spoke volubly and eloquently of the 'awful occasion of his wretched age'. The 'declining years' of mid-life were clearly weighing on him heavily. There was the guilt of the last few days and as Dylan flung himself on his bed his self-pitying cries revolved around the 'filthy and undignified creature' he had become. Dylan was sinking further and further into the pit of his depression and Liz recognised the dangers keenly. Dylan had not been able to lift himself from that pit earlier in the evening and it seemed now that he was going to have trouble lifting himself out of it at all.

Liz's attitude now changed, modified by her new grasp on the innate dangers of Dylan's depressive obsession. Her counselling, she now felt, was not just to be comforting in its principal effect, it was to be stimulatory. Dylan had to do something to help himself. So Liz began to speak – not out of her normal sympathetic communion and 'not gently this time' – 'but out of a grief and impotence to which his alternating gestures of self-destruction and appeals for loving attention had brought her'. Liz in truth was tiring of her role as nurse and aware that nothing she had done while assuming that role had halted the deeper slide in her lover/patient. It was now time for a more direct approach and a more drastic course of action.

Liz began to chide Dylan, almost haranguing him, belabouring him with his apparent inability to do anything to help himself. The atmosphere in the room quickly deteriorated. Dylan might be content to wallow in his depression, pointing out to the world his inadequacies, but he did not particularly want anybody else doing the same and he certainly didn't want to embark on the infinitely more difficult task of actually attending to his recovery. The atmosphere grew tense as Dylan, grim and bitter, listened to the harangue until finally he could stand it no more. Dylan suddenly shouted at Liz to stop, to stop haranguing him, just to *stop*.

This confrontation very nearly achieved what had not been achieved throughout all Dylan's sometimes deliberate, sometimes unconscious treatment of her up to that point. It very nearly drove the couple apart. Liz recalls being 'deeply hurt' by Dylan's outburst, more hurt even than in the aftermath of the Sutton Place debacle. In that instant, perhaps, Liz caught a whiff of the domestic tensions between Dylan and Caitlin back home in Laugharne. For his part, perhaps Dylan felt his relationship with Liz to have come dangerously close to his stormy relationship with the fiery and determinedly unsympathetic Caitlin, and had no wish to travel yet again along that well-worn road.

Liz stood up abruptly and made to leave. She headed for the door and told him 'All right. I'll go.' The relationship between the lovers teetered on the edge of oblivion until Dylan looked across as Liz was about to pass through the door and mustered as near to an apology and an appeal as he was able. 'That won't help my agony,' he told her. So Liz stayed.

Not that averting this crisis seemed to help Dylan a great deal. Liz's decision to remain simply provoked another bout of tears and self-pity. Liz, now alternately determined and overwhelmed, attempted to comfort him. It seems that the ghosts of Dylan's home life were now paramount in Dylan's mind. While Liz comforted him, Dylan spoke of Caitlin and his home in Laugharne. As with many egotistical artists, Dylan always felt that it was inconceivable that anyone in the world could be happy on such a night of personal agony. 'I know she's crying too,' he told Liz. In times of trouble, Dylan's thoughts always turned back to home and to Laugharne. In times of peace and plenty, in the time of his deepest security in Laugharne itself, his thoughts had always turned to escape.

The evening dragged by in much the same vein, with Liz unable to raise Dylan from his real or imagined malaise. Dylan, it seemed, was becoming set on his downward spiral and Liz was not able to risk another potentially catastrophic exchange. The evening was punctuated only by one phone call, from John Brinnin. He was telephoning from his Boston home, at a safe distance from Dylan and from the pressures surrounding the poet.

Brinnin had telephoned to give Dylan his birthday greetings on what Brinnin imagined would be a happy occasion, though why Brinnin should phone Dylan's hotel rather than the Slivkas' party is difficult to see. He should surely have known that on his birthday, of all days, Dylan would hardly have remained virtuously ensconced in his own hotel room. Perhaps Brinnin still felt the unease he had carried into Grand Central Station that night of the Sutton Place party. If Brinnin was experiencing a continuing unease, he was to have that concern confirmed by his phone call.

Dylan, John Brinnin recalls, could not raise his voice above a whisper and Brinnin immediately sensed that Dylan was either ill or drunk. Brinnin tried to lift his friend with an affectionate greeting and by his conventional birthday wishes. But Dylan either could not or would not respond and Brinnin's greetings died on his lips. Dylan seemed 'far away', he has recalled, 'he was out of connection'. Brinnin doubted if Dylan even knew who was calling. Brinnin's impressions here added another dimension to Liz Reitell's concern. Dylan, so it seemed to Brinnin, was not only deeply depressed, he was beginning to lose contact, he was beginning to lose even the most basic abilities to hold rudimentary exchanges. By the time Dylan had completed his mumbling and incoherent conversation with Brinnin, the silent Liz too had registered this new development. Sitting in Dylan's hotel room that night with the poet incoherent and in near-hysterical tears, Liz felt indeed that Dylan's problems had now assumed a far more alarming shape.

From this point on, even though Dylan would make engagements, even though he would fulfil many forthcoming duties in New York and even though there were still some good times to come, some 'peaceful, nice moments', everything was to become progressively more difficult for Dylan. It would all now become more of a 'hardship', Liz Reitell has recalled, and it was all to become more of a struggle for those charged with the task of directing Dylan to his various assignments and duties. 'Everything became more difficult for Dylan', Liz has recalled. 'Getting to a party, for a meeting, to some prearranged event just became increasingly difficult.'

But the picture was not quite so simple as all that. The general trend might be downward but there were individual revivals that may have been of short duration but which did flare and which confused those around Dylan. There were moments of hope as well as stretches of doubt. There were episodes of calm as well as incidents of depressive complaint, often following one on the other. These 'revivals', in distracting attention from the general downward trend, made the later calamity all the more shocking in its seemingly arbitrary and unexpected quality, where the more keen-eyed observer might have seen that calamity as the final act in an inevitable fall.

One such 'revival' took place the very next day. Dylan was scheduled to give a lunchtime reading at the City College of New York and had a later appointment with the Cinema 16 group who had involved Dylan in that great afternoon drinking session earlier in the trip. They were now to involve Dylan in the more official side of their dealings with their symposium on film art.

Dylan, of course, had demonstrated an interest in film from his schooldays in Swansea in the 1930s and indeed had written several articles on film for his school magazine back in the Swansea Grammar School. During the 1940s Dylan had found regular employment for the only sustained period in his life when he was engaged in writing film scripts for the 'War Effort'. But despite his clear interest in, and experience of film, Dylan still seemed a curious choice of guest, given the poet's renowned antipathy to academic 'intelligent' conversation. The signs were not promising, and with Dylan's illness hanging over from the previous evening, the portents began to look disastrous.

Dylan had arisen that morning marginally recovered. He had slept at last, having exhausted himself in his anguished ravings. When he awoke he made clear his intention to complete his day's engagements. This decision was one that was heartily encouraged by Liz Reitell. Liz now believed that a more robust embrace of his duties would certainly provide one key to Dylan's troubles. To that end Liz left Dylan alone while she travelled to the Poetry Center office. Perhaps subconsciously she was relieved that Dylan would be engaged semi-officially for the majority of the day and thus the

107

responsibility of looking after him would fall on other shoulders. But she must also have known that a drinking session would inevitably result, as drinking sessions always resulted from Dylan's engagements. And indeed it did.

Dylan acquitted himself adequately at the City College and indeed now appeared reasonably recovered from the wretched creature of the previous evening. He even seemed to have become imbued with a new and uncharacteristic tendency to husband his resources – he travelled to uptown Manhattan by subway as he told Liz that he wanted to save money. Perhaps the City College itself had infected him with a fresh awareness and appreciation of money. The City College of New York has a reputation for being the 'proletarian Harvard'.

The engagement was a lunchtime reading and the meeting was well attended. It is not a matter of record what Dylan read, but given his lack of time and preparation it is likely that he delivered his usual repertoire of standard Dylan works together with a pot-pouri of works from other favourite poets. He had travelled across the world with the show and there would have been no reason to change it for that one lunchtime engagement in Manhattan.

The lunchtime reading over, Dylan and his new drinking companions moved on to a nearby restaurant for a celebratory party. Here the more promising signs continued. Dylan was drinking only beer and not the whisky that he claimed caused him all his problems. He was also conducting his conversations normally and there was little trace in his bearing or demeanour of the abject self-pity he had hugged to himself throughout the previous night.

Perhaps Dylan had briefly set aside his malaise at the thought of his fateful thirty-ninth birthday and the brooding presence of the much-dreaded fortieth. Perhaps he was feeling the deeper responsibilities of middle age and was acting accordingly. Or perhaps he had no wish continually to scare himself. Whatever the reason, Dylan's ability to flip himself back into normal gear appeared to assert itself once more, though it has to be said that he still exhibited worrying additional symptoms that hinted at a less than complete recovery.

Dylan spent a quiet, settled afternoon in the company of his

new drinking companions and returned reasonably sober and in
fair health to the Chelsea around early evening to prepare for
the symposium on film art later that same night. This was to be
a prestigious occasion, Dylan's fellow participants were Arthur
Miller, the experimental film maker Maya Deren, Parker Tyler
and Willaard Maas as moderator. A delegation from the group
called on Dylan at the Chelsea to escort him to the session.
Perhaps they half-anticipated a reprise of the drinking session
many of them had enjoyed with Dylan a few days previously.
Or perhaps they had been somewhat alarmed at the ease with
which Dylan would abandon his current work (the 'Under Milk
Wood' text) and be distracted by any diversion. In any case,
they clearly decided it would be safer if they escorted Dylan to
the symposium themselves.

The delegation escorting Dylan was just leaving the Chelsea
when Liz Reitell called back from her day at the Poetry Center.
She was relieved to find Dylan comparatively sober and
relaxed, particularly as he was now in the company of those
friends she had herself ejected from Dylan's hotel room earlier
that same week. But this relief turned to concern when Dylan
gave Liz only the vaguest and most perfunctory greeting. She
had the disturbing impression that Dylan did not even
remember that they had arranged to meet. Dylan may have
seemed more settled and more calm but he was exhibiting a
worrying tendency to be swept along by whichever group of
people happened to pick him up. Dylan was moving in a state
of non-responsibility for his actions, much as a rather retarded
child may submit himself to the will of the adult world. Liz,
somewhat subdued by his vague and unconnected greeting,
accompanied the group to the symposium.

Here again, Dylan's powers of recovery asserted themselves
once more, especially as the symposium afforded Dylan the
opportunity for some fine observations and some acute fun.
The fellow panellists were serious and interested practitioners
of the performing arts and keen to offer challenging insights
into the nature of film and its importance. Dylan was mainly
interested in poking fun at these pretensions, particularly the
more obscurely baffling pronouncements of Maya Deren. She
spoke of the 'vertical' nature of poetry and the 'horizontal'
nature of drama and Dylan immediately made some obvious

and somewhat schoolboyish jokes about 'up and down' movements, to the great delight of the audience, who were beginning to warm to the Welshman in their midst and to his irreverent comments on the serious subject under review. Dylan was now playing his much-practised and much-appreciated game of needling the intellectuals. Dylan expressed 'incomprehension and alarm' at the sophisticated notions proffered by his fellow panel-members.

Dylan did speak briefly and apparently seriously about his own view of poetry in the cinema. He said that this poetry occurred 'in the UFA films or something I saw as a child. Or somebody coming down some murderous dark, dark street silent apart from the piano playing, or it might have been that little moment when Laurel and Hardy were failing to get a piano up or down a flight of stairs. That always seemed to me poetry'.

The chairman of the Symposium, Willaard Maas, did not allow Dylan to get away with so simple a statement, but pressed him further. The poet, somewhat self-consciously, embarked on a stumbling explication of his own poetic theory and the relationship of poetry to the cinema. 'As in a poem', Dylan said, 'one image breeds another, I think in a film it's really the visual image that breeds another – breeds and breathes it.' Dylan here was reaching back to the seeds of his own poetic inspiration, to Laugharne and to Wales and to the visual and natural images that fashioned and sustained his own poetry and which constituted its creative force.

But Dylan did not allow himself to teeter on the edge of profundity for long. He picked up on Maya Deren's distinction between vertical and horizontal art and told his audience, 'I'd rather see horizontal films myself. I like stories. You know, I like to see something going on.' This genuine if somewhat unsophisticated statement again elicited laughter and applause from his audience. Dylan the showman knew how to get his audience on his side, and later in the session he was to win them over completely.

Willaard Maas had desperately been struggling to fulfil his role as symposium moderator, as the man who controlled and directed the discussion and who ensured that all aspects of the study were covered. He remarked that in his opinion no-one had yet introduced a consideration of 'love' as a factor in the cinema. This was too much for Dylan, too good an opportunity to miss. With an innocent expression and eyes too wide he turned to Maas and announced 'Oh Willaard! I didn't know you cared.' The rest of the discussion disintegrated as the audience collapsed in giggles at the mock-innocent Welshman who was so successfully rescuing the symposium from itself.

It broke up soon after, and Dylan, with a group from the session, including Liz, retired to the White Horse. Dylan was fired by the meeting and buoyed by what he regarded as a personal triumph during the discussion. He was back in the driving seat, in a new and improved mood and a more buoyant physical state. The session in the White Horse duly turned into a particularly sweet evening after the pain and anguish of the previous night. It was all fitting, of course. The White Horse, Liz has recalled, was not a place that was 'connected with any of the dreadful times'. That night was no exception.

The party, enlivened by the common experience of the occasionally-ridiculous discussion, was riotous, and Dylan continued in his accustomed role of court jester and anti-intellectual. He asked Liz, who was, and remains, an artist of no small distinction (and who indeed earned a professional living in this field as a designer) to sketch the recent discussion group for the amusement of the assembled company. One such portrait survives and is particularly apposite. It shows Dylan insensible on the floor squinting at the audience while a collection of typically bearded intellectuals sit at the table immediately above him.

Dylan did, of course, sketch himself, and while his 'were not too well-structured artistically', Liz has recalled, 'they did have a certain charm.' Curiously, Dylan's drawings always seemed to centre around artistically 'innocent' themes and subjects – a girl scattering cotton, or very small birds, or a small dog. Dylan worked hard on these sketches, but he preferred Liz to draw for him.

Dylan passed the night's caricatures around the company and delighted in them. The party continued with similar innocent enjoyments and Liz's confusion was nearly complete. The man who, less than twenty-four hours previously, had been lying on his bed, wracked with his own internal anguish and telling Liz that he could not possibly continue, was now king of all he surveyed and was holding his own kind of court, in control of his surroundings and completely at ease with himself.

For the moment Liz simply relaxed and revelled in Dylan's new-found wit and humour. Responding eagerly to the poet's demands for fresh sketches and thankful that some key – whatever that was – had at last unlocked his private misery. In retrospect, of course, Dylan's moods were too volatile but hindsight had not granted Liz the benefit of second sight at that stage. For now, Dylan's highs were gratefully accepted and his lows regretfully tolerated in expectation of hope of better times. In the White Horse that night, Liz was aware that the 'flip side' had worked once again.

The night actually seemed to have done Dylan a lot of good. He rose the next morning in the Chelsea well and in relatively buoyant spirits. He was even drawing lessons from the moderately paced drinking session in the White Horse the previous night and vowed to Liz, who had spent the night with him, that from that day on he would drink nothing but beer. She was heartened and gratified by Dylan's new resolve.

She was not to know that there was another cause behind Dylan's new high spirits, over and above the success of the previous night. While Liz was preparing to leave for a day at the Poetry Center, Dylan was preparing to leave for another rendezvous with his 'refugee countess', and for another amorous sojourn with her at Sutton Place. Liz Reitell had left Dylan in the Chelsea on the strict understanding that he would be working on the publication draft of 'Under Milk Wood' for the magazine *Mademoiselle*, for whom Brinnin and Rollie McKenna had been working when they visited Laugharne earlier that year. But Dylan sneaked out of the Chelsea the second Miss Reitell's back was turned. As in his Swansea schooldays, when something remotely more interesting afforded itself, the immediate work in hand was quickly abandoned. The publication draft could and would wait.

Dylan met his countess for lunch and then both retired to the Sutton Place apartment a few blocks away. Dylan might retain a deep affection for Liz Reitell, just as he remained in love with Caitlin back home in Wales, but he wasn't about to lose any opportunity for some easy fun.

The afternoon rolled on and might have continued into the evening had Dylan not already arranged to meet Liz for a dinner date that night. She had spent the day in some concern about Dylan's continued physical recovery. She was not to know that, for that afternoon at least, she need have no worries.

Liz met the refreshed poet early that evening and they went on to a dinner party given by mutual friends: Cyrilly Abels, editor of *Mademoiselle*, and Jerome Winston. The other guests were the Indian writer Santha Ram Rau and her husband. For once the protagonists and the party was congenial to Dylan and he 'participated warmly in a political discussion'. He had little grasp of politics but his vague and woolly socialism would usually go down well in generally liberal company. Later Dylan amused the dinner guests by telling a fund of ghost stories, supported in his storytelling by Miss Rau. Dylan was forever fascinated by the occult and many of his own short stories derived from the folk and ghost tales of Wales. The evening was easy and fun, it was light and comfortable. All in all, the night ended with general good-humour and in general good spirits.

Chapter Seven

Within His Head Revolved a Little World ...

But in truth, the previous day had done little to help Liz in any real sense. She was now deeply confused and most disturbed. She had witnessed Dylan in the depths of depression and despair and then, twenty-four hours later, watched him conduct himself with verve and dash as the life and soul of a roaring crowd and as a relaxed and conversational guest at a Manhattan dinner party. She had seen Dylan deeply ill and wretched and, twenty-four hours later, had seen him restored to the point that no other companion would have suspected that there had ever been anything amiss with his health. He would concentrate obsessively on the work in hand, and then ignore it completely when she left him alone for more than a few hours. She could leave him in the Chelsea one day and find him stupified and incapable with drink on her return. The next day, under precisely the same circumstances, she would return to find him sober and professionally concentrated for the task ahead. Dylan was fast becoming a mass of puzzling contradictions to Dylan's friends, and to Dylan's latest lover he was becoming such a morass of internal tensions that she was finding herself totally unable to cope. She was reduced simply to accepting the good times and enduring the bad.

Liz could not really be blamed. She had had little in the way of any deep experience of Dylan. She had suffered with him through the pain of producing 'Under Milk Wood' and had discovered a love affair between two kindred souls. But she had been totally unprepared for the man who flew back to New York that October. Liz's increasing tendency to leave Dylan alone during the day may have been all part of a continuing instinct on her part to stay away from the poet and to join him only for what she hoped would be a calm evening. She seems to

114

have been backing away from her more disturbing role as Dylan protector, falling back into the more simple state of innocent lover enjoying herself with her new flame and trying to set aside the pain, anguish and heartache of this second trip. It was an answer to her deep confusion and, for the time, the most attractive.

Liz again left Dylan alone the day after the Manhattan dinner party and went to work at the Poetry Center arranging to meet him for another dinner date that same night. Dylan was off to spend another day with his countess in Sutton Place.

But even here matters were becoming complicated. This relationship had changed somewhat on the woman's part, if not on Dylan's. Dylan found his new lover in a far more determined frame of mind. He had anticipated another easy day with his new, glamorous Manhattan playmate, but she was after something rather more committed from the poet now. There is an unconfirmed and rather fantastic-sounding tale from John Brinnin that the countess actually asked Dylan to marry her, and indeed it is just possible that the woman had floated the improbable notion that Dylan divorce Caitlin, leave his three children and settle with her in New York. Dylan, of course, would have run a mile from any such idea, as the shrewd Miss Reitell knew. Liz for her part never attempted to pressurise Dylan into any such action or even suggested it. Dylan needed Caitlin in Laugharne, as he needed Liz in America, and Liz accepted that situation with resignation and grace and did not attempt to force the pace of an already difficult relationship.

Dylan's Sutton Place hostess did not have such insight into Dylan's real inner needs and when Dylan arrived that day she was not content to simply please the ever-eager poet, but wished to place their relationship on a more personally satisfying level. There is every indication that the idea horrified Dylan. He was later to tell Liz that he resolved that very day to see no more of her. Dylan did not object to easy liaisons but his emotional life was complicated enough without his actively embracing any fresh difficulties. He did not want them and he did not need them. His serious affairs were expressions of insecurity and he had found all the security he required, and more, in the capable Liz Reitell. He simply did not need the more emotional Sutton Place hostess.

Thus Dylan spent his day in the midst of a highly uneasy fencing match.

Liz, on the other hand, spent her day in work. Liz had arranged to meet Dylan and Herb Hannum in the White Horse at six, before joining Ruthven Todd, an old friend of Dylan's from London who had settled in New York. Ruthven had arranged a small party for Dylan that night. But when Liz arrived at the White Horse she found Dylan in the company not only of Hannum but also of the Sutton Place hostess. The sight of this latest romantic attachment could not have helped the pre-dinner atmosphere. Dylan, ever-sensitive to mood, was deeply uneasy. He was already suffering the agonies of a one-sided withdrawal from his relationship with the countess and was desperate to escape from yet another difficult situation into which he had precipitated himself. The early evening drink became yet one more painful charade, during which Liz and Herb Hannum watched the poet attempting to dispose of yet another disappointed lover.

The conversation limped on, the atmosphere continually strained. Everybody present began to concentrate on the impending departure for the party at Ruthven Todd's. All the present company, with the exception of the countess, had been invited, and Dylan would either have to leave without her or break his date with Ruthven Todd and the rest of the White Horse party.

As events turned out, the countess made the first move. Before the party began its preparations to leave, she asked Dylan to come back to Sutton Place for dinner, including Liz and Herb Hannum in the invitation. The wretched Dylan mumbled his decline, pleading the excuse of the Todd party. He did not suggest that the countess accompany them and the slight was deliberate. It was obvious that the countess felt it immediately. Looking round at the stony, embarrassed faces, she recognised a hopeless situation. Leaving the others embarrassed and awkward, the woman went home.

Dylan, Liz and Hannum went on to the Todd party. Once again a rebuffed woman had retreated in pain from Dylan's company as Dylan relieved at having made his escape,

accompanied friends to a place of refuge to forget the damage
he had inflicted.

That night's host, Ruthven Todd, was well aware of Dylan's
various weaknesses with respect to women and to drink. He'd
witnessed at first hand Dylan's erratic conduct of various
affairs during several years of friendship in London and Wales.
The trustees of the Dylan Thomas estate clearly felt that he
possessed a special insight into the poet's affairs, as Ruthven
Todd was their first choice as Dylan's official biographer,
though he was later to withdraw and leave the task to the
novelist Constantine FitzGibbon. In all probability Ruthven
Todd had been well briefed by Liz Reitell on Dylan's current
state of health and general instability and was equally well
aware of how to handle his old Welsh friend. It is one of the
minor tragedies of this last trip that Ruthven Todd was not
able to take a more personal charge of Dylan's affairs during
the last few days of the poet's life.

When the somewhat subdued group turned up at Ruthven's
apartment, Dylan was still feeling himself under attack over his
relationship with the 'Sutton Place inamorata'. Liz was
understandably hurt by the continued demonstration of
Dylan's easy ability to jump from lover to lover. Hannum was
still overly protective in his feelings towards Dylan and
ever-mindful of the chilling conversation he had conducted
with the poet in the Chelsea.

But Ruthven Todd, aware of the atmosphere, and
immediately sympathetic to Dylan's ambivalent mood, handled
the trio and the entire evening with consummate skill. First he
deflected Dylan's drinking. On arriving at Ruthven's door,
Dylan had announced his immediate desire for 'whisky', and
the stage was set for the most blindingly drunken night of the
whole trip. But Ruthven Todd was determined that this should
not take place at his apartment. He simply, and with great
charm, refused to serve Dylan whisky and handed him instead
a glass of beer.

Dylan was then propelled from the makeshift bar and into
the middle of the party guests. This occasion was not the great
celebration that his birthday party had been. It was a small
intimate gathering of perhaps fifteen people, and without the
prospect of having to play yet one more major performance,

117

Dylan began to relax. Todd subtly moved the increasingly controlled poet from one guest to another, engaging him in carefully-chosen conversations that centred around writing and prose, conducted not by academics but by its practitioners. These exchanges were easy and free from pomposity and Dylan took part with little more than a glass of beer to sustain him. Dylan soon began to enjoy himself 'hugely'. Away from the schoolroom atmosphere of his college encounters, Dylan relaxed into conversations and company of the type that he might have avoided like the plague in more formal settings.

All the time this was taking Dylan's mind off his obsessive concern with his own health and his poetic abilities and submerging it in a more reasoned and more general concern with the world of literature, to which the poet had dedicated his life or at least his more serious moments. The party lasted an entire evening and there were no lapses on Dylan's part and no abrupt attempts to leave on account of ill-health or depression. To the watching Liz Reitell the score was now two good nights out of two, and that was a significant victory after the scene she had anticipated just a few hours earlier when she walked into the White Horse to find Dylan with his countess in tow. Herb Hannum was similarly reassured, as were Ruthven Todd and his guests who had gathered in a spirit of interested friendship rather than a fascinated concern with the poet's excesses. The night had demonstrated that given the right conditions Dylan could control himself. The task for Dylan's friends was thus clear, and Ruthven Todd demonstrated that lesson for all to see. Dylan could be steered back on to the right course given the right handling. But Ruthven had to demonstrate that lesson only for one night. His other friends had to attempt to reproduce those ideal conditions every minute of the poet's waking days.

The party broke up naturally and late – not prematurely and unhappily – and Dylan, now in cheerful mood, invited Hannum and Liz back to the White Horse for a nightcap. That nightcap continued in the same easy vein and the night ended peacefully. Dylan had come up again for air and was gulping it healthily and heartily. His head and heart seemed clear once more.

To Liz the next day, the puzzle continued. The night had

passed untroubled and peaceful and Dylan suffered no relapse into dependency or depression. Perhaps then, the upset of the previous few days was just a temporary aberration on Dylan's part.

The very next morning Dylan received a phone call that continued the healing process. A mutual friend of Dylan and Liz's called, one of the very best people Dylan could have met after the hugely beneficial Ruthven Todd party. Dylan had stayed with this friend and her husband on one of his previous cross-country tours.

Dylan was delighted with the call, and insisted she meet Liz and himself for a luncheon date that very day. He wanted a small and intimately congenial party and it was soon clear that he also wanted it to be as 'special' as possible. Dylan was not the kind of host who wished to impress by ostentatious display. But on this occasion Dylan wanted to have lunch at Lucklow's, one of the grander establishments on Manhattan.

The party duly met at the Chelsea and moved on, Dylan delighting in the reunion and in the luncheon party. The afternoon passed pleasantly with the Welsh poet wooing his two girls in his most charming manner. Little pressure was exhibited on Dylan's part, and little concern was aroused inside Liz.

But there was one disturbing factor, though Dylan was hiding it well, Liz, though so attuned to his mental state, had missed it too. While Liz and her female friend tucked heartily into the piles of dishes before them, Dylan was hardly touching a thing. He was only picking at the various dishes and was making only a show of hunger. Had his two companions only known it, Dylan had been eating next to nothing for the past few days. His steady diet for some time past had been raw eggs and beer; enough to sustain him on a basic level but hardly enough to allow him to function more effectively. Dylan may appear to have made an effort over lunch in Lucklow's, but his recovery was still far from complete. The signs of future trouble were bubbling just beneath the surface.

The luncheon ended with no break in the general good humour and good spirits. All three guests felt disinclined to end the happy reunion and Dylan proposed that they go on to Costello's for an afternoon drink. Costello's on Third Avenue was one of Dylan's earliest haunts in New York and the bar he had first visited in the company of his original American protector, John Malcolm Brinnin. Liz eagerly agreed. She wanted to stick close by the poet. Once again, the lesson that the right circumstances produced the 'right' Dylan seemed clear. It is just possible, though Miss Reitell has never admitted it, that she herself had arranged the phone call from the mutual friend and planted the idea of a luncheon date to prevent the poet having another dangerously free and indolent day in New York. Whatever the truth, the trick worked. Dylan's time was now being filled with all sorts of distractions designed to lead him away from any kind of trouble.

But once in Costello's, the outside world intruded again. Another of Dylan's friends, Harvey Breit, called on the party to take Dylan to a dinner date. This disturbed the good atmosphere and might have been thought to be one of those unfortunate coincidences without which Dylan would have continued to function reasonably and normally. But the meeting was too pat to be a pure accident. Dylan had presumably arranged to meet Breit in the Third Avenue bar and had proposed that the lunch party move on to Costello's in order to keep that engagement. Liz had not been told about it. The very fact that Dylan could appear so totally absorbed in her company while making plans to leave it, hinted at a worrying ability to dissemble in front of even keenly observant friends. Dylan might appear to be recovering but he may simply have been successful in projecting a convincing public face. The rest of the night was to confirm that much of Dylan's 'recovery' up to that point had been merely a rather successful act. For the night soon degenerated into disaster.

The rest of that night in fact would have been a complete mystery, had it not been for the existence of a private detective from *Time* magazine who was now, improbably, following Dylan around New York. The roots of this unlikely occurrence stretched back to Dylan's previous trip. A *Time* article painted a profile of Dylan that was in fact rather harmless. Dylan's drinking, his unreliability, his propensity to borrow from any and all friends were all highlighted, but the piece was still essentially laudatory in tone and admiring in effect. However, Dylan had not liked it at all. The most 'offensive' section of the article read, 'When he settles down to guzzle beer, which is most of the time, his incredible yarns tumble over each other in a wild Welsh dithyramb in which truth and fact become hopelessly smothered in boozy invention. He borrows with no thought of returning what is lent, seldom shows up on time, is a trial to his friends and a worry to his family.' The tone was schoolmasterly and admonitory rather than investigatively sharp and attacking. But when Dylan returned to Britain with the offending article in his pocket he instructed his Swansea solicitor, Stuart Thomas, to sue the magazine's publishers, Time-Life, for libel.

Dylan's motives here were unclear. The article did little more than report Dylan's behaviour at some of his roaring sessions and there can be no doubt that on occasions that behaviour warranted the descriptions in the article and often a great deal more. Anyone who knew Dylan in America or in Britain would have recognised the portrait with a wry smile. But Dylan decided he was outraged by the allegations. He was appalled, he concluded, by the slurs on his reputation. It should be said that there was one potentially damaging and unwarranted implication in the article: that of unreliability. According to John Brinnin that was definitely misleading and false. Any reputation that Dylan might have had for unreliability was, again according to Brinnin, a fallacy. 'Dylan met 99% of his engagements', Brinnin has said. 'He was incredible, and the one time that he refused to make an appearance ... I never heard the end of it ... the reverberations were as if this happened all the time and it didn't.'

Brinnin, however, was aware that there might have been a degree of substance in the rest of the Time-Life article, though that acknowledgement was cautiously phrased. 'If, incidental to these tours, certain incautious remarks were made or certain kinds of behaviour exhibited, it wasn't taken as scandalous, it just meant that Dylan was alive in a way that a lot of poets weren't.'

But to Dylan there was little of substance in any of the article, or at least nothing that he wanted publicly to acknowledge. Certainly on the question of reliability, Dylan still hoped to earn a good living from the lucrative American lecture circuit and he did not want the influential lecture agents having their deepest misgivings confirmed by an article in a widely-read and widely-distributed popular magazine.

There was of course another motive for this libel suit. Under American law, a successful suit could profit the litigant by some thousands of dollars. American libel suits are notoriously unpredictable affairs and the prospect of immediate easy money would have been heady to the impecunious Dylan. So Stuart Thomas issued a suit for libel against the prestigious Time-Life Corporation and their article of 6 April, 1953.

For their part, Time-Life did not take this suit well. They clearly regarded the article as mild and relatively innocuous in relation to the behaviour of its subject. But they very quickly decided that there might be potential here. Dylan's life and activities made good copy. Here was a chance, in the legitimate defence of a libel action, to wring yet more sensationalism from their initial story. Time-Life decided to defend their story by embellishing it. They hired a private detective to trail Dylan around New York and to report on the poet's 'excesses'.

Time-Life couldn't lose. If Dylan chose to continue his court action, the resultant material would have the case laughed out of court. The events of the previous few days alone would have provided enough material for a veritable series of articles each more lurid than the last. If Dylan had thought about the action at all deeply he would have realised that. It is likely that Stuart Thomas himself realised the flimsy basis to Dylan's suit and would have been aware that at any time any fresh misdemeanour on Dylan's part could sabotage his defence further. But Dylan was implacable. So Dylan found yet another figure watching his every move in New York.

It is not clear exactly when the Time-Life detective began his pursuit but it is certain that he was on the poet's trail as Dylan left Costello's that evening, full of the afternoon's good spirit. He left with Harvey Breit, promising faithfully that he would return to the bar to rejoin Liz and her friend after the dinner date. Liz and her friend then separated and spent the rest of the evening alone, though in mutual expectation of a continued good time when they met Dylan again later that same evening. At eleven p.m. both Dylan's afternoon companions duly returned to Costello's for the anticipated reunion. But Dylan didn't show.

The only news that Liz was later to dredge from Dylan about the events of this 'missing night' was a deeply disturbing item – that in the midst of the poet's confused recollections one memory was clear: he had ejected a woman from his moving taxi, having 'taken a dislike to her face'.

For the full facts of this missing night which were scarcely less dramatic than the ejecting of unwanted women from Manhattan taxi cabs, the notes of the Time-Life detective must be employed. Dylan left for the dinner party with Harvey Breit but the dinner does not seem to have lasted long. He had intended to travel directly back from the dinner to Costello's but at 9 p.m. Dylan, in the company of his erstwhile birthday host David Slivka, a young American friend called David Lougee, and two other companions, arrived at the White Horse. Harvey Breit was not present.

By the time he arrived Dylan was already drunk. When he had left Liz earlier that afternoon he had been comparatively sober. All indications are that Dylan had been drinking fairly seriously from the time he quit Costello's. Worse, Dylan's drinking was now more erratic as well as more voluminous than his previous consumption of beer. The *Time* detective noted that Dylan drank lager, whisky and beer in the space of just a few minutes in the bar, though even here myths surrounding the poet were multiplying: the *Time* detective was informed erroneously by one of the bar-side drinkers that Dylan had been drinking for ten days non-stop.

It was now well into Saturday night in Manhattan and Dylan was in the midst of his usual roaring crowd. He had swung easily and happily into his usual role of party clown and the signs were that he was set fair for an extended stay. As events turned out, he was only at the beginning of a prolonged drinking session.

More drinks were poured down the eager poet's throat as his date with Liz and her friend was completely forgotten. Dylan drank ever more erratically and in ever-larger quantities. Sometime during the evening, one of the company – perhaps David Slivka, keen to minimise the effects of too much alcohol – proposed that they all visit a nearby restaurant, Toppers on Seventh Avenue. Dylan was indifferent but the rest of the company enthusiastically agreed and Dylan was swept along.

The whole White Horse drinking party moved on to Toppers and – so David Slivka hoped – to some kind of antidote to the now-prodigious quantities of alcohol Dylan had consumed.

But Dylan was now beginning to turn maudlin. As so often in the midst of his roaring times, his thoughts were turning to Laugharne. To the tolerant amusement of the assembled company he began to speak of Caitlin and his family three thousand miles away. Dim and gloomy Laugharne was beginning to assume the golden status accorded to New York just a few months previously. Dylan told the company that other women were just a substitute for Caitlin, but he didn't now talk about her 'illumination' as he was to describe her to Liz Reitell. Instead Dylan talked about sex.

He moved on to talk about his first sexual relations (at the reported age of fifteen). Sex was always a source of both strength and weakness to Dylan; a subject of public boast and private indecision. That night the public boast took over and in graphic detail he reported the loss of his virginity in the back of a Swansea lorry. He also claimed that as a teenager he had caught gonorrhaea and that it had taken a month to cure. The status of both stories is extremely difficult to assess. Certainly there is no medical confirmation of the gonorrhaea story, though Dylan did say that he was forced to keep the condition from his family. But none of Dylan's closest friends recall Dylan having this condition – a state of distress that in the sex-starved Swansea of the 1930s would most certainly have conferred upon Dylan a certain status. 'We were after all, the masturbatory generation,' as Dylan's friend Mervyn Levy has recalled and it is unlikely that the ever-boastful Dylan would have kept entirely quiet about this rather exciting complaint.

Dylan's past of course had always been embellished with grotesque stories that had some small basis in fact but which were then twisted, and imbued with a personal application. Now his immediate company listened in a spirit of amused tolerance. All in all, it was not difficult to see why Dylan was being treated increasingly as the 'party clown' in New York. Dylan was once again retreating into public stories to bolster his private inadequacies and using his considerable gifts as a storyteller to boost his self-image in the most adolescent and schoolboyish fashion.

Perhaps Dylan himself felt that that night in Toppers. After a period of sustained sexual boasting, he fell silent. When Dylan spoke again, it was not to boast of wild misdeeds or childhood misadventures. All he really wanted, he told the assembled company, was to be regarded as 'an average human being'. In those last few days of his conscious life, it seemed that the life of the simple and uncomplicated family man in Laugharne, the life that could easily have been his, was uppermost in his desires. Dylan, of course, was not regarded as an average human being because he did not act like one. But the potential for that more settled life was within his grasp and one of the tragedies of these last days was his final realisation that the security he despised was the key to his artistic and personal well-being.

It is not likely that his statement was taken particularly seriously by his companions. The disparity between the Dylan of the American bar-room perception and the stable and settled family Dylan was very great. His statement may well have been taken as even more fantastic than the stories that preceded it. But Dylan meant it, though he had fallen so low and travelled so far that he could hardly expect to be taken seriously by any of those that surrounded him.

There was another and additional cause for concern that night. The *Time* detective's notes state that at 2.30 a.m. Dylan was still in the company of his friends. That is quite possible. The meeting with Liz Reitell had now been missed by over three hours and there is no reason why Dylan should have returned to the Chelsea. But that was not the problem. While Dylan was in the midst of his riotous gathering he was seen, according to the *Time* detective, 'taking Benzedrine'.

There is no other independent confirmation of this. None of the poet's other friends or acquaintances have ever recalled Dylan experimenting with drugs. It is possible that a harmless incident was being exaggerated by the detective in order to provide one more lurid tale for his employers. But it has to be said that the story is worryingly feasible too. It is possible that the drink with which Dylan bolstered his failing personality was being substituted in those last desperate days by a far more insidious agent. The detective's notes that night are exact in their record of the poet's movements and his intake of various refreshments. It is unlikely in truth that he would simply have invented the episode. It is just possible, then, that at the end of his life, Dylan was becoming ever more unstable and irrational.

The last entry made by the *Time* detective is for just after 2.30 a.m. It is likely, therefore, that the Dylan party split up soon after. It had, after all, been a long day. Dylan, in one form or another, had been drinking for some fourteen hours, and had possibly been experimenting with new and unfamiliar drugs. It would have been a miracle had Dylan been able to continue with this punishing pace. Now he travelled back to the Chelsea and it was on this taxi-ride back to Greenwich Village that the discarded woman was reportedly flung out of the cab. Dylan told Liz that he had taken an 'instant dislike' to the woman and had thrown her literally into the street because he could not 'bear her even a minute longer'.

This story worried Liz deeply but in truth it is deeply unsatisfactory. It is perfectly possible that Dylan had intended to take a woman back with him to the Chelsea. Indeed, it would have been surprising had the now-besotted and befuddled poet not been accompanied by one of the 'thieves of my love' as Caitlin had called them – the plentiful supply of young women who would eagerly embrace the opportunity to sleep with the famous and the rich. That part of the story is not difficult to believe and Dylan would have perceived no contradiction between his earlier statement of fidelity to, and love for, Caitlin and his taking another woman to bed later that same night. But the *Time* detective had been nothing if not professional. He had followed Dylan all over New York and had documented his movements copiously, noting every action and presumably delighting in every lapse from the straight and narrow. It is simply not feasible that the detective would not have followed Dylan back to the Chelsea, particularly if he had an attendant woman in tow. It is most unlikely that he would simply have hailed a cab and headed for home. Dylan, after all, had just been seen taking Benzedrine, and if nothing else, the detective would have wished to discover its effects upon the poet's already erratic behaviour. He would scarcely have passed up the opportunity to record yet more outrages.

Given that, it is equally implausible that the detective would have missed the undeniably startling sight of a young woman being hurled out of Dylan's taxi and into the busy New York streets. To a night packed full of incident, that incident with the woman would have been the icing on the cake. Overall, and in the absence of any confirmatory evidence, it has to be concluded that the incident did not take place.

Nevertheless, it was that incident, fictitious or not, that was apparently weighing heavily on Dylan's mind when a worried Liz phoned him early the next morning. He also had a hangover, a 'real horror', he told the solicitous Miss Reitell. Significantly Dylan plunged into his tale of mad night-time incidents and extravagant hangovers the second Liz's voice wafted over the hotel phone, which hints at the deeper motive behind this latest Dylan invention. At its simplest, Dylan knew that he was in for a row. He had kept Liz and her friend – the friend he had made such a performance of meeting once again – waiting in Costello's for a late-night appointment he had had no intention of making. The classic Dylan escape from trouble was into illness and had been, ever since his early childhood when he had quickly learnt the lesson that sickness and illness guaranteed his mother's protection from the harsh outside world. During his time at Swansea Grammar School Dylan was always excused from corporal punishment on the grounds that it might bring on his asthma. 'The greatest refuge of all' as Constantine FitzGibbon wrote 'was sickness, when anything was allowed the little boy'.

It worked again. Liz was ambushed by Dylan's vocal complaints and his frightening recollections. She immediately abandoned all thought of remonstration in her alarmed concern.

Liz herself was immediately unsure if the story was another Dylan fiction, but either way she was worried by it. If true, then the pattern of Dylan's actions had taken a dangerously erratic turn. To the ever-constant fear that Dylan may hurt himself was added the clear additional fear that he might inflict physical injury on somebody else, if he had indeed become uncharacteristically violent. It was possible that the emotional damage he had been inflicting on Liz and Brinnin for the past few days had now exploded into a more physical expression. The results could be catastrophic, if they had not been thus far.

But even if the story was untrue then it had worrying implications. It has to be said that Liz had an immediate and shrewd suspicion that once again Dylan had confused the present and the past and that he had again overbalanced into a drunken and confused 'recollection'. Liz herself had in a great hurry left a taxi that she had shared with Dylan after the disastrous Sutton Place party. She had effectively 'ejected' herself from the cab. It was just possible, as Liz was immediately aware, that Dylan had transferred that incident to the previous night and had cast Liz in the role of the troublesome woman he had thrown out of his cab. But even as that suspicion gripped her, it dragged a fresh implication in its wake. Dylan's inability to distinguish between past and present – between imagined and real events, as with his war ravings in the Algonquin – was a major cause for concern. But if Liz's deeper suspicions were correct, if she had somehow been cast in the role of the irritating and troublesome young woman that Dylan literally could not bear a minute longer, then what did that mean for their own relationship? Was the story prophetic in its hint of Dylan's deeper and perhaps half-submerged feelings towards her? The thought drove all thoughts of recrimination from her mind. When she replaced the receiver, Liz was concerned, worried and in a state of considerable agitation. Dylan, on the other hand, had achieved his objective once again. Potential trouble had been averted and now seemed likely to be totally forgotten.

Liz arrived at the Chelsea a little later and found Dylan once more in the mood for drink. He was still 'disturbed' from the previous evening's encounter, and whether it was true or not, it was again enough that the poet felt it to be true. He was agitated by the recollection and he 'wanted a drink'.

Dylan proposed that they go immediately to the White Horse and Liz found it difficult to object. Dylan clearly needed something and it was just possible, as at Ruthven Todd's party, that a simple glass of beer would be restorative. In any event Liz was now finding it difficult to impose her own confused thoughts upon Dylan. Her concern for his welfare and her indecision over the most effective means of help were rendering her incapable of constructive action.

Dylan and Liz duly gravitated to the White Horse, where

Dylan sat in the middle of yet another crowd of drinking companions and did indeed appear to recover a little of his usual equilibrium. He became relaxed, where previously he had been withdrawn and tense. He was now also lacing his glasses of beer with raw eggs, the first independent confirmation of his story that this had been his diet for some days past.

Lunchtime passed into afternoon and afternoon passed into early evening. During the course of the day the usual White Horse crowd had gathered, and Dylan's table was soon surrounded by the usual mixture of friends and hangers-on. Dylan had now gone eight to ten hours without food, and even if *he* could manage that, Liz Reitell couldn't. Whether for her own sake, or Dylan's, or both, she proposed that they all go on to one of the many restaurants that encircle the White Horse, and while Dylan did not embrace the idea enthusiastically, he did not object when the rest of the company supported the suggestion. Once more he allowed himself to be swept along by the rest of the hungry drinkers.

At the restaurant there was no indication of any fresh excess or indiscretion on Dylan's part and no record of his having conducted himself in any dubious manner. But there is no evidence that the poet ate anything, either. Whatever her intentions, Liz was not finding it easy to influence him in any practically beneficial way. At least Dylan was not volatile. But even here, even after such a Homeric performance the previous evening and after a full day's drinking on top of a 'real horror' of a hangover, Dylan had not had enough. He was still in no mood to retire quietly to the Chelsea and be nursed to sleep. He was looking for kicks, and in ever-active New York he soon found them. Before the meal ended, Dylan had inviegled an invitation to a further event that night – a party to which his journalist friend Howard Moss had been invited in one of the exclusive apartments on Central Park West.

As Dylan, Moss and Liz travelled uptown from Greenwich Village, Dylan's escort impressed upon him that this was to be a quiet gathering, and not the more usual roustabout that Dylan attended. Perhaps the news of Dylan's behaviour in Sutton Place had already done the rounds of his friends. Not that this warning did a great deal of good. From the time he stepped through the door of the select and salubrious apartment,

Dylan's behaviour degenerated alarmingly.

Dylan, of course, had been drinking all day and had eaten next to nothing. The combined effects had not manifested themselves thus far. But they were to make themselves plain now. As Dylan walked in through the door his eye was caught by a young and attractive dancer and he clearly decided, whether she was willing or not, that here was his sexual distraction for the night. The presence of Liz Reitell now seems to have been forgotten. Dylan began physically to pursue the unwilling young woman around the room with all the lumbering subtlety of a great bear.

Dylan had seriously mistaken his environment. This was not a party set up by another 'procurer'. Nor was this a celebration arranged in the poet's honour. Nor were the guests in any particular awe of Dylan himself. Dylan's increasingly clumsy lunges after the young dancer began to excite, not amusement and encouragement, but disgust. The dancer attempted gracefully to dodge the randy Welshman. She moved from group to group, hoping thereby that the poet would be shaken off the scent, but Dylan seemed unable to take the hint. Of course, he had frequently propositioned any and all women, so the pursuit was in a sense automatic, almost a reflex action. But this was not the normal Dylan pursuit, as soon became clear.

Liz Reitell has described the poet's behaviour here as 'messy and unstrung', and the description was apposite. Dylan began physically to stumble around the apartment after his quarry, who was finding it increasingly difficult to dodge him in the small room, just as she was finding it absolutely impossible to convince him that his interest was embarrassing and unwanted. It is possible that Dylan had become so used to easy victories in the States that he could not imagine a situation in which he was refused. But that is not likely. Not even Dylan was so egotistical as to refuse to admit occasional defeat. It is likely now that this new pursuit was but one more symptom of Dylan's instability. His mind had zeroed in on one point: the girl. All the usual proprieties, which he would normally at least have acknowledged, were disregarded. Dylan was finding it next to impossible to focus beyond the immediate.

Eventually the disaster that had been threatening for some

time duly struck. Dylan conducted the final stages of his pursuit so vigorously and so insistently that he bundled the unfortunate young girl to the floor of the apartment. The fall, so John Brinnin records, was no accidental stumble. It was so 'physically awkward that the young woman spent many weeks afterwards under medical care for a concussion'. (It should be said that this was not the first time that Dylan had conducted his drunken lunges with disastrous result. Gwen Watkins recalls an identical incident at a Cambridge literary party in the 1930s.)

Liz Reitell's feelings could not be imagined. All her tenuous theories about the 'right' conditions had just been blown to pieces in the space of that short episode on Central Park West. The party had been small and intimate, the gathering low key and quiet but that had had no effect on Dylan. Dylan's immediate surroundings seemed to have lost all relevance for him, and his actions were becoming ever more dissassociated and ever more distanced from the desires of his company and his closest friends.

Howard Moss, who was responsible for Dylan's disruptive presence at the party in the first place, quickly proposed that the Dylan party move on, a proposal that the rest of the gathering greeted with relief. Dylan himself did not protest, so it is possible that even he was aware he had overstepped the mark, and that it would be better to quit while his offences still fell short of actual murder. The Dylan group hurriedly left the somewhat devastated apartment and made their way to Howard Moss' apartment for a night cap, Dylan still being reluctant actually to return to the Chelsea. Sadly, the night's list of disturbing incidents was still incomplete. Already Liz had witnessed his lack of appetite, his physical onslaught on an unsuspecting young girl and his dulled mental responses. Now she was to witness his delusions too.

Howard Moss' apartment, while it may have been a little less elegant and exclusive than the apartment on Central Park West, was by no means a slum. Nevertheless, with the guests grouped around the room and Dylan sitting alone on the sofa, the poet suddenly stiffened. He sat rigid and stared at a point just beneath the apartment door. Music was playing gently in the background but Dylan's anguished voice cut through that and through the desultory conversation. 'I just saw a mouse,' he suddenly announced. 'Did you see it?'

Dylan's eyes sought Liz Reitell and then the rest of the gathering, which had now frozen, less in horror at the unlikely possibility of vermin in the apartment than in concern at the state of mind that could produce such hallucinations. Dylan persisted. 'It went under there,' he indicated, pointing towards the front door. Dylan was suffering an early version of what Liz was to later call 'the horrors'.

A silence descended on the gathering as the poet's crazed eyes sought them again and again, demanding a response. Liz was the first to react. It was obvious that no other guest had seen Dylan's 'mouse', and all shared her immediate suspicion that there had in any event been nothing to see. But Dylan's insistence was frightening in its intensity, and so vehement in its force that Liz felt an immediate and overpowering need to reassure him. She stepped forward and told Dylan that she had indeed seen the mouse too. If the rest of the guests were inclined to contradict her, Dylan's obvious relief was eloquent testimony to the humanity if not the accuracy of Liz's support and to the collective wisdom of their keeping quiet.

Dylan immediately relaxed and became more settled. He may or may not have seen a mouse but he did not want to add to his list of troubles the possibility that he might now be suffering delirium tremens. Liz was absolutely correct in not confirming this new tendency any earlier than was absolutely necessary.

The rest of the party, however, were not likely to indulge Dylan's delusions all night, and some diversion was clearly required. Like all good hosts, Howard Moss quickly stepped into the breach. He suggested to Dylan that he might entertain the party with a few readings, and supported by the enthusiastic requests of the rest of the guests, Dylan agreed. His choice of reading matter was made without hesitation – W.H. Auden.

John Brinnin has said that, to Dylan, Auden's later poems 'were the greatest of all modern poems and had become increasingly the models of what he himself strove toward'. Certainly Dylan's association with Auden went back a long way. In his early Swansea days Auden was one of the poets Dylan had read with his childhood friend, Dan Jones. When

Dylan embarked on his professional reading career, Auden was one of the poets he joined in a BBC broadcast from Manchester in England in 1938. It cannot be said that Dylan was in great awe of the older poet, however – for the BBC broadcast Dylan had demanded his rail fare in advance on pain of his own non-appearance. Over the years Dylan had written film scripts that rang with a distinctly Audenesque note, perhaps in deliberate parody. Nevertheless, the fact remains that Dylan used Auden's work continually in his American engagements and in many of his British engagements, and there can be no doubt that his regard for the poet was genuine.

This was now to be the last poetry reading that Dylan was ever to give and inevitably the list of his final readings is of some special interest. Among the poems that Dylan read to the small appreciative gathering were 'News for Delphic Oracle', 'Long Legged Fly' and 'John Kinsella's Lament for Mrs Mary Moore'. The last poem that Dylan Thomas read on earth was 'September 1, 1939'. This reading seems to have been accomplished and professionally competent, and Dylan, in his concentration on his performance, seems to have overcome his earlier messy and unstrung behaviour. The reading ended with nothing more dramatic than general applause and quiet acclaim.

Perhaps because he feared another outbreak of 'delusions', Howard Moss now suggested that Dylan and himself take the air on the terrace of his apartment. Dylan agreed and the two friends went out. It was said that Moss made his suggestion so that Dylan could inspect the last blossom of summer on one of Howard Moss' rose bushes. It is difficult, however, to see why Dylan – never an avid gardener – should have found that of any great interest and, if the story is true, then it was a singularly inappropriate suggestion. Dylan was overtly susceptible to any reminders of fading powers, and for a poet whose work was so closely allied with the natural landscape, he would hardly have welcomed the reminder that the natural world was preparing for its descent into aridity and winter. But whatever the motive for the balcony visit, it was on this balcony that Dylan was said to have suffered his most famous 'accident' of the whole tour. The still unsteady Dylan stumbled towards the rose bush in the half-lit darkness, bent to catch its last fragrance, and scratched his eyeball on a rose thorn. The pain briefly flared and Dylan drew back with a curse. The sensation then subsided and Dylan made no more of the incident.

It is noteworthy that there are no direct witnesses to this 'accident'. Dylan had his back to Howard Moss, while the balcony itself was lit only by the light spilling from the main lounge onto the terrace. If Dylan really had 'scratched his eyeball on a rose thorn', then it is likely that the pain would have been far more considerable and the effect more immediately apparent. An inflamed eyeball would even have burrowed through the anaesthetising effects of the drink Dylan had been consuming since lunchtime. It does seem that, once again, Dylan was playing his accustomed part to the full. The incident with the rose thorn, in any event, is a singularly apposite encounter for a poet as others have noted, certainly more romantically redolent than many of the more factually accurate accidents that Dylan had suffered in his youth. On one famed occasion in Swansea for example, the poet had been suspended by some older boys upside down in a bucket of lime; hardly the type of incident that associated itself with a sensitive poet. The rose thorn story was far better.

Dylan and Moss rejoined the main party indoors and the 'night cap' staggered on till 5 a.m. Liz then accompanied Dylan back to the Chelsea and stayed with him for the remainder of the night. It was still not beyond the bounds of possibility that Dylan – despite the fact that he had been drinking solidly for seventeen hours – could have become involved with some of the late-night drinkers in the bars around Greenwich Village, ever willing to start afresh with the visitor from Wales.

The next day Dylan was, unsurprisingly, unwell again. He now had another huge hangover from the previous day's drinking and his eyeball, he claimed, was throbbing badly from the previous night's encounter with the rose bush. He was, however, in a relatively stable state mentally. He never left his bed all day, and demanded that Liz nurse him for the duration, but he was able to entertain visitors throughout and kept them amused with witty and acerbicly lugubrious comments about his own physical distress.

Among the visitors that day was Ruthven Todd, who has recalled Dylan drinking beer only. There was a bottle of whisky on the bedside table – Dylan's favourite brand, 'Old Grandad' – but this was unopened. Dylan's hangover seemed to be such that he had no desire to consume more of its principal agent, for the time being at least. Besides, all the time Liz Reitell was watching him like a hawk.

By early evening the poet had achieved a 'semblance of normality'. He was not only beginning to feel better, he was starting to feel like getting out and about. The inactivity of the day had repaired his immediate physical distress but now it was becoming counter-productive. As his mental concentration became less engaged with his improving physical state, so he came more and more to contemplate his mental anguish. He would have welcomed any diversion.

As things turned out, there was an engagement that night to which he had been invited, the unveiling of a statue of Sir Thomas Lipton by the sculptor Frank Dobson at the nearby Wildenstein Galleries. Dylan suddenly decided that he wanted to go. Liz instantly opposed the idea but Dylan was absolutely insistent and, as ever when Dylan absolutely insisted, Liz found it enormously difficult to withstand his determination. It was only later that Liz would fully realise that Dylan only ever followed her instructions – or anyone's instructions – when that counsel coincided with his own desires and intents. The objections to Dylan venturing out to another engagement were various. Most particularly, the gathering would inevitably end up in some bar or restaurant and Dylan would once more drink, while a few short hours earlier he was vowing that drink was the cause of all his troubles and that he would not drink again.

Less importantly, but no less practically, Dylan now had no clean clothes. His laundry had not been attended to for some days past and he now had no clean shirts or suits appropriate to the occasion. But this last objection was easy to overcome. On one of his roustabouts around Greenwich Village one of his drinking companions had persuaded Dylan to buy a cheap and ill-fitting suit from a late-night bargain emporium. The fact that he cut a ludicrous figure in the shapeless, baggy garment did not prevent Dylan from immediately donning it to stand by the hotel door like an instantly happy schoolboy who has found the means to have his treat after all. Liz was aware that if

135

Dylan was prepared to do all this, he would not be dissuaded from attending, and she reluctantly agreed to accompany him, if only to minimise the potential damage.

Dylan thus made the engagement, albeit cutting a strange figure in his ill-fitting cheap suit, his soiled shirt rescued from the hotel laundry basket, and no socks. But Dylan's behaviour excited no comment. Though Liz held herself in readiness the whole time to steer Dylan out of trouble, he seems to have relaxed, content to let another take the limelight, and exhibited no desire to impinge himself – as he had the night before – on the common attention. The ceremony over, the publicist Ben Sonnenberg (who had originally arranged Dylan's invitation) invited Dylan and Liz for a celebratory drink at the rather fashionable Colony restaurant. Famous faces then, as now, seemingly counted for more than their ostensibly curious apparel.

In the restaurant Dylan began to drink once again, but he was clearly not intending immediately to re-embrace his role as Welsh clown and womaniser, much to Liz Reitell's personal relief. Indeed, the poet acquitted himself competently in the elegant dinner-table conversation and appeared at ease in the grand surroundings. Liz watched him closely, grateful for the outward stability but uneasily aware that there was a deeper disquiet behind the Dylan facade and fearful that it would once more claim him.

Dylan, however, still ate absolutely nothing, and there is no evidence that he had eaten anything during the whole of that bedridden day.

The party began to approach its close when Dylan spotted the famed Southern novelist William Faulkner at a nearby table. While there is no record of Dylan having read Faulkner voraciously – as he certainly had read Dickens – there were enough intriguing similarities between the two artists to suggest that a successful friendship would have issued. Faulkner was an innovator in his field, as Dylan was an innovator of a different type in his. Faulkner, moreover, had been tempted into the lucrative Hollywood film world as Dylan had been inveigled into the smaller British film world and Faulkner had subsequently combined an artistically interesting career in novel-writing with a financially lucrative and extended spell in the commercial world of Hollywood movies. Dylan could have learnt a great deal from the old Southern master.

Perhaps Dylan felt that, too. On this occasion he was able only to exchange the briefest of greetings with Faulkner before accompanying his departing party but he told Liz that he hoped Faulkner and he could have 'a real conversation' one day. But for now there was no time to talk. From that time on, sadly, there was destined to be no time left.

Dylan now announced that he wanted to go on to Costello's, the scene of his missed appointment with Liz and her out-of-town friend a couple of nights before. Perhaps again Dylan wanted to revisit the bar in a spirit of 'reunion'. The choice of bar, in any event, coupled with the less than riotous day, was significant. Dylan was not looking for a rousting time.

In Costello's he asked Liz yet again to entertain him and the rest of the gallery guests with a few more cartoons and Liz, delighting in Dylan's enjoyment of apparently innocent pursuits, eagerly agreed.

The healing process continued. The evening ended with Dylan proposing that they all buy food from a nearby delicatessen and take it back to the Chelsea for a midnight supper. Again this was all music to Liz's ears and she eagerly supported Dylan's suggestion. In that brief instant she may have dared to hope that Dylan's famed 'flip side' was finally beginning to assert itself. The group left Costello's and headed into a nearby delicatessen where Dylan bought 'huge' quantities of food. The stage was set for a typically British midnight feast.

Back at the hotel Liz set out to prepare the food for a late supper. But perhaps it would have been better had Dylan been able immediately to eat. In the short time it took to prepare the simple meal Dylan lost his appetite. As the food was placed before him Dylan suddenly announced that he could not possibly eat it and he ended the evening consuming nothing more substantial than a bowl of soup.

The revival was thus clearly not anywhere near absolute. The night ended, not on the anticipated high note, but on the familiar depressed and low note that was coming to characterise all of Dylan Thomas' days. The party split up soon after and he retired to bed.

The next day was 3 November 1953 – a fateful day for Dylan and a fateful date in this tale. It was also an important day in America. November 3 was Election Day, though that would hardly have interested the politically naive Dylan. Though he fashionably embraced Communism in the 1930s, Dylan's political commitments were always imperfectly focused and naively conceived. He professed a woolly socialism that would not have stood up to any but the most superficial scrutiny. In his letters to friends in the 1930s, Dylan seemed to decry politics as a distraction for the artist and an exercise which led to propaganda rather than meaningful artistic activity.

Now with election day in the US upon him, Dylan's comments upon the whole exercise were caustic. Dylan once more began to receive visitors as he lay in bed in the Chelsea, one of those visitors again Ruthven Todd. Todd noted that the bedside bottle of 'Old Grandad' was still unopened. Dylan was still not succumbing to the early morning shot while he was in the company of the ever-vigilant Miss Reitell. This bottle was to be opened later that day, but only for the refreshment of the maid who arrived to clean Dylan's room. Dylan was always willing to play his role of ever-hospitable host.

Ruthven Todd, Herb Hannum and Liz talked with Dylan throughout the morning in a conversation that was constantly punctuated by the poet falling asleep. As the afternoon approached, Liz told the company that she was going off to vote, a prospect that Dylan viewed with the utmost cynical hilarity. Dylan even sought actively to dissuade Liz from travelling to the polls but she was adamant. Perhaps Dylan had now come genuinely to regard politics as an irrelevance; it will be remembered that when he arrived in New York he was quite prepared to break a union picket line at the Idlewild bar until restrained by the politically more sophisticated Miss Reitell. Or perhaps by now, Dylan had come to resent anything that was not specifically connected with himself.

Liz left for the polls in the company of Ruthven Todd. Herb Hannum also left the Chelsea for a short time and that short absence was enough. By the time Liz returned to the Chelsea Dylan had been visited by three more drinking companions, and another riotous drinking session was under way.

The implications were now more than usually catastrophic. Dylan was in danger of upsetting not only his constantly fragile health, but his very future. Later that day Dylan was to meet the lecture agent whose offer of a lucrative trans-American tour had been one of the primary reasons for his undertaking the trip. The sight of the drunken poet stumbling around his bottle-laden hotel room would have confirmed all the worst stories about Dylan's reputation and could easily have led to an immediate cancellation of the whole venture. Dylan was threatening the very lifeline on which his future fortunes and thereby his future equilibrium hung.

Liz swept into the assembled company like a veritable whirlwind and despatched them with even less ceremony than the unfortunate visitors from Cinema 16. The drinking group stumbled out of the hotel room while Dylan cheerily waved them goodbye. Dylan probably anticipated Liz's reaction and would have been aware that inevitably this latest session would be of short duration. He then fell immediately into a deep sleep while Liz cleared the room of all offending evidence and banished the lingering smell of alcohol and cigarettes.

The lecture agent arrived an hour or two later. In truth the lecture agencies were just beginning to realise that they had missed a prize in Dylan Thomas. The attraction of such a public personality on the lecture circuit would be considerable – and certainly would have proved powerful enough to offset any stories about his unreliability. In any event a little original research would have shown a determined lecture agency that this reputation was undeserved.

For Dylan's part, the attraction was also considerable. It was true that Dylan would have been moving away from his smaller and more intimate college audiences but he had little affection for the academics who made up the bulk of his listeners. Dylan would read to anyone, so long as the fee was right. And in these instances the fee would indeed have been exactly right.

It did not take the lecture agent long to play his most compelling card: should Dylan agree to the lecture the agency would guarantee earnings of one thousand dollars per week, undertaking to make up any shortfall should the sum fall below that figure. One thousand dollars a week was a fortune in 1953 – as John Brinnin reflected thirty years later, it was a not inconsiderable sum in the 1980s. More than the specific figures it meant that Dylan held within his grasp the ability to resolve his financial difficulties once and for all. He could finally, as John Brinnin has said, lift himself out of the 'humiliating position of having to point out what the house needed, what the children needed, he could have moved into some kind of dignity, at least on a financial basis'. Brinnin further had no doubts whatsoever that this is just what Dylan wanted. 'Maybe he didn't want to hear that,' Brinnin has said, 'but I doubt it.' Thirty years after the event Brinnin stopped for a second in his recollections and then emphasised his keen insight into Dylan's true desires. 'There was a deep bourgeois element right in the heart of Dylan,' Brinnin averred, 'and Dylan would deep down have liked a life that he despised.' On the very edge of oblivion Dylan had been offered the one lifeline he had sought throughout his adult life.

There is a sense in which the meeting with the lecture agent may however have complicated the picture. First, the strain such a series of engagements would have imposed upon his time and his ability to concentrate single-mindedly on his opera assignment with Stravinsky would have been considerable. Secondly, Dylan also may have realised that he was now committed to spending even more time in the United States, and by implication more time away from Laugharne, from Caitlin and his family.

The possibility that Dylan may indeed have signed himself into another trap just as he was celebrating a form of release, is given credence by his immediate reaction to the agent's visit. As the agent left he lay back on the bed, not exultant or even relieved, but 'inordinately depressed'. He insisted that he could not keep that night's engagements – a cocktail date with Santha Ram Rau arranged in the light of the successful dinner party – and fell instead into a deep sleep. Liz made no move to persuade or dissuade him. She was still holding on for the ride.

Dylan awoke an hour or so later and once again his now-characteristic volatility had reasserted itself. He felt marginally better and with his mental energies disengaged from contemplation of his physical ills, he once more craved distraction. He announced that he now wanted to go to the Santha Ram Rau party and Liz simply agreed. She had decided that there was now little she could do but accompany the roustabout poet; though in truth he seemed in little mood for any more drastic behaviour.

Dylan drank only moderately at the Rau apartment and appeared to enjoy himself hugely playing with the hostess's young son. Perhaps the boy recalled more settled times home in Wales and the little boy of his own that Dylan would never see again, Colm.

This cocktail date lasted only a short time and Dylan then announced his intention to visit the sculptor Frank Dobson at his hotel. This had been pre-arranged in the light of the previous successful evening at the Wildenstein Galleries and the Colony restaurant. Again Dylan acquitted himself with decorum and none of the other guests would have suspected there was anything amiss. But Dylan could only keep going for so long. It had been intended that the Dobson party visit a Broadway theatre to see 'Take a Giant Step'. But at the very moment of departure, Dylan suddenly announced that he could not possibly go. Liz, now accepting all the poet's decisions with a resigned fatalism, did not try to persuade Dylan, and the couple made their excuses to the Dobson party and headed back to the Chelsea. Weariness of body and spirit had suddenly overtaken Dylan. He now wanted a place of refuge, a place of safety. He wanted to return to the comfort of a mother's arms.

The short taxi-ride intensified Dylan's sudden collapse and as he stumbled onto his hotel bed he fell into another sleep, apparently exhausted, that in its immobility approached a form of paralysis. Had that situation continued and had he been able to sleep off his distress, events might have turned out very differently. As it was, Dylan's mental anguish, whatever form that might now be taking, was militating against any normal repose and his periods of unconsciousness lasted a regrettably short time.

Yet again, in times of deepest trouble, Dylan's thoughts were returning to Laugharne. The prospect of separation from Caitlin raised by the lecture agent's offer and the echoes of Colm wafted across the Rau apartment by their little boy were too much, and in the first few moments back at the Chelsea, Dylan's conversation was foreboding.

As he threw himself on the bed his physical distress had clearly proved too much for him. He told the increasingly alarmed Miss Reitell that he had now 'had enough', that he now wanted 'to go to the Garden of Eden', that he now 'wanted to die'.

The 'Garden of Eden' was, of course, a particularly apposite symbol for Dylan to employ. Phillip Burton had remarked on the 'Garden of Eden' aspect to his 'Two Streets' idea the month previously in London. But there the BBC producer had used the phrase to describe a theme in occasional opposition to the poet's usual poetic preoccupation: that life is stronger than death. Dylan was employing the metaphor now in its opposite sense. In the Chelsea Hotel on that 3 November, the emphases were reversed. He wanted, he told the appalled Liz, to 'die, to be forever unconscious'.

But even as he spoke the image of the small boy in the Rau apartment was floating up from Dylan's subconscious. Jerking back and forth between sleep and tormented consciousness, he told Liz that he 'adored' his little boy back home in Wales. Thoughts of his family were once again returning him to a more reasoned state of mind. However, it all brought a fresh anguish of its own. From his conviction that he was about to die and from his apparent embrace of that conviction, he now swung again to an abhorrence of the prospect. Dylan told Liz that he couldn't bear the thought that he wasn't going to see Colm again and he told Liz further that his family 'didn't deserve this'.

He had swung back again. Liz, now deeply disturbed asked Dylan, 'He doesn't deserve what?' Dylan's answer was matter-of-fact and deliberate. 'He doesn't deserve my wanting to die.' As Herb Hannum in the Chelsea Chop House, Liz didn't know what to say. Dylan paused for a few seconds and then emphasised once again, 'I truly want to die.'

But even here, in the depths of his anguished disintegration, Liz still insisted that Dylan was not actively embracing his own demise. 'He had a death wish', she agreed, 'but he also had a life wish. He was ambivalent, but the life wish actually was stronger and I think if it hadn't already been too late in a medical sense, that he would have gone on a regimen.'

Dylan once more began to talk of Caitlin and Laugharne.

Again trouble was leading Dylan back to his original security and that night confirmed Liz in her belief that in the end Caitlin would always prove the strongest pull. Liz was robbed of any illusions about Dylan's true fidelity, if she had dared to harbour them. Dylan was always 'spiritually faithful' to Caitlin, she has acknowledged, though she was to add wryly that this 'didn't mean that he couldn't be spiritually close to someone else too.' Even in the throes of her most intense rivalry there was an acknowledgement on Liz's part that Caitlin was always going to win. 'There is an illumination about Caitlin,' Dylan told Liz. 'She shines.'

· But for now all thoughts of rivalry were far from Liz's mind. Her task was simple and overpowering in its urgency and magnitude. It was left to Liz, alone in the room with Dylan, to convince the raving poet that his life was not automatically coming to an abrupt end, that his destruction was not preordained. Liz gripped Dylan's hand and tried to convince him, if only by the force of her insistence. His end was not approaching, as Dylan clearly felt, with the inexorable pace and ruthless steadiness of some giant express train. He had the means to frustrate it within his grasp. He could lift himself once more from his self-imposed pit.

But Dylan seemed no longer able to accept this truth. The escapeologist was lost in contemplation of his own trap and had seemingly forgotten how to escape it. Told by Liz that he did not have to die, that he could rise again if only he chose to, if only he would stop his ceaseless assault upon his own mental and physical self, Dylan began to weep uncontrollably, as if in recognition that such a prospect was beyond his reach.

At last he fell into fitful sleep, emerging into consciousness only for more agonised outbursts about his own approaching end. For her part, Liz simply sat and waited, unable to influence the poet's thinking but hopeful as ever that the outbursts would burn themselves out and leave a restored and reasonable Dylan in their place. She was aware, deep down, that at some point the restorative process might not take place and a more reasoned Dylan might not emerge. At this stage, however, she was not to know that such a time was most definitely upon them.

Chapter Eight

Before We Mothernaked Fall ...

Dylan kept to his bed until 2 a.m. the next morning. He could sleep only fitfully and when he woke his talk was agonised. His body continually tossed and turned. It was clear to Liz, looking on, that there was to be no rest for either Dylan or herself that night. There was, in fact, to be no peace or rest for her for the next five nights. She was not to know then, though perhaps she was dimly to suspect, that Dylan would soon embrace his own peace. Dylan was a soul in torment, seeking release. That release was tragically close at hand.

Under normal circumstances Dylan would have remained in the Chelsea until his bouts of depression had burnt themselves out. But that night the pattern changed. Dylan could find no peace in the security of the Chelsea and could not remain in his retreat as he was wont to do in times of pain. His usual self-protective instincts that had served him so well through so many adventures appeared to desert him, and instead of remaining in his place of safety until the crisis had passed, Dylan suddenly reared up from his bed and announced that he had to, just had to, have a drink. There was a now-familiar insistence in his tone and Liz observed him with a sinking heart. Once more there was little she could do. She was aware that once Dylan was out in the New York night, the potential for self-damage was enormous. But she knew that now, as ever when Dylan really wanted something, he would prevail.

Not that she abandoned all efforts to dissuade Dylan from leaving the room. There is some evidence that she even attempted physically to restrain the poet from rising from his bed, and the tussle seems to have lasted some time. But Dylan was desperate and Liz was merely scared. He manoeuvred past his nurse and the only scrap of comfort Liz could extract from the situation was a vague promise that he would be back 'in

144

about half an hour'. He just wanted air, he told her, he wanted just one late-night and restorative drink. Liz dimly recalls Dylan saying that he was just going 'to the corner'.

Liz was now aware that the simple act of rising for a late-night drink had implications beyond its stated intent. In retrospect she has come to see it as the final nail in the coffin, the final twist in the mad dance Dylan had been conducting for some days past. Other events were to contribute to his final downfall, but that fateful decision set in train the tragic events that followed. That simple exit from the Chelsea was the final confirmation that Dylan had indeed lost control. He overstepped every mark, it was true, but he had never abandoned his basic lifeline, whatever that lifeline might be and whatever form it might take. But that dark night in New York he came to confuse escape with flight; flight, as it turned out, into the teeth of approaching disaster.

Liz Reitell stepped out of Dylan's path in the Chelsea, defeated as Caitlin had been defeated at the start of that long summer back in Laugharne when she too had opposed a Dylan decision on the grounds of her husband's best interests. One great irony of this whole last story was the common frustration that Caitlin and Liz were to share concerning the activities and antics of their mutual charge.

Once Liz had abandoned all hope of preventing the poet's flight, Dylan hastily dashed past her, down the long wrought-iron staircase of the Chelsea and out into the still-vibrant New York night. Liz waited alone in the hotel room for the poet's return, hoping against hope that his half-hour forecast would be accurate for once.

Inevitably there has to be speculation as to just why Liz did not accompany him. She was after all already primed with her fears about his erratic behaviour. It is likely, of course, that Dylan would not have wanted her and that he made no bones about his wish to embark alone on his late-night drinking spree. But that in itself would not have been enough to deter her. If she had insisted on sticking to Dylan like glue, then there is no possibility that he could have left her in the Chelsea that night.

But human endurance only stretches so far. Liz had already exhibited John Brinnin's tendency; the instinct to withdraw on key occasions from Dylan's company, if only to save her own

sanity and equilibrium. It had after all been an enormous day.
Liz had suffered through Dylan's fitful and disconnected
ravings and his restless sleep. She herself had enjoyed little rest.
The effect was draining. The prospect of accompanying Dylan
on yet one more round of the Greenwich Village bars or the
seedier taverns that bordered the Chelsea on 23rd Street was a
nightmare too awful to contemplate. She could not endure it.
So she let him go.

There is one other motive here. Had Liz accompanied Dylan,
it is likely that the poet would have stayed out all night. With
Liz by his side his sense of security was complete. With no-one
with him save his own tormented presence Liz could at least
hope that the late-night company he would find would simply
cause him pain and he would return to her, as he had returned
home to Caitlin in Wales so many many times before.

Liz lay on Dylan's bed in the Chelsea, too weary even to
sleep. Painfully alert, she listened to every footstep on the stairs
and every echo sounding down the corridor in the hope that it
might herald the poet's return.

What happened next has become the subject of deep and
widespread speculation. There can be no doubt that when
Dylan left the Chelsea, he drank, though the scale of this
drinking has caused disagreement ever since. For his part,
Dylan would claim on his return that he had just drunk
'eighteen straight whiskies'. Most biographers agree that this is
probably an exaggeration on his part. It has indeed been
questioned whether Dylan actually left the room at all, given
that there was drink there already. But Dylan certainly left the
Chelsea. The events of that night are burnt into Liz Reitell's
memory and thirty years later its every detail was recalled with
perfect clarity. The fact that, as one biographer has noted,
Dylan could have drunk in his room is irrelevant: the flight was
as much the motive as the drink.

Given that Dylan did leave the Chelsea, where precisely did
he go? He did not say when he returned. He was absent for
roughly one and a half hours, which makes a taxi trip to the
White Horse feasible. It is unlikely that he could have walked
to Greenwich Village and back in that time. Besides, if that
were the case then it is curious that no voluble New York taxi
driver came forward after Dylan's death to claim his place in

the cabbie's roll of fame as the man who transported Dylan Thomas on his last extended drinking session.

If Dylan did not go to the White Horse, then he could have dived into any of the bars that surround the Chelsea, in which case his extended absence could have been devoted solely to drinking. His 'eighteen straight whiskies', in that case takes on a frighteningly plausible ring.

There is a report that he had been seen in the White Horse, though the proprieter could only substantiate this story by checking with his whisky stocks. Presumably he hadn't been in personal attendance. That means that any other corroborative evidence would have derived from the late-night drinkers at the White Horse bar, and times could have become dangerously confused for the 2 a.m. night-cap brigade. It seems inevitable now that Dylan's exact whereabouts on that last night are destined to remain a matter of speculation.

But there is also a mystery about the quantity of drink itself. Liz did not believe Dylan's eighteen straight whiskies. 'I'm certain,' she has said, 'that he didn't count them.' Thirty years later, indeed, she could not be sure if Dylan had said eighteen or seventeen. John Malcolm Brinnin believes that the statement was just a typical Dylan fiction and bore little connection with the actual truth. Later Brinnin was to reflect, 'It took me not very long to see that he knew what was going to happen, very precisely. It was spelled out. He then challenged it in the bravado of his last night when he turned and said "I've had eighteen straight whiskies". The challenge, he was meeting that challenge.'

To Brinnin, then, the whole statement was a last defiant gauntlet. To Ruthven Todd the statement was simply typical Dylanesque exaggeration. At least one biographer has noted the fictional equivalent to this claim in Dylan's 'Adventures in the Skin Trade'. In the manuscript version, a character says 'I remember once I drank twenty-nine Guinesses straight off', and a later draft added another twenty to that figure. The boast of excessive alcoholic consumption is still regarded as an important status symbol in Dylan's native Wales.

But to Liz the precise amount of whisky that the poet consumed was an irrelevance. The salient point was that Dylan 'had had far too much to drink, and whether that was eighteen or eight it didn't make any difference.' Even eight whiskies would have been equivalent to sixteen British measures. Consumed over a very short time, the effect would still have been acute.

Liz lay on the hotel bed trying to listen for the sounds of Dylan's return. After an hour and a half she was rewarded, a relief in itself. There was no reason, after all, why Dylan shouldn't have stayed out all night. This wasn't Laugharne where life closed down at midnight.

Dylan stood in the hotel room doorway and swayed. Characteristically he made no apology for his extended absence. He was drunk, but he was coherent, though that in itself meant little. He could usually function on one level or another even when totally stupefied with drink. Dylan moved to the centre of the room and spoke – the sentence that has since passed into common mythology: 'I've had eighteen straight whiskies. I think that's the record.'

Liz sat bolt upright on the bed watching him, waiting for what would happen next. What actually happened next was that the physical effort of walking up the Chelsea stairs and the effort at articulate delivery – Dylan was forever the actor – suddenly took its toll.

As Liz watched, he stumbled across the room and laid his head in her lap. Dylan the child was returning to his mother. His flight into the New York night seemed to have done little for his morale. 'I love you,' he told Liz, sinking deeper into her arms, 'but I'm alone.'

Now, Dylan seemed to be telling Liz, there was no real comfort that he could find or she could bring. On that night, after years and years of so many, many such nights, there was little that anybody could do, little practical help that anybody could offer. It is possible that Dylan himself now realised the extent of his fall and the danger that lurked all around but the time to avoid that danger had now past.

Even as he considered the question Dylan may have been aware of a more general despair. For what, for example, would recovery bring? More of the same agony in Laugharne? More of the same oppressive doubts about his failing powers? More of the same complicated emotional tussles pulling him to opposite sides of the Atlantic? As Dylan lay in Liz Reitell's lap he groaned and cursed for a short time and then his breathing became more regular and his curses fewer and less intense. Then the drink seemed at last to have an effect, and soon the sleep that had proved so elusive finally descended, courtesy of exhaustion, mental torment and an indeterminate amount of whisky.

While Dylan slept a fresh concern gripped Liz Reitell. Had Dylan really drunk the amount of whisky he claimed, the clear possibility arose that he would not wake up. He may have indulged in some spectacular drinking sessions in the past, but none had assumed the intense and feverish character of this last escapade if its reporting was accurate. The equivalent of thirty-six whiskies (British measure) in the space of just ninety minutes was a feat that had not been seen even in the more manic sessions in Laugharne's Brown's Hotel and that institution had witnessed some spectacular feats in the past. Death would certainly have been a distinct possibility. Though Liz immediately suspected exaggeration, the claim could possibly be true. In that case ...

In the event Dylan did wake. He revived from his deep and apparently untroubled sleep around mid-morning, making this one of the longest unbroken stretches of rest the poet had enjoyed on that last American trip. But when he revived on that fateful morning it was clear that the sleep had done little to restore him. He was beyond all that.

When he awoke he was once again immediately ill. He told Liz that he could not breathe, which was precisely the sensation he had experienced the previous night and indeed at other times on that last trip. Perhaps as his end approached, Dylan's subconscious mind was making its fateful connections with Houdini. The escapologist would bury himself in sealed tanks beneath hundreds of gallons of water. Had anything gone amiss with his escape route, he too would have suffocated.

Dylan told Liz once again, that he had to get out, and as so often, Dylan had his way. Liz had lost control in any event and if she could not have prevented Dylan escaping from the Chelsea the previous night she certainly could not prevent his setting off for the White Horse later that same morning. This time, however she decided to accompany him. In the morning light she felt a little more able to face a drinking tour; and it also probably occurred to her that her lover would face a greater potential for self-destruction during the course of a full day in New York than on the tail-end of the night. Once again Liz was simply hanging on for the ride. She attempted to direct Dylan into the Chelsea Chop House but he refused, and again dispensed with breakfast altogether. He had now finished with his last food on earth and would eat nothing during his last few conscious hours.

Liz and Dylan left the Chelsea and headed downtown, walking the not inconsiderable distance between 23rd Street and the White Horse. The walk was accomplished without apparent difficulty and it did not seem that Dylan's physical powers had been impaired by the previous evening's claimed excesses. He was also outwardly calm and there was no repetition of his famous impersonation of a wild and erratic lunatic accosting the bemused passers-by. Dylan was still asserting a measure of physical control over his imminent mental collapse. But then his physical abilities were considerable; Dylan's oldest friend, Dan Jones, had concluded his first impressions of Dylan's apparently frail appearance with the note that the thin, fragile-appearing boy was in reality 'very tough'. That strength was now to be tested beyond its limit.

Perhaps it was fitting that Dylan took his final drink in the White Horse. Dylan's favourite bar in New York was the correct setting for such a poignant occasion and thirty years later, the place was still a source of fond memories for Liz. As the couple entered, the bar was not full and Liz noted with relief that many of Dylan's more regular drinking companions had not yet arrived. Dylan recognised some acquaintances, however, and inevitably he fell into conversation with them. A series of photographs taken that day show him talking to two men who may well have been the 'truck drivers' Liz recalled drinking with Dylan that day. The two men are happy and relaxed, posing for the camera and grinning up at Liz. But Dylan is clearly sick. His smile is fixed and frozen, he seems to be unsure of where he is or what she is doing. Dylan looks like a grotesque puppet searching for those who are controlling the strings at the end of which he is so ineffectually and purposelessly dancing. These are the last pictures of Dylan

Thomas alive, and are doubly tragic, both in their content and in the context of the proximity of Dylan's fateful coma. The signs of his approaching doom are burned deep in Dylan's haunted eyes and for once this is not hindsight. Approaching disaster was now clear for anyone to see.

Dylan only stayed in the White Horse for a relatively short time and Liz is adamant that he drank no more than two glasses of beer; an innocuous amount and one that could not have set in train any of the day's fatal events. Dylan had taken exercise, he had drunk only a small amount of alcohol, but he was still suffering 'agonies', he told Liz. Liz was in despair. If Dylan suffered agonies in a congenial setting and among people he liked and with whom he felt happy, then what was she to do? The answer, of course, was absolutely nothing but for now that course was not considered.

Liz decided that she had simply had enough. It was clear that, left to his own devices, Dylan would simply wander around New York desperately seeking fresh distractions and substituting yet more as each one failed to work. She was not prepared to do that for a minute longer. Dylan said that he wanted to head back to the Chelsea and Liz accompanied him silently, even meekly, but in a highly determined frame of mind. Dylan had left the White Horse so many times before in such varying states of health that the proprietor and the rest of the regular White Horse clientele did not notice his departure. They weren't to know this leavetaking was special. Dylan and Liz now took a cab. They did not break the journey at any of the usual bars on the way back to the hotel.

As they entered his room Dylan threw himself down on the bed, once more in the throes of sickness and Liz immediately announced that she was going to fetch Doctor Feltenstein. When Dylan made a show of dissent she told him that he could not and would not go on like this. He made no further protest. Perhaps he had come to the same conclusion.

Doctor Feltenstein arrived at the Chelsea within the half-hour. One look was sufficient to tell him that his advice, sternly delivered to Dylan a few days earlier, had been ignored. But for now he did not embark on yet another lecture but contented himself with simply administering some medication – the exact nature of which is not known – and settling for a more temporary solution to the problem of getting Dylan back on the rails. He may have hoped that at least the medication would revive the poet to the point that he could endure once again the stern Feltenstein admonitions. He instructed Liz on how best to care for her patient and then left. It seemed that Liz's day was to be spent once again caring for the largely insensible form of her lover.

For the time being Dylan slept, though the sleep was fitful and troubled, and did not seem likely to afford Dylan any more genuine rest. Liz sat on the bed beside him, alert for any danger signals.

By mid-afternoon, Dylan was awake again. He was in severe discomfort and there seemed to be several strands to his distress. There was the previous night's heavy drinking: his continued lack of food; the meagre lunchtime beers which may have stimulated the alcohol consumed the previous day; his more conventional illness – gastritis, from which he had suffered for several years. The combined effects were acute and led now to a huge and racking bout of vomiting. This in turn aggravated Dylan's old condition of gout.

Dylan was never the man to stand pain with fortitude. As he went into the first of his 'ghastly racking spasms', Dylan immediately demanded that Doctor Feltenstein should be summoned again. Liz obliged and Dylan soon wished he had not made the request. For on arrival, the stern doctor could withold his lecture no longer. He knew that Dylan had not heeded his advice. The results, as far as the good doctor were concerned, were plain for all to see. He was at once alarmed and angry – Dylan was characteristically shifty.

Feltenstein began by stressing once more to Dylan that he simply had to begin *now* on his much-needed regime of self help, bolstered by a steady course of medical supervision and treatment. But Dylan could not face the thought of such a regime, let alone contemplate sticking to it. The fact that his best interests were involved was, as ever, irrelevant to the debate. In any event, even in the depths of his physical distress, it still seemed to be Dylan's conviction that all this was just a temporary difficulty. Added to that, he had engagements to fulfil and commitments to meet. He could not possibly embark on any strict medical programme aimed at purging himself. He had after all abused his body for the past two decades, had fallen ill and had recovered before.

Round and round the circle of prevarication and self-deceit continued as Feltenstein desperately tried to make Dylan see some sense. As far as Feltenstein was concerned Dylan had no choice, his options were closed. The alternatives were simple in the doctor's view and they were irredemably bleak: a programme of recovery; or an inevitable end. As Dylan continued to prevaricate Feltenstein asked him with great force and bluntness, 'Do you want to go on being sick?' For once Dylan responded equally clearly and without prevarication. 'No,' he said quietly.

The doctor took this as a turning-point in that particular interview and motioned to Liz that she should join him outside. Dylan lay back on the bed, subdued for once by Feltenstein's stark warning. Liz accompanied the doctor into the corridor for a more confidential discussion about their common charge. Though Feltenstein here stopped short of any sensationalist predictions of imminent collapse, he did impress upon her the potential disaster that could befall Dylan if he continued to ignore his own warning symptoms. Then the doctor left the Chelsea and a thoughtful Liz re-entered the room.

She was to find Dylan equally thoughtful. The interview had clearly impressed him. It had also ushered in a new and – despite all his previous ramblings – a frighteningly distinct possibility.

'What did he say to you?' Dylan demanded when Liz appeared. 'Did he say I was going to die?' Dylan had talked about his own death many times but it is likely that he had never properly considered it as an actual and approaching fact.

Liz was now in a quandary. She wanted to repair the damage that Dylan had already inflicted on himself, and that would not be most effectively achieved by concentrating his mind on any awful possibility. On the other hand she did not want to reassure Dylan to the point that he began to disregard the doctor's dire predictions. She phrased her response carefully. She told Dylan that while the doctor had said that Dylan's life was not in imminent danger, he had also said that the poet must begin to do something about his potentially disastrous physical condition and right away. She could not resist giving more force to the warning than to the note of reassurance.

Dylan lay back, still quiet. Perhaps for the very first time, when he was already beyond the point at which such knowledge might help him, Dylan realised the full extent of his predicament and was beginning to glimpse its most logical outcome.

'All right,' Dylan said suddenly. 'I'll do whatever you wish.' But Liz was now too wary to let that sentence pass, with its classic shifting of responsibility. She turned on him. 'Is that what *you* wish, Dylan?' she asked. Dylan registered the question and its real meaning. He looked at her and nodded. 'Yes,' he said. 'I truly, truly do.' At that Liz let him rest and he slipped off to sleep.

Liz decided to keep one major fear strictly to herself. His principal concern, Feltenstein had told her, was that Dylan might slip into a coma. Deep down the doctor was aware that he too was now on the Dylan Thomas rollercoaster, hanging on behind and wondering what was going to happen next.

But by now the doctor had also found Liz Reitell's own physical condition to be of some concern. It should be remembered that she had stayed awake throughout all those fitful bursts of sleep that had claimed her lover over the past few days and had thus had virtually no sleep of her own for two or three days. Thirty years later she estimated that she had probably had three or four hours sleep in the previous seventy-two hours. The days too had been anything but easy. Liz had been dragged round behind Dylan, from one bar to the next, constantly on her guard and forever fearful that her charge might do or say something that would harm either him or someone else. She was exhausted by her care and totally drained by the constant responsibility.

Feltenstein had recognised the strain evident in Liz as they had talked in the hotel corridor. He told Liz that Dylan could not be left alone, but he also suggested she find some friend to help shoulder the burden. For now, however, Liz resisted. She felt just about able to continue. Dylan, it seemed, was content to stay safe in his hotel room. If he would just stay there, Liz felt, she could pull him through, everything would be fine. She would not need anybody, she felt.

Dylan slept on while Liz desperately tried to resolve the practical difficulties attendant on Dylan's latest illness. Her principal concern lay with the poet's approaching engagements. She did not wish him to have any excuse to rise from his hotel bed once he woke. She used the bedside phone to contact John Brinnin in Boston. She asked him to cancel their planned weekend meeting, and to place a very large question mark over Dylan's next reading engagement the following week at Wheaton College.

Liz also sought moral support. Dylan's closest American friends had demonstrated a clear tendency to cling together in times of trouble and to derive a great deal of mutual comfort from the exercise. Liz needed Brinnin's sympathy and fellow-feeling.

Brinnin heard the reports of Dylan's illness with considerable alarm. He immediately cancelled the weekend's plans and from that point on, held himself in unconscious anticipation of the call that would confirm all his worst fears. That may well have been Liz Reitell's real motive in phoning him. There was comfort in the thought of another sharing the suspense.

That practical detail taken care of, Liz attended to others. Dylan had slept through the phone call and seemed set to sleep for a while longer. Liz calculated that she could now leave him alone for a short time in order to collect some of the medical supplies prescribed by Feltenstein, including foodstuffs to be used in Dylan's new diet. Liz stepped out onto 23rd Street.

In late afternoon Liz returned to find Dylan still asleep. She prepared a simple meal, determined that if he was to begin a new diet then he would begin immediately.

But when Dylan did wake, food was the last thing on his mind and his new diet would go the same way as many earlier attempts. As Liz moved around the room she heard Dylan stir and she crossed to his bedside. Dylan stumbled into consciousness and almost immediately retched and vomited. Liz sat by his side, resigned, and waited for this latest attack to pass. He lay back exhausted on the bed. Liz hoped that he would now return to sleep. But rest was now far away. His erratic health had taken another turn, a development anticipated in Howard Moss' apartment just a couple of days before. Once more he began to experience delusions.

Perspiration suddenly broke out all over his forehead and began pouring down his face. He was seeing things again, but this time it was worse. Now he *knew* he was seeing things. Now it was not possible to fool himself, as he had fooled himself in Moss' apartment, that he had actually seen a mouse. The illusions that were dancing before Dylan's eyes that afternoon in the Chelsea were not of such convenient shape and were not so easily explained or dismissed. Dylan was not now seeing animals or figures or even recognisable human shapes. Dylan was now beginning to experience 'abstractions'.

The precise form of these abstractions is difficult to determine. There were certainly circles and triangles and squares swimming in front of the poet's fevered vision. But the shape of those delusions mattered less to Liz than the fact. Liz knew now, beyond all shadow of a doubt, that Dylan's brain was beginning to give way. There was no possibility of pretending that Dylan was not in the grips of delirium tremens.

Dylan began to retch again and this fresh attack of physical nausea, multiplied his mental anguish. He began to rave about the shapes that were now filling every inch of his room and was fast becoming literally uncontrollable. His erratic actions were degenerating into pure derangement. Liz, alarmed beyond measure, immediately telephoned Doctor Feltenstein. She was desperate for something that would calm Dylan's morbid terror. She needed help.

It seems now that Doctor Feltenstein may also have half-expected another urgent summons back to the Chelsea. Within a few minutes of Liz's call he was back at the hotel. It was just as well. Even those few minutes had seen a marked deterioration in his patient and an increase in tension inside his Chelsea hotel room. Dylan had moved from a state of terror to unbalanced anger. He was beginning to rant and rave against the visions that were haunting him.

Doctor Feltenstein immediately gave Dylan a sedative in a now-desperate attempt to quell his lunatic ravings. The problem, as it had been from the start, lay in the fight for Dylan's mind, and his physical distress would not be resolved until that major victory had been achieved. The doctor was anxious that his patient should be placed on a stable mental plane. Dylan raved on for a few more minutes while Liz, beside herself with alarm, waited for the injection to take effect. Perhaps she believed that he was already beyond all medical aid. But then Dylan began to lapse back on his bed and did indeed begin to seem more peaceful.

With Dylan now significantly calmer and subsiding into sleep, Doctor Feltenstein now turned his attention to Liz herself. In addition to her obvious physical exhaustion, Liz was now totally drained by the experience she had just undergone, and with the cessation of Dylan's ravings had come a relief that expressed itself in physical and mental exhaustion. Feltenstein hardly needed to be a trained physician to recognise that Liz was at the end of her tether and he had no desire to begin treating two patients in one hotel room in the Chelsea. Where before he had suggested that she call somebody to sit with her, he now positively insisted that she do so, and insisted further that she do so immediately and in his presence. He did not know just what Dylan might do next, Feltenstein told her, he could not even speculate on the next road his illness might take Dylan down, and he was not prepared to risk leaving her alone with the ailing poet. The possibility was now distinct that Dylan might lapse into a coma, and he was reluctant to commit his charge to an exhausted and amateur nurse who might at any time lapse into a sleep that given her state, might approach a coma of its own. The doctor was also concerned that Dylan might experience another attack of the delirium tremens, might panic himself to the point that Liz would not physically be able to control him. Feltenstein feared that Liz might find herself in actual physical danger, with Dylan locked in his own private hell: he made it a further condition that this friend should be a man.

Liz, at a loss who to suggest, made several unsuccessful attempts to locate various mutual male friends in New York. Her obvious first choice, John Brinnin, was still miles away and out of reach, in Boston. Eventually Liz managed to contact Jack Heliker, the New York painter. Heliker, alarmed, instantly agreed to help out, and arrived at the Chelsea within a few minutes of Liz's call. Somewhat reassured, Feltenstein now left and Liz and Heliker began their vigil at Dylan's bedside.

But Feltenstein's reluctance to leave Liz alone may have

reflected a larger insecurity on his part. This insecurity related to the nature of the sedative with which he had just injected his patient. It now appears that the doctor injected Dylan with one half of a grain of morphine sulphate; a curious choice and potentially catastrophic. This conclusion is not mere hindsight. Paul Ferris, who has mounted a special investigation into the details of this medical treatment, has established that even at that time, the injection of such a comparatively large amount of so powerful and addictive a drug was highly incautious. As indeed it proved.

Dylan had a history of asthmatic attacks that stretched back to childhood, and he was a renowned and heavy smoker. Liz Reitell would certainly have told Doctor Feltenstein that Dylan had claimed to have been on a heavy drinking session the previous evening. The combined effect, allied to the attacks of nausea, should have warned the doctor not to give Dylan anything that might possibly affect his breathing. Yet he injected Dylan with a drug that could do just that.

After Dylan's death all Feltenstein would say, in explanation of his action, was that Dylan was 'in pain'. His injection was clearly intended to relieve that pain but its side effects seem never to have been considered. Indeed the doctor would neither confirm nor deny, up to the time of his death in 1974, that he actually injected Dylan with morphine. It seems he may have realised his lack of caution. The puzzle that remains, is just why it did not dawn on him before.

There has been speculation that Doctor Feltenstein may unconsciously have been attempting to rid himself of a troublesome patient, but this is an unsatisfactory notion. It should be remembered that this was only the third time that day that Feltenstein had been called to the Chelsea and only the fourth occasion on that entire trip that he had attended Dylan. The first appointment was actually in his own surgery. Before that he and Dylan had met just once, six months earlier, and had got on well on a personal level. Dylan had even sent his greetings to the doctor in one of his letters in the summer. Four consultations, even with three on the same day, hardly constitute an intolerable burden and the doctor would have needed to have operated on a very short fuse had his patience snapped.

Liz was later to describe him as 'wild', and there seems little doubt that, from the first, the doctor demonstrated an easy willingness to inject his patient. He may have wished, in depressing Dylan's metabolism, to make sure that existing engagements would be cancelled. It is possible that he regarded Dylan's physical distress as secondary to his mental problems, and believed that he should address himself to the latter before attending to the more physically based distress. It is equally possible that he simply panicked.

These possibilities are all plausible but none are entirely satisfactory. For his part, Doctor Feltenstein maintained a constant refusal to answer all questions on the matter or even to discuss it with colleagues and took that refusal to the grave. When he died, the mystery of that last injection died with him.

Liz Reitell and Herb Hannum were unaware of the nature of that injection and would have been little the wiser had Doctor Feltenstein acquainted them with his every move. They simply sat in the Chelsea by Dylan's bedside with the layman's blind faith in the medical fraternity.

Dylan had actually been conscious when Heliker arrived, and had even managed some attempt at a joke. 'This is one hell of a way to greet a man, isn't it?' he challenged Heliker. Heliker smiled back. That was the old Dylan poking fun at his own physical distress, and the signs may briefly have seemed hopeful once more. But Dylan could not now sustain it and he soon fell into his now-characteristic fitful sleep. As he slept Liz acquainted Jack Heliker with all the details of that disastrous day and the previous night. By their side the visible evidence of those sorry tales slumbered on.

Dylan, however, was not destined to sleep for long. His physical distress was now frustrating his attempts to rest. He was perhaps experiencing difficulties with his breathing by now, though not to the extent that would have alerted him or alarmed Liz and Jack Heliker. For her part Liz had become well used to Dylan complaining of 'suffocating'. But now that breathlessness was a genuine physical condition rather than a mental one.

Presently, then, Dylan awoke again, quickly and abruptly, jerking upright, tense and alarmed as befits a man in the grips of some private nightmare. It was true that he was gulping for air but this could still have been induced by mental distress rather than anything else.

It was immediately clear that the large dose of morphine had not achieved its purpose: to calm the poet to the extent that he would be able to control his delusions. Dylan was still suffering from delirium tremens; they were assuming precisely the same form as before, and as before, were taunting him anew with their obvious unreality.

Once again these delusions were 'squares, circles and triangles' and Dylan now began to call them 'the horrors'. Years earlier, on the Gower cliffs, Dylan had talked of 'taking my devils for an airing'. But now the devils were real and uncontrollable. They were claiming him as Dylan had always feared that they would. Once more he raved and ranted, while the distressed Liz and the helpless Jack Heliker looked on. There was, of course, nothing that either attendant could do other than trust that the attacks would burn themselves out. For her part Liz could now feel herself on the point of the collapse that had been imminent for some days past. Liz herself has said that after Heliker arrived, 'the atmosphere was a little better, simply because there was someone else there. I was less frightened.' She would not have given in had Heliker not been present. But with the capable painter beside her, even with Dylan still raving and ranting, she could begin to contemplate some form of rest. As Heliker took her place by Dylan's side, providing a receptive if silent audience for Dylan's ravings, Liz curled up on a nearby chair and managed to grab an hour or so of disturbed and interrupted sleep. It could hardly be peaceful with Dylan punctuating her descents into oblivion with his outbursts of shouting and swearing. But it was something, and it meant that when Feltenstein called again he was to take just one patient to a New York hospital rather than two. Thirty years later, Liz Reitell still did not know just what that sleep cost her. When she woke, as she later recalled, she woke 'to what was to be only a minute more of Dylan's conscious life'.

Dylan, almost incredibly, was still mentally alert and was still lucid in his delusion-free moments. Liz had had a strange dream which, echoing Dylan's 'accident' in Howard Moss' apartment, had revolved around roses. As she emerged from sleep, she told Dylan that she'd had 'such a strange dream, I kept dreaming about roses'. Dylan seized on the grammatical ambiguity and the poet, 'word grafter to the end', asked Liz if she meant 'roses' as in 'bunch of flowers' or 'something belonging to Rose?' A flash of the old characteristic Dylan which made the next few days even more painful to bear. To the very end, it seemed that Dylan's brain was still quick-silver sharp and his only real distress that of physical excess and medical misadventure. Thirty years later, Liz Reitell could still 'not bear that thought'.

Liz now lay fully dressed on Dylan's bed by Dylan's side. Jack Heliker sat on the nearby chair. There was some of Dylan's writings on the table. Heliker thinks they were lines from Dylan's unfinished *Elegy*. It was now past midnight on the 4 November. Dylan asked for a drink but Heliker obstinately refused to give him one, and must thus take credit for not hastening Dylan's already fast-approaching end.

But that end was now at hand. Dylan began raving about the 'horrors' once again. He was still lying on the bed, Liz beside him, holding his hand. She was not looking directly at him in this position but was simply trying to give comfort as she had done once before in the Algonquin. Jack Heliker was sat opposite the couple, watching the poet intently.

There is now a discrepancy between the two witnesses as to Dylan's last words. According to Heliker, those last words came as Dylan lay staring at the ceiling and remarked, 'After thirty-nine years, this is all I've done.' They really do seem remarkably apt and perhaps just a little too stagey. It is possible that Heliker had become infected by the general atmosphere surrounding Dylan and had elevated a chance remark to the status of 'Dylan's last words'. Many others would similarly recall their last sight of Dylan and would produce their own versions of Dylan's 'last words'. If all were correct, Dylan would have been anticipating his death six months before its actual event.

Liz Reitell's recollections are different, and are probably more reliable. Through thirty years her memory has remained steadfast and consistent with the account she first gave John Brinnin in 1954. Liz was lying with Dylan on his hotel bed. She was attempting to comfort him, to reassure him that his condition was only temporary, that this new anguish was not some general backcloth to his life but was an aberration in his normal well-being which time, medical help and his own endeavours would cure. Dylan seemed to accept it, which also made the immediate events all the more difficult to accept. Dylan had relaxed but not into hopelessness. He relaxed, so it seemed, into a more resigned peace. Liz said to him, 'Dylan, you must know about the horrors – they go away – they do go away.' Dylan replied as if he had just seen the truth for himself and would now act on the knowledge. His manner was calm and reassured and he squeezed Liz Reitell's hand as he spoke. 'Yes,' he said, 'Yes, I believe you.' Liz lay with Dylan on the bed hardly daring to hope that the poet had just resolved on a fresh start. But those were Dylan's last words. As Liz then recalled events, there were next some moments of quiet, and she began to look forward to a new and changed Dylan. But the end was now too close. Liz Reitell, more calm and inwardly settled, suddenly felt Dylan's hand stiffen in hers. It took a few seconds for the implication to sink in. She wasn't looking at Dylan's face, which would have alerted her immediately that something was terribly wrong.

But Jack Heliker from his vantage point on the chair was watching their common charge and he was frozen by what he could see. The poet had stiffened his grip on Liz's hand because he was suddenly experiencing the most acute difficulty in breathing, unable to catch his breath. The injection of morphine sulphate was beginning to have its disastrous effect. As Liz realised that Dylan's hand was stiffening in hers, Heliker saw Dylan's face beginning to turn blue as the poet struggled for air. A couple of seconds later both heard a gasping sound emerging from deep inside Dylan's throat. The end was indeed upon them.

Liz Reitell has described this 'dreadful gasping sound' as a 'stoppage of Dylan's normal breathing', which seems to indicate that the drug was the primary trigger of Dylan's new distress. But all such speculation was for later. Now Dylan desperately needed medical help. In those few panic-stricken moments in the Chelsea it did not seem beyond the bounds of possibility that Dylan might die there and then while they helplessly looked on.

Liz and Heliker sprang into action. A phone call was

hurriedly made to Doctor Feltenstein and the doctor once again appeared within minutes. When he arrived at the Chelsea sufficient to tell him that his patient was beyond the reach of any help he might bring. Dylan now needed urgent hospitalisation. Indeed, he should have been hospitalised many hours before. Doctor Feltenstein called an ambulance from the nearby St Vincent's Hospital and within minutes Dylan was being carried out on a stretcher attended by a near-hysterical Liz Reitell. It was now shortly before 2 a.m.; twenty-four hours after Dylan had risen alone and unaided to embark on his last great drinking session.

Doctor Feltenstein accompanied the ambulance and his unfortunate patient. Later, in partial explanation of his curious actions of that day, he told a colleague that Dylan was suffering from 'acute liver failure' and that this condition would have proved fatal whatever sedatives were used to quieten him. This may well have been so. But it still leaves the question as to why the doctor, recognising that from the start, did not commit Dylan to intensive medical care immediately, rather than waiting for the poet to succumb to the effects of his diagnosis. A doctor who studied Dylan's hospital treatment was to say later that Doctor Feltenstein's failure to have Dylan admitted to hospital earlier, was even more culpable than his controversial course of injections.

St Vincent's Hospital records that Dylan was admitted at 1.58 a.m. on the 5 November. It notes his history of 'heavy alcoholic intake', and also notes the recent injection of one half grain of morphine sulphate.

Chapter Nine
Do Not Go Gentle ...

On arrival at St Vincent's, Dylan was immediately wheeled to the Emergency Ward where a deputation of doctors and nurses began a round-the-clock vigil in an attempt to save him. From the time of his admission however, Dylan would be beyond the best and most sophisticated of medical endeavours. Liz Reitell and Jack Heliker had accompanied Dylan in the emergency ambulance. They were now left alone in the private Roman Catholic St Vincent's Hospital, bereft of their charge and suddenly at a loose end. Where earlier the full horror of the situation had been held at a distance by the more immediate need to care for Dylan, now it was beginning to impinge. Liz suddenly had nothing to do other than reflect on what she had just witnessed and to speculate agonisingly on what it all might mean for Dylan. She woke up with a jolt to the surroundings of the white well-scrubbed clinic. It all embodied her own private nightmare of what might befall her lover. Now it truly had befallen him.

A few feet away in the emergency ward, the doctors treating Dylan had noted first his 'acute alcoholic encephalopathy' – the source for the much-quoted and typically inaccurate phrase 'an insult to the brain' – but also that Dylan was exhibiting 'no response'. In those first few minutes, the hospital staff tried everything to elicit that response.

For their part, Liz Reitell and Jack Heliker sat in the hospital waiting room for a few more minutes. For Jack the immediate future was bleak. He was about to lose a close friend and the circumstances of that loss made it all the more difficult to bear. But for Liz the prospect was unbearable. She was about to lose a lover, a lover who had come to claim all her waking moments, and with whom her very self had come to be

164

inextricably linked. Dylan had formed the backcloth to all her thoughts for weeks past.

There was of course a great deal to do, and it is likely that this saved Liz from descending any further into despair. There were friends to contact, arrangements to make and relatives to inform. There were a thousand details to attend to, and there would be a thousand more should the unthinkable happen and Dylan not recover from his latest collapse. Liz now needed help and predictably she turned to the one man who could sympathise at the deepest level with the agony she was experiencing and who shared her love for the errant poet. For the second time that night, John Malcolm Brinnin found his sleep disturbed by a phone call from Liz Reitell in New York.

John Brinnin has recalled that this call came through at approximately 2.30 a.m., which means that it took half an hour for Liz to rouse herself from the shock of Dylan's hospital admission. Brinnin was awoken by the 'insistent ringing' of the phone, and indeed probably Liz would have kept his phone ringing all night had Brinnin proved a heavy sleeper. Brinnin was needed as he had never been needed before. But it is likely that Brinnin had passed a fitful night thus far too. The earlier phone call had wakened his fears. This second phone call confirmed them.

By now Liz had managed to glean from the hospital staff some more details of Dylan's condition and her report to John Brinnin was remarkably full and accurate, as if Liz were making a desperate attempt to attend to the details of Dylan's illness rather than allowing herself to be overwhelmed by that illness. But her voice gave her away.

As far as Liz could determine, Dylan had been given a spinal tap in order to establish whether or not he had suffered a cerebral hemorrhage and that he was also being administered oxygen to aid his difficult breathing. It took a few seconds for John Brinnin to absorb the news and to realise the full implications of the 'cerebreal hemmorhage'. In that terrifying instant the possibility was raised that Dylan may be permanently brain-damaged. Brinnin said nothing lest his voice give him away. But Liz could not remain silent. The burden suddenly became too much to bear. Her immediate duty discharged, Liz now broke down completely. Her voice throughout the conversation had been 'shrill' and 'barely controlled' but once she had completed her message her voice collapsed just as she herself collapsed into a bout of almost hysterical weeping. The despair that had threatened all evening now finally claimed her and Liz simply broke down. The distraught John Brinnin could not hear her and could make no sense of her disconnected hysteria. Eventually Liz managed to regain control of herself for just a few seconds and she blurted out the most chilling sentence of all thus far. 'John,' she sobbed, catching her breath between each word, 'he may be dying ... he may be dying.' Within three hours John Brinnin was on a plane from Boston and was flying down to join Liz in New York.

In the meantime the news of Dylan's hospitalisation had begun to spread around his immediate network of New York friends. Liz contacted some friends after her call to Brinnin and those friends contacted others. Soon a veritable chain of contacts was waking up in the early hours of 5 November to the news that the errant Welsh poet may finally have overstepped the mark.

It seems that Ruthven Todd was the first to arrive at the hospital and that he must have arrived within a few minutes of Liz's call to John Brinnin. Liz stumbled through the story of Dylan's collapse and committal, aware that this was already beginning to become a routine. She would say her piece again and again over the next few days, and indeed would rehearse it for the next thirty years.

Ruthven Todd's presence meant that Jack Heliker could now be relieved of his duty and there was a more positive way in which he could be useful. Liz had arranged with John Brinnin that he call her at her Charles Street apartment on his arrival in New York. The arrangement was curious and illogical. Liz could surely not have expected to have been at her apartment within the next couple of hours, while things in St Vincent's were poised so agonisingly between life and death. The fact that the normally clear-sighted John Brinnin agreed to this arrangement, rather than insisting on proceeding direct to the hospital, is a measure of the derangement in his own usually well-organised state. Brinnin would have telephoned an empty apartment, so Liz now arranged that Jack Heliker should take up temporary residence in Charles Street while Ruthven Todd took on Heliker's role as friend and comforter to Liz.

As yet, no other Dylan friend had made their way to St Vincent's and the circus that normally accompanied all Dylan's appearances had not yet materialised. Sitting with Ruthven Todd in the bleak early hours, her immediate duties discharged, Liz had a few moments to attempt to collect her thoughts. This was the last period of extended quiet and peace that Liz would know for the next five days.

As far as Dylan's immediate condition was concerned, Liz and Todd had received no more information. The doctors were frantically trying to repair the immediate damage and had little time to spare for near-hysterical friends or lovers. The only information Todd had been able to glean was that the doctors were still attempting to establish what had caused Dylan's condition, as well as dealing with the effects of the morphine injection that had been administered late the previous evening. It is possible that even at this early stage the doctors were having doubts about the wisdom of Doctor Feltenstein's treatment – later a doctor was to tell Dylan's friend David Lougee that Feltenstein was not allowed 'near the case' once the hospital had realised what course his treatment had taken (but this is contradicted by John Brinnin).

It was now approaching 6 a.m. and New York was beginning to wake up. Brinnin was at that moment flying over Long Island 'in a numb suspension', concentrating only on the details of the journey and not allowing himself to think at all of the fact of Dylan's illness. He was, he has recorded, 'leaning against a wall of apprehension that would give way if I moved so much as an inch'.[1] Thirty years later, Brinnin could recall every detail of that journey, 'as though my attention would fix on anything but the one fear that obsessed it'. Liz Reitell's voice had warned him, if nothing else, that at least one calm head would be required when he arrived in New York.

In keeping with his earlier arrangement, Brinnin immediately telephoned Liz's apartment and found Jack Heliker at his lone duty, waiting by the phone. Liz had promised Heliker that in the event of any catastrophe she

[1] For much of the factual detail here I am indebted to John Brinnin's account in *Dylan Thomas in America*.

would call. Gathering, correctly, that Dylan's condition had at least not worsened, Brinnin hurried to St Vincent's. He had been preparing himself so carefully for the worst that the news that Dylan was still alive came as a deep relief; it was a much happier Brinnin who took a cab from the airport. His relief was to be short-lived.

The cab dropped Brinnin off at the hospital at around 7 a.m. St Vincent's was still mercifully free of any other Dylan friends though Brinnin was well aware that the hospital would probably be inundated within the next few hours. He dashed out of the cab and into the hospital but the sight that immediately greeted him stopped him dead in his tracks.

Liz Reitell had been at the hospital all night, poised in an agony of waiting, and was now in a state of imminent collapse. As Brinnin hurried into the hospital, he could see his assistant being led away down the hospital corridor, leaning for support on the arm of Ruthven Todd. It looked as if Todd were comforting her, where in reality he was physically supporting her. But the sight was enough for John Brinnin to believe the very worst. He was immediately convinced that he was too late, that the end had come for Dylan. He called out to Liz and Todd and they stopped and turned to him. Liz's dazed expression seemed additional confirmation of the disastrous turn events had taken. Brinnin hurried up and put his arms around her. She seemed beyond all words. Liz broke down as she had broken down on the telephone a few hours earlier. Brinnin still believed that he could read the fact of Dylan's death in her dazed expression and for a few minutes contented himself with simply comforting her. But then, looking past Liz, he made a silent enquiry of Todd, who told him that Dylan was still alive. There was a moment of immediate relief but that feeling was at once muted. In his arms Brinnin held the most eloquent testimony to the true status of Dylan's existence and the weeping Liz Reitell was banishing any thoughts he might have entertained of a Dylan recovery.

Ruthven Todd steered Brinnin and the weeping Liz to a nearby waiting-room. In fits and starts Liz brought Brinnin up to date with the medical situation. In her earlier distraught phone call to Boston, Liz had told Brinnin that Dylan 'may be dying'. Now she told him that the hospital feared death at any

moment. The only hopeful sign that had emerged in the time
between the phone call and Brinnin's arrival was that the
spinal tap had confirmed the absence of a cerebral
hemmorhage, but even that had been outweighed by a new
suspicion – that Dylan was suffering from diabetes. Liz,
Brinnin and Todd watched the door of the waiting room,
united in apprehension, waiting for the news they had all begun
to dread as inevitable.

The recriminations had also begun. Liz was now beginning
to blame herself for the events of the previous night. For some
reason she had fixed on the notion that she should have called
the police, and that they might have escorted Dylan back to the
hotel if only she had thought of it. Again the notion was
curious and illogical but in that fevered early morning madness
in St Vincent's mere logic held little sway. Brinnin attempted to
comfort her. 'No-one ever thinks of the police,' he told her, but
Liz was beyond all comfort now and merely repeated her
self-accusation again and again, until Brinnin finally let her
burn herself out.

It was now breakfast time in New York which made it
mid-afternoon in Laugharne. The shadows would be drawing
in, the night settling over the sleepy Welsh town. Brinnin was
aware that he had a duty to inform Dylan's family and close
friends in Britain of the poet's distress, but he was at a genuine
loss as to how best to accomplish that. Most importantly,
Caitlin had to be told, but Brinnin did not relish the idea of
shouting the devastating information across a crackly phone
link from New York to Laugharne. In his indecision, Brinnin
decided to postpone any action until he himself had spoken
with one of the physicians attending Dylan and had more
definite and first-hand news. He was also aware that, through a
slight delay, he could spare Caitlin the agony of uncertainty, of
not knowing whether her husband was alive or dead, though
this might be achieved at the expense of an even greater agony.

After another hour the swing doors of the hospital corridor
burst open. But instead of the lone doctor they had all feared,
face professionally composed for the communication of bad
news, there was a veritable flurry of activity. Doctors and
nurses hurried through the swing doors with Dylan,
outstretched on a hospital trolley, at the centre of attention.

His face was covered in an oxygen mask and all they could see of him was his flushed face, his skin blotched in great scarlet patches, his hair matted. Dylan was wheeled past the standing group and into a nearby elevator where he was transported to the St Joseph's division on the third floor of the hospital. No-one spoke to Brinnin, Liz or Todd. But at least that sight offered a kind of hope, a desperate prayer in the face of all that had promised otherwise. Dylan was still with them and they had now seen him. He had also been removed from the emergency ward and surely, each told the other, he would not have been, had his physical distress still threatened his very existence. The next few minutes were passed in a fever of speculation. The mood, where earlier it had been depressed, now swung towards a cautious though heartfelt optimism. Shortly it would switch back to despair once more.

Doctor Feltenstein had been at St Vincent's since the time of Dylan's admission. With Dylan's removal to routine nursing care, Feltenstein was now about to leave for home himself. On his way out he made it his business to acquaint Liz and John Brinnin with the current state of Dylan's health.

As the trio eagerly discussed the implications of Dylan's removal from the emergency wing, Feltenstein joined them. The true state of affairs, which they would have realised had they been thinking rationally, was not good, he told them. Dylan was still in grave danger and death was an ever-present possibility. The doctors were searching for clues to his coma and Feltenstein now urged his three closest US friends to dredge their respective memories for events or incidents, conversations even, that might hint at some past condition that might have led Dylan into his present state. But they could offer little help. None had any idea that Dylan might be a diabetic. Brinnin repeated Dylan's stories concerning his 'cirrhosis of the liver', but as Dylan had told many stories concerning illnesses real and imagined Brinnin had long since ceased to view them with other than amused tolerance. Alcohol was certainly a potent cause of Dylan's distress, but beyond that the trio had little to offer. For his part, Feltenstein was careful not to say anything that would raise any false hopes on their part.

Feltenstein left. Brinnin, Liz and Todd went back to

speculating on Dylan's condition. Half an hour later there was a development. They were told that they could now look at Dylan if they wished, though they were warned that he had still not recovered consciousness and that they would not be allowed near his bed as the hospital staff were in constant close attendance. The offer was accepted gratefully. Any sight of the poet still alive was welcome. They had all prepared themselves over the past few hours for his death.

The three friends followed a nurse upstairs and then crowded into the small room that contained an inert Dylan and the bevy of doctors and nurses attending him. From their vantage point they could see him encased in an oxygen mask and could hear his laboured breathing.

The medical staff were engaged in giving a blood transfusion and had little time or inclination to advise the anxious group on the health and prospects for their distressed friend. However, they duly hung around in the room until it was obvious that there was nothing that they could do, and nothing further they would learn of Dylan's condition. They agreed to abandon their vigil. The prospect of continuing to listen to Dylan's difficult breathing was intolerable. They were impotent and could only withdraw. It was by now a feeling of helplessness fast becoming familiar. From that time on they were all condemned to their roles as mere spectators.

Brinnin and Liz then left the waiting room to visit Dylan once more, but this time they were not allowed into the room. The last thing the St Vincent's staff wished was a constant stream of visitors disrupting their care for a patient ill. Watching from the door of the hospital room they could only observe that Dylan was at least still alive. But there was now a noticeable increase in activity around the poet's bed.

Brinnin and Liz returned to the ever-growing band of friends and well-wishers and practical issues now began to surface. The position was clear. Dylan was ill. Dylan would remain ill for a good time to come and the only hope of an early release lay in Dylan's death. Such a state of affairs could not now be allowed to continue without Dylan's family being informed and certainly Rose Slivka would have insisted that Caitlin be told of her husband's illness as soon as possible. In addition to Caitlin there was also an enormous list of people who should be told, and it is likely that Brinnin now welcomed the prospect of activity after the ceaseless and largely useless speculation that had occupied him since his arrival. By now Brinnin wanted to do something and his more accustomed role as organiser and helpmate came itself as a blessed relief.

Various friends were contacted and Rollie McKenna has recalled one such telephone call early on the Friday morning and remembers that John Brinnin did not attempt to raise any false hopes of Dylan's ultimate recovery.

In the meantime, as he talked with other Dylan friends, John Brinnin wrestled with the problem of contacting Caitlin. He still did not relish a shouted transatlantic phone conversation, buffeted by intercontinental interference. It is also likely that he simply did not know what to say to the woman who had so vehemently opposed this trip in the first place, and he was also aware that, in aiding the poet in the arrangements for this trip, he shared some responsibility for Dylan's current desperate predicament. Eventually he decided not to phone Caitlin direct but to relay the news of Dylan's illness via Dylan's London agent, David Higham. David Higham would in any event be in a better position to make any travel arrangements that might be required and could look after Caitlin in a more immediately practical way than Brinnin could hope to do, three thousand miles away across the Atlantic Ocean. However, it is likely that the most pressing consideration was Brinnin's reluctance to face Caitlin with the confirmation of her own worst fears.

Brinnin returned from his marathon telephone session to find Rollie KcKenna newly arrived at the hospital along with Howard Moss and the ever-dependable Herb Hannum. Hannum felt as if a nightmare prophecy had come true.

Within minutes of Brinnin's return, Doctor Feltenstein joined them and introduced Doctor James McVeigh, the staff physician now in direct charge of Dylan's case. He had gloomy news to impart. They were examining the triggers that had provoked Dylan's coma and it looked as if alcohol was the most likely. Dylan had consumed a large amount within the previous twenty-four hours. It looked as if his careless boast to Liz Reitell contained some degree of truth. At this stage nothing was said to Brinnin or to Liz concerning the likely effects of Doctor Feltenstein's morphine injection.

172

It was now noon in New York, which meant that night was most definitely closing in on Laugharne. Caitlin was preparing to attend a radio talk recorded by Dylan before his departure for the US, in which he would paint an affectionate picture of his adopted home town. The dignitaries of Laugharne had decided that this broadcast should be the feature of a special evening in the local Church Hall. The residents were to gather to hear themselves described.

By this time David Higham had been informed of Dylan's desperate condition and he too had decided that Caitlin must be told personally and not through a telephone message. Accordingly he instructed a 'local' – whose name does not now survive – to carry out this task. It meant that, by a strange quirk of circumstance, Caitlin was actually told of her husband's last illness while she was sat in a hall in his home town, surrounded by all his friends and neighbours and listening to his voice booming from the loudspeakers that sat on the stage in front of her.

Caitlin's reaction could have taken many forms. She had become innured to Dylan's succession of illnesses and well used to Dylan's using his illnesses to dodge even the most basic of his responsibilities. But this time it seems she did not doubt for an instant the seriousness of her husband's position. She did not even need that one night to decide what she would do: she would fly at once to the US to be with him.

Caitlin made immediate arrangements to travel to London, where Higham was instructed to find her a seat on an American-bound plane. Her children were despatched to the care of their bewildered grandmother, to whom the news of Dylan's illness came as the third blow in less than a year: a year that had started with her daughter's death; continued with her husband's last illness and decline; and was now being concluded with her son's fight for survival.

In New York the anguish continued. It was now mid-afternoon and the media were beginning to pick up the story. The New York evening papers carried a bulletin that the famous British poet Dylan Thomas was ill, but there was little in that first account to indicate either the nature, or the severity, of the illness. But it was a start. News was beginning to travel.

The situation changed a little just before midnight. The medical authorities requested that Brinnin and Liz, who had become established so far as the hospital was concerned, as Dylan's two closest friends, should attempt to make some kind of contact with him. Having restored some semblance of physical stability, the doctors were now anxious to penetrate Dylan's coma, and were willing to experiment with key friends in an attempt to reach the unconscious poet. Brinnin and Liz duly made their way to Dylan's room, where they began to speak to him, repeating key words and phrases, recalling past events that would mean something to him and which might provoke some kind of response. Occasionally, very occasionally, Brinnin believed that he caught 'the flicker of a response' though it is more likely that this was simply an interruption in Dylan's laboured breathing. A nurse in constant attendance encouraged these attempts until it was finally clear that little was being achieved. The poet was blind, unconscious and out of touch with his surroundings.

Liz Reitell left the room in some distress and Rose Slivka took her place. John Brinnin remained. With Liz absent, John Brinnin may have felt a little less inhibited in his choice of subject matter, he immediately began to talk of Caitlin. Caitlin's closest friend in the US, and perhaps in the world, Rose Slivka, supported this flow of recollection and reminiscence.

Brinnin told Dylan that Caitlin was on her way, that she was at that moment looking for a flight over to the U.S. and to his side. Suddenly, as Brinnin was speaking, there came a definite and unmistakeable response. It could have been yet one more electrical interruption to the brain. But then Dylan uttered a sound, the first since he had entered St Vincent's. The atmosphere was charged and the nurse urged Brinnin to try again. Dylan repeated exactly the same sound and Brinnin became convinced that Dylan was actually trying to say something, that he was frantically attempting from the very depths of his coma, to communicate with Brinnin, a response triggered by associations Brinnin's words had aroused. It was a brief moment of exhilaration and acute pain for all in the room while they waited for the exchange to be continued, but then the moment passed. Dylan sank back once more into passive unconsciousness while Brinnin watched, helpless and hopeless. Later he was to find comfort in the doctor's reassurance that this 'response' was merely a muscular spasm. The other alternative – that somewhere inside the inert body was trapped an alert and aware Dylan – was perhaps too painful to contemplate.

More friends were now beginning to pour into St Vincent's, alerted by a simple report in the New York evening papers. As he maintained his vigil by Dylan's bedside Brinnin had already spotted the odd recognisable face gazing through the glass door of the hospital room. These included John Berryman, the poet and critic from Princeton, and David Lougee. Liz Reitell forced her way through the new swarm of visitors to rejoin Brinnin in a vigil that was now to last till the early hours of the following morning.

But St Vincent's, as Liz recalled, 'wasn't one of those hospitals in which a whole family or a whole group comes in and gathers and makes a lot of noise.' Thus of the gathering crowd that began to assemble within the precincts of the hospital, very few were allowed anywhere near the poet and this comparatively tight security was the principal factor which prevented the whole affair from degenerating into a circus; the circus that always surrounded Dylan on his trips abroad from Laugharne and which now threatened to engulf him at the very point of his death. 'Occasionally,' Liz has recalled, 'if the hospital thought it might help, selected people were brought in very quietly' and allowed to remain. But of course 'there was nothing one could do when they came in ... he was in a coma, so nobody stayed long'. However, this denial of access soon began to breed tensions of its own.

As strangers and less-than-close friends were denied contact with Dylan, sinister rumours began to circulate, particularly in the wake of the hospital staff's refusal to issue constant statements about the poet's condition or even its likely prognosis. The ambiguity that surrounded his condition now encouraged the wildest speculation. More rumours multiplied, all revolving around the 'facts' of Dylan's collapse and the efficacy of his treatment, and soon the most ludicrous stories began to circulate around the hospital, spreading to the wider New York community to form the basis of the thousands of stories that were to pass into common mythology and become accepted as fact after Dylan's death. Thirty years later John Brinnin still refused even to repeat them. 'They're too obscene,' he decided, 'and to call them black comedy would be to elevate them.' Brinnin understood his friend's propensity to generate rumour and counter-rumour. 'Dylan', he refleted, 'had this ability to generate stories which had nothing to do with him ... he became identified with certain kinds of behaviour ... people went ahead and made up what he actually said.' That process began in St Vincent's before Dylan even passed away, but Brinnin was determined thirty years later that he would still play no part in their dissemination. (That impulse was the crucial factor in persuading him to write his own version of those years, in his book 'Dylan Thomas in America'.) More friends arrived throughout the night, including many that Brinnin didn't recognise at all, drawn to the hospital either by some secret past association or simply by a fellow-feeling. The nurses were consulted by ever-increasing numbers of Dylan friends, all of whom demanded more and more attention and exhibited an ever-greater propensity to get in the way. By 4.a.m. the ward sister, Sister Consilio, decided that enough was enough. She began to clear the hospital waiting room, and then she turned her attention to Liz Reitell.

By now Liz had not slept in any effective sense for the best part of four days. The past twenty-four hours had been a particularly acute strain. Doctor Feltenstein had probably alerted the medical authorities to his own fears concerning Miss Reitell and it is certain that the doctors at the hospital would not wish to deal with another collapse through default.

The hospital decided that she must have some rest and that this rest should be away from the confines of St Vincent's. Sister Consilio assured both Liz and Brinnin that Dylan was now in no immediate danger and that Liz's most fruitful course of action lay in grabbing some much-needed rest. But the idea was anathema to her. Her whole being had focused down to one point: that hospital room and Dylan himself. The prospect of a separation was simply too much to bear. She refused point-blank to leave, not only the hospital premises but also Dylan's actual room.

She had reckoned without the adamant determined Sister

Consilio. Brinnin had been equally reluctant to leave, but faced with the redoubtable Sister, had decided that discretion was the better part of valour and had meekly left the room. Liz allowed herself to be shepherded as far as the hospital entrance but then refused to go any further. She showed every sign of actually squatting down in the hospital doorway and defying the nurses to drag her out into the street. It was left to the diplomatic Brinnin to convince her of the wisdom of leaving St Vincent's to get some rest. He led Liz, weeping hysterically, back to her Charles Street apartment. This was the first time that Liz had left Dylan's side for four days.

Friday morning now dawned, and the news of Dylan's illness was beginning to spread internationally. In Swansea, working at his usual post in the bank, Vernon Watkins was shown a local newspaper report of Dylan's illness. It said that Dylan was suffering from a 'serious brain ailment'. At this stage it did not report that Dylan was in a coma and indeed stated that the poet was 'showing signs of recovery'.

In London David Higham was now frantically engaged in the search for a plane seat for Caitlin, who was herself trying to compose a telegram to be despatched to the US in advance of her arrival. She hoped that, in the event of his recovery, the telegram would be the first sight that would greet Dylan as he awoke.

Back in New York, after just a few hours sleep, Liz Reitell and John Brinnin arrived back at St Vincent's. It was now just after eight a.m. New York time, and Brinnin and Liz found no change in Dylan though they were greeted by one piece of mildly hopeful news. They already knew that the hospital's first choice of brain specialist, Doctor Leo Davidoff, was not available, but an equally distinguished surgeon was due to arrive at St Vincent's that morning, Doctor C.G. de-Gutierrez-Mahoney. The news revived hopes that some miracle was still possible, and they settled down to await his arrival with some hope. Brinnin and Liz were now allowed to remain in Dylan's room, though they were ushered outside whenever a new doctor or nurse wished to attend him.

By now the news had also reached Dylan's closest friend in Wales, Doctor Daniel Jones. Dan Jones had already suffered through an overly dramatic announcement of Dylan's condition from a journalist who wished to record the impact on

177

Dylan's oldest friend. Years later it still clearly gave Dan Jones some satisfaction that he simply stared at the journalist soberly and neutrally as the grave announcement was being conveyed. He permitted no response to flicker across his face. But inside, there was turmoil. Dan Jones' first instinct was to help, and this instinct was spurred by his role as custodian of special knowledge concerning Dylan. One incident in particular he felt might be of help to the doctors in New York. Earlier that summer, so Dylan had told Dan Jones, he had become involved in a fracas in a London nightclub and had sustained a severe cut on his forehead. Aware that the New York doctors were searching for clues to Dylan's condition and feeling that this might be significant, Dan Jones immediately sent a cable to New York, detailing the injury and speculating on its possible implications. Perhaps Dylan had suffered some delayed brain damage. This was presumably the same injury that Roy Poole had noticed while walking with Dylan in New York. On that occasion Dylan's explanation was different. This cable was one of the first communications to greet Dr de-Gutierrez-Mahoney when he arrived at St Vincent's later that morning.

Dr de-Gutierrez-Mahoney spent an hour closeted with Dylan and the staff physicians of St Vincent's before descending to the hospital waiting-room to meet Liz and John Brinnin. He won them over immediately. Brinnin has described the doctor as a 'soft-spoken man who knew Dylan's work and understood its worth'. He also had a fresh approach to Dylan's particular problem.

The doctor told Liz that he was working on the theory that the most crucial factor in Dylan's coma was the 'direct alcoholic toxicity in brain tissue and brain cells'. The possible diabetes, concussion and even the effects of the morphine injection were now being relegated to contributory, secondary factors. Brinnin and Liz were only too well aware of Dylan's heavy drinking. To questions concerning prognosis the soft-spoken de-Gutierrez-Mahoney pulled no punches. In his opinion, surgery should not be attempted because the condition was not reversible. Dylan was to die.

The doctor did not tell the stunned couple that it would be infinitely preferable that Dylan should die. No patient had been known to survive more than eighteen hours in a deep alcoholic coma without that coma leading to irreversible brain damage.

Brinnin attempted to mount some feeble protest against the inevitable. He asked the doctor whether the fact of Dylan's continued survival was not a hopeful sign in itself. The doctor hesitated before his reply. He did not want to spell out the full horror of Dylan's condition, merely wished that his closest friends accept it as inevitable. He contented himself with telling Brinnin that while it was true that Dylan's body was functioning adequately, that was largely irrelevant to the primary damage to the poet's brain.

The hospital was now in a virtual state of seige. Friday afternoon brought more and more visitors, stimulated by ever more detailed and occasionally lurid media reports. Many friends and fans turned up hoping for a last glimpse of the poet, while the switchboard quickly became jammed with hundreds upon hundreds of calls. St Vincent's made a policy decision: the list of people allowed to visit Dylan's room should be restricted to just two: John Brinnin and Liz Reitell were duly issued with passes for the purpose.

But there was another reason for this new severity, over and above the fresh crush of visitors arriving on the hospital steps. The staff physician, James McVeigh, told Brinnin and Liz that the next twelve hours would see the genuine crisis in Dylan and would determine his fate one way or another. The hospital wanted to be ready for that crisis and did not want hordes of visitors getting in the way when it came.

Brinnin and Liz maintained their vigil by Dylan's bedside, their minds concentrated on the approaching crisis and unable to think of anything else. Around the bedside nurses busied themselves with a thousand preparations.

Back in Wales Dan Jones had again been active. He had already enlisted the services of a journalist friend, Jack Jenkins to communicate to Dr de-Gutierrez-Mahoney salient details of Dylan's past which he felt might be of use. These included Dylan's history of very heavy drinking which confirmed the New York doctor in his theory. But Jones also asked his own doctor in Swansea, Charles McVie, to telephone Dr de-Gutierrez-Mahoney to offer what specialist help he could. The call was made from the Swansea doctor's surgery with an anxious Jones looking on.

Freed from the constraints of soothing a close friend's pain, de-Gutierrez-Mahoney spelt out the situation in New York with all the frankness of a normal medical exchange. Jones watched while McVie listened with a stony expression on his face. He caught the echo of the odd ominous-sounding medical phrase but was not enlightened by it. The conversation ended with the news that the Dylan crisis was expected within the next few hours and that the New York doctors were about to perform a tracheotomy. McVie replaced the receiver and communicated the essence of the conversation to Dylan's oldest friend, if not its every gruesome detail.

It was now late afternoon in New York on Friday 6 November. Brinnin and Liz were asked to vacate Dylan's room while the tracheotomy was performed. This was the crisis that the hospital had expected and the staff did not want any distraction at all. Dylan's breathing had become progressively clogged and he had to be allowed to breathe more freely if he were to avoid death by suffocation. The operation had not been performed before because of its attendant dangers. But now the hospital had little choice.

Brinnin and Liz rejoined the large group of friends and well-wishers in the waiting room and together endured the vigil that contained Dylan's crisis. An hour or so passed, and then Sister Consilio entered with a grave expression on her face. The news was devastating. The tracheotomy had indeed ushered in the much-anticipated crisis and in those few highly charged moments the hospital did not expect Dylan to survive. She asked Brinnin and Liz if they wished to enter the hospital chapel to pray, and while some of the friends present in that room took that offer, Brinnin and Liz remained glued to their seats 'in a silence that was itself a prayer'. The minutes ticked by agonisingly, and then Sister Consilio appeared at the door once more. But she did not bring the news of Dylan's expected death. Instead she told them that the unendurable waiting was to continue. Dylan had survived the crisis.

Brinnin and Liz immediately hurried to the poet's bedside. He did indeed now seem to be breathing more freely. But by now both had come to a fresh acceptance of the facts of their friend's illness. To Brinnin, Dylan now seemed a man kept alive by medical invention alone. The crisis so recently surmounted had merely postponed the inevitable.

On the table beside Dylan now lay the cable from Caitlin containing her last tender message to her husband. Dylan would never read it, as Brinnin and Liz, now knew. They sat with Dylan throughout the long night and it was left once again to Sister Consilio to consider their best interests. Shortly before dawn she once more insisted – with more gentleness now, and less force – that they leave the hospital for some rest. She gave them her personal assurance that with the major crisis passed, Dylan was expected to continue living for at least the duration of that night. Brinnin and Liz would not miss Dylan's end through default. Brinnin and Liz duly left to grab a few hours' sleep.

Saturday morning dawned in New York which made it Saturday lunchtime in Wales. Vernon Watkins, finishing work in the Swansea branch of Lloyds Bank, read with alarm the latest report of Dylan's illness in the South Wales *Evening Post*. Under the headline 'Dylan Thomas Worse' the report stated that Dylan was now in a 'deep coma'. Watkins immediately climbed the town's Constitution Hill to visit Dan Jones in an attempt to glean more details.

At Jones' house, the news was not good. Jones had not had the full position spelt out to him by McVie, but he was perceptive enough to realise the true state of affairs. He told Watkins that neither of them were likely to see their friend alive again. Back in New York, even as he spoke, that diagnosis was being confirmed.

Dylan was getting visibly worse. His breathing, which had been aided by the recent tracheotomy, was now causing problems again, and the poet was experiencing sudden rises and falls in temperature; those very symptoms that had assailed him in the Green Room of the Kaufmann Auditorium just a few days before.

This fresh crisis ushered in a fresh problem for John Brinnin. Keeping in close touch with David Higham in London, Brinnin had learnt that Caitlin had managed to locate a seat on the 3 p.m. flight from London. She was thus due to arrive in New York early the next morning. As time passed, with Dylan apparently sinking ever faster, Brinnin was assailed with doubts as to whether Caitlin should come at all. It was intolerable for her to travel to America to be greeted only by the news of her husband's death.

So Brinnin telephoned David Higham once again, and impressed upon him the imminence of Dylan's demise. But Higham told Brinnin what he already suspected, that he would not be able to influence Caitlin's decision one way or another. Mere reason was not about to stand in her way.

It is difficult now, of course, to establish Brinnin's real motives for that phone call. He may indeed have wished to spare Caitlin the pain of a fruitless and agonising trip to the US. But it is likely that he also wished to spare himself and Liz Reitell the pain and anguish her arrival in New York would necessarily bring. Liz Reitell's position in particular was invidious. It was clear that once Caitlin arrived there would be no place for her by Dylan's side and all contemporary convention dictated that Liz surrender her lover to another's charge. While Brinnin would most certainly not have denied Caitlin her last access to Dylan, it is likely that he would have not wished Liz to suffer any additional pain. Higham told Brinnin that he would cable as soon as Caitlin had boarded her plane to confirm that she was indeed on her way. That call came through later the same day. Caitlin was on her way to New York.

While they awaited Caitlin's arrival, Doctor de-Gutierrez-Mahoney had one more conversation with Brinnin and Liz. He had clearly decided that there was now little point in shielding them from the full facts of Dylan's illness. They had both had time to absorb its reality and now they should know its details. He impressed upon them the full implications of Dylan's brain-damage and went so far as to tell them that even if Dylan should ever recover – which was highly unlikely – there would be nothing left of the personality they had both known so intimately and loved so fully.

The effect on the couple was acute. Brinnin's attitude in particular now changed completely. 'When we comprehended this,' he has written, 'when we could grasp the idea of Dylan's mind brought into some half-articulate and crippled distortion of itself, we could only wish that death would come soon.' Dylan's end was now being anticipated, not with dread but with the prospect of release. Not that it made the prospect any easier to bear.

The endless Saturday limped on. More visitors tried to cram into the waiting room and in the fevered atmosphere, ever-wilder rumours began to circulate about the nature and extent of, and background to, Dylan's injuries. Ever more fantastic stories claimed that Dylan had been mugged, that he had fallen intoxicated from some great height. They began to be taken seriously by many who should have known better. When Brinnin made his brief forays into the waiting room, he found himself having to deal with one fantastic rumour after another, aware all the time he was trying to deny them that they sprang largely from the individual grief of the rumour-monger.

There was one more practical detail to be attended to. For better or for worse Caitlin was on her way and every minute was vital, if she was to see her husband alive. It was essential that Caitlin should not be delayed in her progress through customs or be impeded by some petty immigration procedure which she had likely not observed in the course of her mad flight from London. Brinnin did not want Caitlin trapped at Idlewild while twenty miles away in Manhattan her husband slipped into death.

Brinnin immediately embarked on a circuitous series of phone calls, desperately trying to raise off-duty officers of the British Embassy to arrange for a speedy passage of the poet's wife through US customs. The whole business took close to three hours and was only accomplished finally by the intervention of a high ranking friend in Washington. But finally Brinnin achieved his objective. Caitlin would not be delayed.

By this time it was approaching 2 a.m. on Sunday morning, New York time, and Brinnin reeled from the phone 'half-blind and useless from fatigue'. One look from Sister Consilio despatched Brinnin from the hospital in the care of Howard Moss for some much-needed sedatives and sleep.

All this left Liz Reitell on her own for the large part of that evening and it was a particularly poignant evening for her. She was now aware that Caitlin's arrival would be the signal for her own withdrawal. There was simply no emotional room for them both in that small hospital room. In a real sense that evening and that night would be her last time alone with Dylan before he was claimed once more by the woman who would always have the first call on him. Liz sat quietly by Dylan's bedside, while Brinnin busied himself with the details of Caitlin's arrival, and tried to deal with the personal implications of that arrival.

When Brinnin left the hospital at 2 a.m. Liz adamantly though quietly refused to accompany him, and for once Sister Consilio did not press the matter. Dylan's condition was worsening – his temperature at one time touched 105.5° – but even that did not cause Liz to withdraw. It is likely that Sister Consilio glimpsed something of the pain behind Liz's last vigil and she did not oppose her decision to remain. Liz stayed at Dylan's side throughout the whole of the night and was still there when Brinnin returned to the hospital at eight the next morning. A few minutes later, Caitlin arrived.

Her actual entry was dramatic. Caitlin had been met by Rose and David Slivka at Idlewild and had been whisked to St Vincent's flanked by a posse of police motorcycles. The only news Caitlin had been able to glean from her two American friends was that there was 'no change', and Caitlin was hungry for more. She duly swooped on the New York hospital.

Later Rose Slivka was to say that Caitlin hoped that the dramatic nature of her arrival would somehow galvanise Dylan into consciousness, as if the sheer energy of her performance would provide the key that would unlock his coma. But this is perhaps a charitable interpretation. It is equally likely that the pressure of waiting in London had simply and understandably unbalanced her. In the hospital Brinnin looked on, dazed, as Caitlin marched up to him. They embraced. For a second they stood, silent, in the hotel corridor, and the first words were spoken by Caitlin. Characteristically, they were sharp.

'Well? Is the bloody man dead or alive?' Caitlin demanded. She could have been affectionately despairing of a favourite child. Perhaps after all Caitlin could not really comprehend that Dylan had now fallen into a real trap, as distinct from the myriad number of false alarms sounded at various times in London and in Wales.

By way of reply Brinnin led her upstairs to Dylan's room. From that moment on the 'island of quietness' that Liz experienced around Dylan's bed was to be irrevocably breached. Brinnin and Caitlin had to wait a few moments at Dylan's door while a nurse finished bathing him and that wait was unfortunate. At the far end of the corridor, having left Dylan's room but not the hospital, sat Liz Reitell. Rose Slivka was to say later that they had attempted to keep Caitlin away from Liz but in that brief pause outside Dylan's room the women were within clear sight of each other and a tense and uneasy silence fell. Then the nurse allowed them in to see Dylan.

By this time Dylan had been placed in an oxygen tent, and it is unlikely that Caitlin would have been prepared for such a stark demonstration of the seriousness of her husband's condition. But she remained in control for the present. She took Dylan's hand and began to speak to him.

Brinnin left her alone and hurried to join Liz, ousted from her special place at Dylan's bedside both physically and emotionally. They did not expect Caitlin to emerge from the room for many hours, and were surprised and disturbed when she left Dylan's side just fifteen minutes later and began to walk towards them along the corridor. The drama continued. As Caitlin drew level with them she stopped and looked at them silently and then turned and slowly and deliberately began to smash her forehead against a nearby window. That the window did not break was solely due to its reinforced netting. Brinnin and Liz were helpless, frozen to the spot. Rose and David Slivka were the first to act and they dashed from the other end of the corridor, took charge of the clearly distraught Caitlin and rushed her to their own apartment and away from St Vincent's.

For Liz's part, she had now come to a definite decision that Caitlin's actions had only confirmed. While Caitlin was in St Vincent's she could have no place there. Her presence could only strain an already fraught atmosphere. She had no right to be there while Caitlin was in attendance and she decided that she must leave at once. Brinnin reports that she was 'calm' now she was resigned to her decision and 'to a circumstance too complex to unravel'. He believed that her decision was the correct one. But with Liz gone, problems would multiply for John Brinnin.

Liz left and Brinnin was alone. His closest friend in New

York, his confidant, had gone and he now had Caitlin to deal with. In that moment Brinnin truly felt that Dylan too had gone from him already.

Brinnin stumbled into Dylan's room, irresolute and lost. He records that he has never experienced a lonelier moment in his life and for the first time since he arrived in New York he gave way to his grief. No-one was there to see him or to comfort him and anyway Brinnin would not have wanted any comfort. As Dylan's immobile form lay before him, Brinnin simply wept.

Brinnin remained in the small hospital room for some time while his immediate grief burnt itself out. When he arose he took comfort in more action on Dylan's behalf.

It was now well into Sunday morning and Britain had woken up to more serious bulletins concerning Dylan's illness. Dan Jones and Vernon Watkins held themselves ready in Wales for the news they dreaded, though Watkins resisted the notion of Dylan's death to the very end. Thirty years later, Vernon's wife Gwen can still remember his anguished cry that Sunday morning when a caller from the London *Times* asked her husband to prepare an obituary for Dylan. Vernon's protest rang through the house. 'But he's not dead yet!' Nevertheless, Vernon sat down to the task, which took him most of that Sunday. His obituary was to be rushed into print less than twenty-four hours later.

Later that same day, and now apparently more calm, Caitlin returned to the hospital in the company of David and Rose Slivka. She looked, so Brinnin recalled, radiant, but Brinnin could also tell that she had been drinking, and when she embraced him she clung to him for more than a minute. Brinnin sensed that physically she was now unsteady through drink rather than through grief. Then she left Brinnin to join Dylan on his death bed. It would soon become obvious that her new calm was only skin-deep.

Caitlin had always believed that 'Dylan was never his proper self till there was something wrong with him'. But the sight that had greeted her on arrival and with which she was about to be re-acquainted, was horrific. Dylan, she recorded was 'basely humiliated with the disgusting things he dreaded most; not one organ in his body working in its own right, without mechanical assistance, intravenal feeding, tubes attached blatantly to each vulnerable shy orifice; the head encased in a transparent tent, pumping oxygen into him; the eyes turned up bulging, unseeing; the breath roaring like a winded horse pounding up a slope; and no Dylan there, no contact.' The obscenity of Dylan's position led her naturally to the logical but hopeless conclusion: that this was 'a farcical artificial prolongation of what had already gone'.

This perception, her acute awareness of Dylan's 'humiliation', and the drink, all conspired now to bring Dylan to the edge of a premature end at the hands of his wife. Caitlin decided to take matters into her own hands. She tried to embrace her insensible husband. When restrained by a somewhat distraught nurse, Caitlin calmed herself by lighting a succession of cigarettes within dangerous proximity of the fragile oxygen tent.

The nurses attending Dylan were now alarmed beyond measure, and they hurried Caitlin away from Dylan and into a private room. But this only became the setting for more torment. Someone had brought a bottle of whisky into the hospital and Caitlin immediately drank deeply. Others of Dylan's friends joined her in the private waiting room, including Rose Slivka, Rollie McKenna, David Lougee and John Brinnin. Caitlin eyed the assembled company and drank some more. Her attention, as she continued to drink, became fixed unwaveringly on Brinnin.

It seems now that Brinnin had come to embody all Caitlin's problems and that she was beginning to associate all Dylan's present difficulties with the hapless Director of the Poetry Center. Was it not Brinnin who had enticed Dylan across to the US in the first place and who arranged the details of this very trip that had led him to the edge of oblivion? Caitlin's tortured thought processes twisted themselves into a sudden and vicious hatred of Brinnin.

Without warning Caitlin flew at him. She physically attacked him, biting and scratching. The other visitors attempted to intervene, but they were turned on with equal ferocity. Rollie McKenna hastily suggested that Brinnin, as the object of Caitlin's rage, should leave the room in the hope that his absence may soothe her. Brinnin duly removed himself and rejoined Dylan next door. But when Brinnin returned to the assembled company a few minutes later, the torment had still not subsided.

Rollie McKenna met Brinnin at the door. She urged that he now call a doctor, as Caitlin was rapidly becoming uncontrollable. She had smashed up the room and had now turned her attention on the unfortunate nurses who had been despatched to investigate the disturbance. Brinnin summoned a doctor, who arrived complete with a burly attendant and a wheel-chair. This sobering sight quietened Caitlin momentarily, but as the attendant escorted her out she flew into another rage, biting the attendant, who attempted to restrain her, and kicking out at the surrounding doctors. All this was Caitlin's escape valve, as she later admitted. She hoped 'through the sheer weakness of excessive excess, to escape the consequences lying viciously in store for me'. Caitlin was eventually bundled into a strait-jacket and rushed to the emergency ward. Within twenty-four hours of her arrival, Caitlin was thus as physically helpless as her incapacitated husband a few yards away. Neither, it seemed, was responsible any longer for their actions. At that moment Vernon Watkins back home in Wales was putting the finishing touches to his obituary tribute to Dylan and its last sentence could have encompassed both husband and wife. 'Innocence is always a paradox,' Watkins wrote, 'and Dylan Thomas presents, in retrospect, the greatest paradox of our time.'

Caitlin was taken to the emergency ward hopefully to enjoy a recovery. But within minutes there was a fresh Caitlin crisis. Doctor Feltenstein hurried from the emergency ward to tell Brinnin that Dylan's wife had become totally uncontrollable and that the hospital could no longer take any responsibility for her actions. Her hysteria, he told Brinnin, was 'extreme'. St Vincent's had neither the facilities nor the inclination to take care of Caitlin. Neither could they permit her simply to walk free into the New York streets in her present condition. They also distrusted certain of Caitlin's friends – there was an unconfirmed report that Rose Slivka had encouraged her attack upon one of the nurses. The hospital were unsure what could be done with Caitlin but on one point they were agreed: Caitlin could not remain in St Vincent's.

Brinnin knew that he could not assume any personal

responsibility for Caitlin and indeed feared for his own safety, should Dylan's wife be released to his care. The only possible solution was staring them in the face and Feltenstein had no hesitation in spelling it out: Caitlin must be committed to an institution more able to deal with the deranged.

This idea repelled Brinnin. As far as he was concerned, Caitlin was in the grips of an understandable grief rather than a more deep-rooted psychosis. He insisted that a staff psychiatrist from St Vincent's examine Caitlin to confirm Doctor Feltenstein's recommendation. This procedure was hastily arranged, but once complete it brought no comfort to Brinnin. Caitlin, the staff psychiatrist concluded, was simply not rational: she needed professional care and that care was beyond the scope of her friends and of St Vincent's. A private institution – a mental institution – was required. In New York that meant only one thing: Bellevue, Manhattan's renowned mental asylum. Brinnin continued to resist the idea, though he was now on considerable weaker ground. As a last-ditch effort, he proposed that they choose some other institution than the notorious Bellevue. Reluctantly he proposed that Caitlin be despatched to the Rivercrest Clinic on Long Island.

Caitlin was duly sent to Rivercrest in the care of hospital attendants and in a hospital ambulance. Brinnin was later to learn that Caitlin calmed down and became quite reasonable in the wake of her departure, which may have been due to a final sedation. There may also have been another cause, though this is unconfirmed. David Lougee has said that before she left St Vincent's, Caitlin had been told that her husband was dead. (This statement has not been supported by any other witness in St Vincent's).

With Caitlin absent, Brinnin was able to turn his attention to more immediate matters and to take some personal comfort at the thought of rendering practical aid. Freed from distraction, Brinnin's organising zeal reasserted itself. Caitlin's arrival had raised the question of money.

Dylan certainly had no money to pay his hospital bill, which was likely to be considerable, and he had no money either to provide for the future care of his bereaved family. A trust fund supported by contributions from friends and well-wishers had to be started immediately, and Brinnin set about its establishment. To that end he contacted Liz Reitell and asked her to bring Dylan's American publisher James Laughlin to St Vincent's for an immediate conference. It is likely that he told her that Caitlin was by now out of the way, which would have been a condition of Liz's return. Even in those few moments outside Dylan's hospital room, Liz had felt the waves of hostility flowing toward her from the implacable Caitlin, and even months later, back home in Laugharne, Caitlin was still deeply suspicious of Liz's part in this whole last episode. Despite Rollie McKenna's later assurance of the essential sincerity of Liz's actions, Caitlin was not convinced.

Laughlin duly arrived at St Vincent's and a New York attorney, Phillip Wittenberg, now joined him. Brinnin, James Laughlin and Phillip Wittenberg then sat down in St Vincent's to devise ways in which a trust or memorial fund could be established to take care both of immediate expenses and of Dylan's dependants.

The discussion was deliberately business-like and brief, concentrating on essential details and eschewing any useless speculation. It was agreed that a fund should be established, that it should be called the Dylan Thomas Memorial Fund and that a list of literary sponsors should be approached to lend their names, their support and their money. It was further agreed that the first of the necessary letters would be sent out the very next day. The Dylan Thomas Memorial Fund was not even to wait for the death of the man it was to commemorate. Events had moved a long way in a very short time.

It was now a waiting game. Liz Reitell was back at St Vincent's, when earlier she thought she had left the hospital for good. There was little she could do but look on helplessly as Dylan's life ebbed away. Brinnin, too, now sensed that Dylan had entered the final phase. They sat beside Dylan's bed and waited. Caitlin, under sedation in the Rivercrest Clinic also waited. Back in Britain and all over America thousands of Dylan's admirers waited. In Wales Vernon Watkins had finished the obituary he never wished to see in print. Dan Jones was preparing listlessly for a recital that had been planned for months previously but which now had lost its earlier keen attraction.

Liz was sitting by Dylan's bedside and as much to comfort

herself as him, was talking to Dylan constantly. She was talking, so she recalled thirty years later, 'of Montana'. Dylan 'adored Montana though he had never been there,' Liz recalled. 'He loved the name, which was beautiful and he had flown over it several times and looked down at the mountains.' It seems that Montana was a fantasy land for Dylan. 'Welshmen and mountains are inseparable,' Liz has said, 'and we had fantasies about leaving this world and its troubles and ... living in Montana on a ranch by the mountains.' Montana would indeed have represented for Dylan a fantasy escape had he been able to heave his protesting body there now. But Dylan had already made his escape, and Liz was merely awaiting its confirmation.

Brinnin telephoned the Rivercrest Clinic later and heard that Caitlin would not be released for at least two or three days. He also learnt with some concern that she was alone, and he immediately arranged for Rose and David Slivka to visit her. Brinnin the tireless organiser was organising tirelessly to the last.

Monday dawned – 9 November – with Dylan sinking ever deeper into the bottomless pit of his illness. Inactivity reigned, though there was one brief flurry of activity later that day; one event that was to raise a last flicker of hope before hope was extinguished for ever.

A specialist in alcoholism, Doctor James Smith, who headed the alcoholism unit in Bellevue, called at St Vincent's. Liz and Brinnin became aware of an increase in the activity around Dylan's bed as Doctor Smith suggested some new treatments. For a brief second Liz and Brinnin may have dared to hope that the poet's condition might not be irreversible after all, that perhaps Dylan might cheat death at the eleventh hour. But deep down Brinnin and Liz knew that any treatment was too late. When Liz was herself to talk with Doctor Smith, it was not to speculate on a possible Dylan recovery, but to determine whether alcohol was the primary factor in the poet's inevitable death.

Everyone continued to wait. It was now mid-day on Monday, early evening back home in Wales. Dan Jones was practising for his recital the next day, his fingers moving automatically over the keys in a parody of rehearsal. Caitlin was in the Rivercrest, 'the one undeniably sane freak among the chattering starlings'. Brinnin was still actively employed on the details of Dylan's Memorial Fund. The rest of Dylan's world held their breath lest they missed the end.

As things turned out, Dylan died when neither Liz, Brinnin nor Caitlin was by his side. Around mid-day Liz came out of Dylan's sick-room for a short break, and joined Brinnin who was busily making his final arrangements in the waiting room. Only John Berryman was with Dylan, watching a nurse wash him. There was nothing to indicate that this would be Dylan's last moment, and the end when it came was not dramatic.

As the nurse scrubbed Dylan's unresisting body, Dylan gave a small gasp. Berryman might not even have registered it. The nurse had been just about to turn Dylan over, but now she stopped. She checked his breathing and his pulse. Berryman, his disbelief growing, looked on. Then she looked towards the anguished Princeton poet and academic and her expression betrayed her. Dylan was dead. Berryman could not believe that, in the end, it had all been so simple.

Berryman stumbled from Dylan's room to find Brinnin and Liz. Brinnin was at that moment emerging from the waiting room to take up his own vigil by Dylan's bedside. Berryman hurtled down the corridor towards him and Brinnin stopped, arrested by Berryman's expression.

'Where were you, where were you?' demanded Berryman. Liz had now come to the door of the waiting room and knew too what was to come. 'He's dead,' said Berryman. 'Dylan's dead.'

Brinnin did not move for a few seconds and when he did it is to his credit that it was back towards Liz Reitell. He took her hands in his own. Neither spoke and the rest of the assorted visitors watched them, waiting for direction, to be told how to act. Brinnin simply nodded to her and both understood the signal, their private signal that would denote Dylan's death without either of them articulating its fact and thereby forcing it into a kind of existence. They both then pushed through the crowd that had stood up around the door and made for the elevator.

In Dylan's room the nurses were already clearing away the hospital instruments and Dylan's body had been disconnected from its life supports. Brinnin and Liz watched from the door, and then approached. Neither spoke and neither wept; the time for talking and for tears was past, or for the future and that time was not now. Brinnin now felt that Dylan was at peace. For her part Liz Reitell did not feel anything at all, and would not feel anything until others forced the reality of Dylan's death into her conscious mind. Dylan was even more of a public figure in death than in life, she was to discover.

But for now there was one last private exchange. Liz approached Dylan's bed for the very last time before his body would be claimed by others, and kissed him on the forehead. She bade him goodbye and whispered to him that she would see him in Montana, on their mythical ranch. As the nurses then crowded around the body and the news of Dylan's death began to be flashed around the world, his two closest American friends, the two people most intimately involved with his tempestuous stay in the US, stood by the foot of his bed in silence. As Brinnin has recorded, there were no tears.

Chapter Ten
Return Journey

By late afternoon on Monday 9 November, everyone connected with Dylan Thomas knew of his death. So did everyone else. Its long drawn-out prelude had ensured the maximum amount of media interest in his struggle for survival and the news that he had lost that last fight was flashed around the world.

Dan Jones was interrupted by his mother as he practised for his recital the next day. She didn't waste time in considering his feelings. 'Dylan's dead,' she announced. Vernon Watkins sought refuge in a grief that was frantically searching for a more positive expression. 'What a good job he managed to meet Ceri Richards,' he exclaimed. Dylan's London agent, David Higham, communicated the grim news to the rest of Dylan's English and Welsh friends.

In New York, friends and colleagues either received phone calls from those intimately involved with Dylan's struggle or heard the news themselves on television or radio broadcasts. Roy Poole, then working as an usher at the Poetry Center, answered the telephone that Monday afternoon to hear Liz Reitell's voice. She too wasted no time on preliminaries. 'Roy, we've lost him,' she said. Thirty years later Roy Poole can still remember his immediate reaction of disbelief. It did not seem possible, that anyone so alive could now be dead. All over the country and all over the world, friends and fans shared that same sense of disbelief and shock.

The tributes began to flood in. In London every newspaper prepared its own special testimony to one of Britain's favourite literary sons. Victor Herbert in the *Daily Herald* described Dylan as 'the most prominent poet in our literary landscape' while the *Daily Express* and *Daily Mail* both described him as an 'absolute genius, a genius who loved life and talk and saloon bars'. Two newspapers concentrated on the poet's vul-

194

nerability. The *News Chronicle* told its readers that 'with the death of Dylan Thomas, we have lost a born poet. There has never been any doubt about his gifts. Plenty of people tried to tell him how he ought to use and husband them, but he never seemed to listen.' For the *Manchester Guardian*, Dylan had 'established himself as one of the major British poets of this century – he was a master of vocabulary. He thought in images where lesser mortals were content with phrases.' But it admonished its readers, 'The age that knew him may have appreciated him, it cannot flatter itself that it made life easy for him.' The *Manchester Guardian* concluded its tribute with the observation that Dylan 'should have been born in the age of patrons'.

The two principal New York papers also carried immediate tributes. The *New York Times* wrote that 'There is little doubt that the young Welshman was among the foremost poets of our generation. In addition to his poetic gifts, Dylan Thomas possessed a remarkable flair for making himself liked and admired by those with whom he came in personal contact. His affable and sincere personality projected itself through his readings ... Those for whom his poetry added a little to life's fresh beauties will be grieved by the silencing of his ... young voice.' The New York *Herald Tribune* speculated that 'There is no saying what might have been the extent of his literary accomplishments had he had the time our age allows most men ... His unfinished book is closed now and it stands with the poetry of Keats and Marlowe as an excellent but poignantly half-filled promise.'

In the US it was immediately decided that the American community should hold a memorial service in advance of Dylan's transportation to the U.K., at which that widespread sense of loss and grief could be expressed.

Caitlin had been released from the Rivercrest Clinic immediately after her husband's death and was taken into the care of Rose and David Slivka who had now assumed complete charge of Dylan's widow in the US. She was taken back to the Slivka's Greenwich Village apartment.

Rollie McKenna visited Caitlin on her return with the Slivkas, and discovered now a very different character to the one who had tried to demolish St Vincent's. While heartbroken,

195

Rollie has said, Caitlin now seemed able to cope with the 'reality of her loss'. Perhaps the immediate opportunity for some constructive action was soothing her as it soothed John Brinnin. Caitlin had decided that she herself must compose and despatch to his mother and to her own children waiting back home in Laugharne the telegrams announcing Dylan's death. Much of Monday was spent in that task.

The next day the opportunity arose for Caitlin to view her husband's body as it lay in a Manhattan funeral parlour and she eagerly embraced the offer. Rollie McKenna accompanied her, and for once her renowned coolness deserted her. Rollie was unable to face the sight of Dylan, inert and lifeless in his coffin, and it was left to the implacable Caitlin to stand alone and stare at the deceased form of her husband. On returning to the Slivkas' apartment Caitlin first learnt of the planned memorial service for Dylan that had been fixed for that approaching Friday, 13 November.

Caitlin immediately resisted the idea; it would all be an intolerable trial, she announced. But Dylan was no longer her private property – he had not been that for some time – and in the extremity of her private grief, Caitlin was not able to dictate how the public grief should be expressed. It was clear that Dylan's friends wished to hold a memorial service and that they would do so. Faced with the inevitable, Caitlin agreed, though she made her own private arrangement with Rollie McKenna for the photographer to take charge of her throughout the ordeal and to 'rescue' her from the inevitable crush of well-wishers and sympathisers.

As it happened, an advance deputation arrived the very next day. In the Slivkas' apartment Caitlin received a visit from the Welsh Society, a solemn New York-based group that had come to offer their condolences to their countryman's widow. The audience confirmed Caitlin in her renowned antipathy towards the pretensions of the 'respectable Welsh' and her later description was characteristically hostile. 'Even in that state of abysmal disadvantage I could not help being impressed by the endearing cardboard formality of their pinstripe suits, their industriously polished shoes, their squeezed-to-extinction collars. After several generations in America they had not lost one intonation of the guiding Welsh principles, nor contaminated with a drawling slur their chanting up-and-down accents.' Caitlin's clear-sighted hostility continued. 'After a tremendous amount of palavering, and skirmishing round the fragile, handle-with-care subject, they solemnly presented me with a small cheque, collected from the extensive Welsh community.'

It was partly to avoid such situations that Caitlin had resisted the initial proposal of a memorial service. But now it was fixed.

For the next two days that memorial service became the focus for all the public and private grief being expressed in countless newspaper articles, radio broadcasts and more intimate conversations in apartments up and down Manhattan. The service was scheduled to take place in the St Luke's Episcopal Church of Trinity Parish.

In the period between Dylan's death and his memorial service, Liz Reitell and John Brinnin had done little save deal as best they could with their own private and individual experience of loss. Brinnin had left New York after Dylan's death but had returned later that week to meet Caitlin. Liz had anguished over whether she should leave New York but had decided that she must attend his farewell American service whatever form that might take and however her presence might offend against the contemporary proprieties. Perhaps she suspected that no-one would notice her in the inevitable crush and that she could thus pay her own private tribute to Dylan within the context of that public expression without offending against convention.

The day of the service found four hundred people milling outside the St Luke's Episcopal Church and Liz was indeed lost in the crush. In strict observance of the ritual of such ceremonies, Caitlin and the principal mourners stood at the front. Liz huddled in at the back, feeling herself to be 'the loneliest person in the world', distanced from the immediate orbit around Dylan and apart from her dead lover in every possible sense. By her in the congregation was another close friend, who sensed the waves of loneliness and despair flowing from the unfortunate Miss Reitell. He took her hand in silent sympathy and she gripped his hand back and held it throughout the service, as the hymns were sung and the lessons read and Dylan slipped further and further away from her.

The service ended. At the front of the congregation Caitlin avoided the crush of mourners and headed for Rollie McKenna as they had previously arranged. She delivered herself into the care of the capable photographer and in her charge extricated herself from St Luke's and went back to the Slivkas' Greenwich Village apartment; her duty in America had been discharged and the trial back home was yet to be faced.

For her part, Liz hesitated outside the church. She had now said her final goodbye. She would not be travelling to Britain and would be taking no part in Dylan's funeral ceremony to be held in Wales. After the weeks of caring so intimately for Dylan, her charge had gone and she was alone.

The experience was cruel. Dylan had been part of her existence. Her days had been his days throughout that last dramatic and desperate passage. Later, in television interviews, Liz was to express her sense of personal loss as bleakly as she had experienced it. 'I feel,' she was to tell a reporter, 'as though the sunlight has been maimed.' the days of Dylan Thomas had passed and gone and from that moment on her own days would be irremediably lacking in some way, 'as if I knew that never again,' Liz was to say, 'would the sun shine so brightly for me, never in all my life.'

Liz and hundreds of other friends and fans continued to stand around the doors of St Luke's, reluctant to leave, to bid farewell to each other and thus to mark the end of their mutual association with the Welsh poet and to embark on their own more private expressions of grief. Once that party finally broke up, Liz well knew, there would be no more Dylan for her and any future events would pass her by, as they would pass any spectator, forever excluded. It was one of the cruellest consequences of her peculiar position. Dylan's death had cut her off even from participation in the full and proper expression of grief.

It was now intended that Caitlin should escort Dylan's body back to the U.K. aboard the SS *United States*, due to sail from New York to Southampton that very afternoon. Back to the Slivkas' apartment she seemed apparently more composed, with one of her hated trials at an end. There was now little time to live through in America before she took Dylan back to where she had always wanted him – home. The only remaining task was to collect Dylan's small and motley collection of possessions.

These effects contained jottings for Dylan's last poem to his father, his *Elegy*, a copy of the radio script 'Return Journey', letters from Stravinsky, Phillip Burton and Caitlin among others, an inhaler, a tube of pills, a fountain pen, a box of cigars, four suits, four shirts, two vests, two hot-water bottles, an empty cheque book with blank stubs, and a few pounds in cash. There was also a letter from Dylan's bank manager. It all amounted to very little and provided a poignant reminder – if Caitlin had needed any – that from that point on finances threatened to be even more stretched than before. Caitlin now faced the prospect of bringing up three children with no money. This had been John Brinnin's constant concern from the time of Dylan's illness, and the indefatigable Director of the Poetry Center had been highly active behind the scenes. First the Memorial Fund itself had been launched under the signatures of some of America's most prestigious literary figures: W.H. Auden, E.E. Cummings, Marianne Moore, Arthur Miller, Wallace Stevens and Tenessee Williams. The appeal addressed itself to 'Dylan's friends', and opened, 'I am sure you have read in the Press of the sudden and tragic death of Dylan Thomas. Thomas died of encephalopathy at St Vincent's Hospital in New York after an illness of four days. He was only 39 years old. He was attended by one of the best brain surgeons in New York and everything possible was done to save him.' The letter made one reference to the more general and widespread loss Dylan's death occasioned. 'Thomas' death is an incalculable loss to literature. His work was growing in stature every year.' But it soon moved on to its real theme. 'But there is a personal tragedy – he leaves a widow and three children – which gravely concerns his friends and admirers.' The appeal then made its request for money to aid Dylan's dependents. 'As spokesmen for a Committee of his friends we are making this urgent appeal to you for a contribution to the Dylan Thomas fund which we have hastily organised which will be used to meet his medical bills and funeral expenses and, if the response is as generous as we hope, to tide his family over the next difficult months.'

One of the first responses to this appeal was one of the most remarkable. Within a few hours of the appeal being launched, the St Vincent's medical authorities let it be known that they had cancelled all charges for Dylan's treatment and care. It was a quite remarkable gesture and one for which the trustees were most immediately thankful. The medical fees alone would have constituted a heavy drain on the fledgling fund and would have inflicted a blow from which the fund would have had difficulty in recovering. Thus one of the last acts connected with Dylan Thomas in the US was one of extraordinary generosity.

The afternoon rolled round. Caitlin left the Slivkas' apartment and travelled the short distance to the Hudson River to embark on the SS *United States*. Dylan's body was loaded into the hold and Caitlin accompanied the coffin into the hold itself before making her way to her own cabin. Crowds of assorted well-wishers, on-lookers and friends gathered on the quayside to bid farewell. Liz Reitell was still in New York, though not by the Hudson River. But she would have heard with a heart too full for expression the mournful hoot of the great liner's whistle as it pulled away from the Hudson quayside. A few short weeks earlier Dylan had arrived in the US. She had met him at the airport, heart bursting with excitement. Now she stood in a New York street while Dylan's body sailed out of the Hudson in the company of his grieving wife, and knew that she had lost him forever. The only emotion left was a dull pain that thirty years later was recalled with as much intensity as Liz experienced at the time. The SS *United States* steamed down the Hudson and out into the open sea. Dylan's body was going home to Wales.

Back in the U.K., Dan Jones had become the self-appointed Master of Ceremonies. His duties were various and they were onerous. In the first instance, there was a British Trust Fund to establish, to supplement and complement the work of the American project. To that end Jones contacted some other of Swansea's famous sons and, in the company of Vernon Watkins and Alfred Janes, he called on the Mayor of Swansea to set the new fund in train. The mayor's appeal was published in the South Wales *Evening Post* on Friday, 13 November, the day of

Dylan's memorial service in New York. After reminding its readers of Dylan's Swansea connections, the mayor wrote, 'In accord with my promise to do whatsoever I can to assist in these tragic circumstances, I am asking for your generous support to the fund to give financial aid to the dependants of Dylan Thomas. Let your contribution be an expression of your sympathy for the family and a tribute to the memory of a great citizen of this town.' Contributions began to pour in from the day of its establishment, headed by donations of ten guineas apiece from Vernon Watkins and Alfred Janes. A boost to the fund in its flagging later stages was to be provided by a huge injection from Jones himself, of £52.10s.

Jones had already participated in a memorial programme in honour of Dylan, broadcast on the Welsh Home Service the night after Dylan's death at which he played a piano piece and Vernon Watkins read some poetry. Earlier in the evening Saunders Lewis had given an appreciation in Welsh. Jones also made it his business to care for Dylan's mother, struggling with Dylan's three children in Laugharne. He told Vernon Watkins that she was 'bearing the news wonderfully'.

Out in the Atlantic, Caitlin was dealing with problems of her own. She had already suffered through a nightmare farewell to New York. Resting in the Slivkas' apartment after the memorial service, Caitlin had found that she literally could not move, that she could not coax her legs into action. Rose Slivka physically forced her upright and a group of friends escorted the unwilling widow out of Rose Slivkas' safe apartment and into the frightening bustle of the Hudson Docks to face the prospect of a long, lonely sea voyage back to detested Laugharne with the dead Dylan.

The nightmare continued. A group of friends insisted on accompanying Caitlin right into the cabin. David Lougee, presumably in dubious honour of Dylan, was bearing a bottle of iced champagne. Determined that she should not be left alone for a moment, the group piled into the cabin and started to drink. Soon the cabin was in disarray, as were Caitlin's guests. At one stage Herb Hannum ended up on the deck of the small cabin, clinging to Caitlin's legs.

Her one real friend in New York, Rose Slivka, stood silently at one end of the cabin while Caitlin stood at the other. Caitlin wanted to scream, but no sound came.

The hooter sounded for the visitors to scramble ashore and Caitlin embraced the new peace and relative calm. She still could not escape a bitter suspicion that her friends were scrambling away from her dark cabin with a sense of relief, with a sense of a duty finally and thankfully discharged. Caitlin was left 'mad; drunk; heartbroken; and, for the first time, horribly alone; in the middle of the morning; in the middle of the sea; and in the middle of Dylan and me; me and my box, down below, that I was bringing home.' But Caitlin was given little time to indulge in such feelings. There were more immediate difficulties to be faced.

Despite Caitlin's requesting a single cabin, she had been given a cabin mate. Not 'a nice ordinary woman' moreover, 'but the kind that terrifies me most: young, suavely polished, metallically smart, always possessing just the right casual garment to change into.' The young cabin mate loomed in the doorway and Caitlin stared at the apparition as if she could not believe it. She willed the woman to disappear; but the visitor was determined to stay.

Caitlin immediately decided that the prospect of sailing for a week with this 'creamily elegant woman' was more than she could stand, and she left the cabin, determined not to return. She decided that she must stage a scene to convince others that she required a degree of privacy for her own sake and for the other traveller's. She chose the most public place on deck and then staged a much-practised and horribly convincing attack. As Caitlin has recorded, 'I was getting accustomed to the role.'

The ship authorities immediately agreed that Caitlin could not share a cabin with any of their fellow-travellers and found a change of venue for the apparently hysterical widow. But events did not go entirely to plan. For the first three days of the voyage Caitlin found herself locked in the ship's hospital, deep in the bowels of the ship. The crew had decided to take no chances.

Caitlin was let out on the fourth day of the voyage, but more nightmares were to come. As Dylan's wife wandered into the hold to visit her husband's temporary place of rest, she noticed a group of sailors drinking beer and eating sandwiches. Their sandwiches and beer were strewn across a coffin top. It had to be Dylan's, and it was. Caitlin was not angry, more bitterly amused. If Dylan had been alive, she has recorded, 'if it had been possible for him to have enjoyed it,' he would have done.

Two days later the voyage ended at Southampton. Dylan and Caitlin were to be met, inevitably by Dan Jones. Caitlin was still bitter and distraught. In an interview on board she told a reporter, 'I was determined to bring Dylan back to Wales. I would not have him rest in America because I would hate to think they they might ever have cause to nominate him as one of their own poets.' She disembarked with relief to a Jones depressed at his task and irritated with its details.

By one of those unfortunate accidents the only helper free to travel with Jones was Ebie Williams, landlord of the Brown's Hotel in Laugharne. The two men had never got on, and the trial of a two-hundred mile trip exacerbated their mutual dislike. At the Southampton quayside they encountered members of the Southampton Cymrodorian Society and a mutual friend of Dylan's and Jones, Vera Bevan, who had been at school with the two men and was then a Southampton school teacher.

Jones greeted Caitlin and attempted to shield her from the expressions of grief being rehearsed by the Welshmen-in-exile on the quayside. He then supervised the unloading of Dylan's coffin.

Here more difficulties arose. It had been planned to embark on the long homeward journey immediately, but it was discovered that the coffin had been sealed in a huge casket, far too large for the English hearse. In desperation, Jones directed the coffin to a private mortuary where workmen were found who were able to open the sealed container in which the coffin had been placed. The cortege finally began its homeward journey at 9 p.m.

Dylan's body arrived back home in Laugharne at 5 a.m. the next morning. Six Laugharne residents had stayed up all night to greet the returning party and to carry Dylan's coffin into the front room of The Pelican, Dylan's mother's house in the middle of Laugharne. It had been decided that the Boat House would have proved too inaccessible a resting place. Caitlin relaxed for the first time in days. Dylan was home.

It was Monday 23 November. For the next day Dylan's body

would remain on view in The Pelican while an assortment of various friends, relatives and curious Laugharne residents filed in to pay their last tribute to the man who had immortalised their village. The American morticians had done a good job on the dead poet. His face, so Dan Jones recalled, was plastered in make-up and bore little relation to the more care-worn visage the poet had worn for the past thirty-odd years. He was also wearing a particularly vile red tie, so Jones recalled. The tie had been an object of note back in the US too. Ruthven Todd had told friends that he wouldn't be seen dead in it.

The day of Dylan's funeral inexorably approached. The majority of Dylan's last guests were to view his body on the morning of the funeral itself and the coffin lid was open from early morning. Ebie Williams walked across the road from Brown's Hotel and placed a red carnation inside the coffin. It had been Ebie and Dylan's pact that whoever should survive the other should place such a token inside the burial casket. Ebie had clearly not forgotten. More friends filed in and stared at Dylan who, fixed and mute in his American mask, stared back. Some took pictures of Dylan in his coffin. One such picture is reproduced in the worst possible taste in one of the poet's biographies. None of these last glances did Dan Jones a great deal of good. 'However much I reproached myself,' he has written, 'I could summon up no feeling for the object at the foot of the bookcase or for anything now connected with it.' But Dylan's mother was pleased with the job the morticians had done on her son. Dylan, she told Dan Jones that morning, 'looked nice'.

Vernon Watkins did not see Dylan in his final resting casket. Indeed he nearly missed the entire funeral. His bank was reluctant to allow him leave to attend the ceremony and they finally agreed only grudgingly. He was to face more disappointments on the day of the funeral service itself. Watkins wanted very much to have one last look at Dylan. Years later his wife felt that the heavily made-up face of Vernon's Swansea friend would not have upset her husband. Vernon, she felt, would have perceived it as one more mask behind which the real Dylan hid, and would have delighted in it. But even this was to be denied Watkins.

The car driver, Huw Griffith, decided that in honour of

Dylan their car should stop at every pub from Swansea to Laugharne. He proceeded to do just that. By the time the party finally made it to Laugharne the coffin had been closed. Worse, the coffin was in St Martin's Church and the service had begun. Watkins was not only denied his last look at his friend, he was nearly cheated of his opportunity to bid his own more formal farewell.

But if the atmosphere in Watkins' car was wild, the atmosphere in Laugharne was even more so. Dan Jones witnessed the general deterioration with a sinking heart. Louis McNiece dashed into The Pelican to tell Jones that an attempt had been made to break into Dylan's workhut. Sure enough, the strong padlock showed unmistakeable signs of having been forced. Fred Janes, drinking quietly and soberly in Brown's Hotel, had six pints of bitter thrown over him simply because he looked quiet and sober – and thereby offended somebody's prejudices as to what was 'fitting' on such a day. Fights broke out on the village square and an old Dylan flame was making herself available to all comers, presumably in some kind of tribute to her sexually indefatigable lover. A variety of callers visited The Pelican with a variety of suggestions, some simply foolish, some obscene.

Someone suggested that Dylan's coffin be sanctified by pouring a pint of bitter and a jar of pickled onions into it. Another problem arose with the grave itself. There is an unconfirmed report that the first gravedigger delegated to the job – a deaf mute who knew only one thing about Dylan; that his favourite fruit was a banana – dug the original grave in just that shape.

The problems continued as the funeral procession finally ground into motion. The front door proved too narrow for the coffin, emerging from the front room at an awkward angle, to negotiate. The coffin had to be carried in an undignified fashion through the front window of the house. Mrs Thomas, Dylan's mother, also decided that she could not attend. She was not up to the service and contented herself with standing at the door of The Pelican and watching, as her son's coffin was loaded into the hearse. Crowds of friends and drinkers watched from the other side of the road, spilling out of the door of Brown's Hotel. Dan Jones and Caitlin had been assigned the

roles of chief mourners and sat in the front of the car, both aware
in their own respective ways that the ordeal would soon be over.
The hearse lurched into motion and then rolled off down the
short hill and through the winding streets up to St Martin's
Church on the very edge of the village.

As the hearse moved away, the rest of the mourners walked
behind it the short distance to the church. The journey took
about ten minutes and the mourners blocked the narrow Laugharne thoroughfare. The crowd then proceeded through a stone-
roofed gateway and up a steep path to the church itself. It was
soon packed to overflowing with friends, relations, family,
drinkers and hangers-on as well as the cream of contemporary
British writers, broadcasters, poets and artists.

The service itself was simple. The Vicar of Laugharne,
Chancellor S.B. Williams, officiated, assisted by the Rector of
Pendine, J. Pockford Williams and the Reverend D.T. Owen of
nearby Llanddewi-Brefi. Dylan's casket lay in front of the
candle-lit altar.

The congregation first sang a hymn, 'Blessed are the Pure in
Heart'. At the front of the crush Caitlin endured the ordeal as
she had endured the trial ten days earlier in New York. At the
back Vernon Watkins just managed to squeeze into the over-
crowded church. Outside, the Laugharne public houses stayed
open all day. After the hymn the Rev J.P. Williams read a psalm,
before the whole congregation listened to the Laugharne vicar
read St Paul's remarks about death from 'Corinthians'. The
whole service then closed with one more hymn.

Dylan's body was then taken from the church through the
vine-deep churchyard and across the stone bridge that separated
the church itself from the hillside graveyard. One hundred yards
up the hillside the cortege stopped at a simple, plain grave
marked by a white cross inscribed with plain black lettering. It
recorded Dylan's name and his dates of birth and death. It
eschewed any more verbose last message, contenting itself with
the simple legend 'R.I.P.' Once again the day's witnesses claimed
a special significance to apparently innocent incidents. John
Davenport records that as Dylan's body began to approach the
open grave a nearby cock began to crow vigorously. Bill Read
heard it too. It was as if, he said, 'to announce a beginning to
which Dylan was going for as long as forever is.'

Farce continued side by side with genuine sentiment. It is said that Louis MacNeice, passing Dylan's grave for a last look at the poet, intended to drop a bunch of flowers onto the coffin lid. He dropped his sandwiches on it instead. Throughout it all Caitlin merely observed and suffered. She was beyond everything that anybody could inflict upon her. She knew now it was all inevitable. From the day of Dylan's death there had been no peace and there would be no peace. Dylan was public property and she was going to have to get used to that.

The day did not end with Dylan's funeral service, of course. Dylan's British mourners seemed as reluctant to mark the end of their association with the Welsh poet as his American admirers had been ten days before. Vernon Watkins could not return to Swansea but instead walked about Laugharne in the brilliant autumn sunshine, aimless and lost. But he found that he could not escape Dylan. So much of the countryside *was* Dylan, as were the local sights. There was no escape and no resolution in Laugharne. Later Caitlin was to feel the same and was to seek her own escape and her own resolution thousands of miles away from Laugharne, in a new life in Italy.

Vernon Watkins returned to The Pelican to find Mrs Thomas entertaining a host of different visitors with assurance and aplomb, fielding with ease their assertions of sympathy and naive professions concerning her son. As Vernon arrived she was reading to the latest group of well-wishers selections from an assortment of telegrams she had received. One seemed to please her particularly. 'He lived only a short time,' it read, 'but how he lived!' Mrs Thomas kept repeating that last line over and over again. 'But how he lived!'

Vernon Watkins headed across the road to Brown's Hotel. Caitlin had also retreated into Brown's from The Pelican for a drink. Here the atmosphere had degenerated alarmingly. Near-hysteria seemed to have gripped the drinkers; accusations and counter-accusations flew, taunts were exchanged, stories challenged, repeated and challenged again. The chaos and the hysteria that Dylan always trawled in his wake was being well and truly culled forth in the wake of his funeral. The Brown's crowd, in some subconscious way, were gathered together in commemoration of Dylan and they were going to recreate some of the atmosphere that Dylan himself had always engendered.

Caitlin once more observed and did not intervene. It may have been thought that she was past it all, that now she was past caring. But she was not. Dylan's widow leant her head silently on Vernon's shoulder as he joined her. She rested there for a long moment that embraced eternity for Watkins. No words passed between them in a communication that went deeper than words. His wife Gwen Watkins was to describe it later as 'for him, the saddest moment in a bleak day.'

Dylan had gone and Watkins was aimless. Dan Jones took refuge in an activity that betrayed a deep sense of loss. Dylan's mother took comfort in just one thought which she held to her tightly as a talisman that would banish all her mother's pain; Dylan might have burnt briefly but he burned bright. For the rest of the crowds, the drinkers, that feeling of aimlessness, of betrayal almost, continued. Dylan was the kind of figure that gave definition to a group. His life had been so remarkable that many in Laugharne clearly felt that something equally remarkable should commemorate the day of his death. Edith Sitwell, dealing with dozens of phone calls from distracted Dylan friends, concluded loftily that the poet really knew some 'awful people'. She missed the point. Dylan provoked that behaviour with his presence. In his absence the wildest reactions substituted for the roaring times. Dylan was gone and Caitlin's insane grief, measured out in a trail of destruction at St Vincent's Hospital in New York, became the prelude to an even more extensive and even deeper trail of lies, myths, larceny, violence and theft that ambushed the day of Dylan's farewell.

In the middle of everything, of course, was Caitlin, and as the day progressed, she seemed to retreat into bitter and sardonic observation. Perhaps this formed the basis for the later stories circulating around Laugharne, that Caitlin did not care about Dylan's death. But Caitlin had still not truly absorbed the fact of Dylan's end, nor its manner. The sight of her husband so 'basely humiliated' in New York had still not struck home. Caitlin once again erected her defences, and there was more than one Dylan admirer, that sad funeral day, that felt the sharp edge of Caitlin's ironic tongue. Caitlin had never behaved like a normal wife, sometimes to Dylan's own chagrin, and now she was not able to act like a normal widow. She retreated into anger, as she had so often retreated in the past. That anger expressed itself in an air of detachment that was taken more as uncaring disengagement. That was unfair. But in the atmosphere of that wild and abandoned day, anything became very quickly believed, every story was instantly accepted and any rumour or chance observation became immediately elevated to the status of immutable truth.

This single story involving Caitlin's detachment was only the prelude to many more stories that arose from that day and from many subsequent days. Dylan's funeral celebrations limped on, punctuated by fights and tears, grief and mad hilarity. Many newspapers reported the day's events but few caught its more important atmosphere and it was this atmosphere that would persist in the dozens of stories – some true, some half-true – that the day provoked. The funeral of Dylan Thomas confirmed one major effect; Dylan had already become the fulcrum of dozens of private myths. Dylan was fast becoming a symbol and this symbol was to assume a life of its own that was to persist. In a sense, Dylan's death freed the myth-making process. Dylan was now public property and could neither confirm nor deny those stories by the actual fact of his presence. Again this was not malice – Dylan supplied something to his many admirers, in his work and in his perceived life-style, and the myths this engendered were more than deliberate attempts to distort Dylan the man, they were attempts to perpetuate Dylan, to guarantee him some immortality in his continued importance in the lives of those he touched. At the time of his death Dylan became born again, into a myth. In life he had demonstrated that potential for years, and he fulfilled it totally in death. There is a real sense in which Dylan's next life began on that funeral day and it was to become a life more potent than anything in his physical existence. The myth of Dylan Thomas began with his death, and the myth was to prove stronger than any mere facts of the poet's life.

Chapter Eleven
After the Funeral

Across the Atlantic the American connection had been all but forgotten. So much attention was focused on the details of Dylan's burial there was little left for the poet's American friends, staring helplessly from across the sea. This was accentuated by a reaction against all things American on the part of Dylan's British friends. A belief grew up that in some way America had 'killed Dylan' and it proved a remarkably steadfast delusion. One could still detect the same prejudice in the comments of Dylan's Welsh friends thirty years after the event.

Perhaps for Caitlin that reaction was understandable. She had always distrusted the easy temptations that lay in America. She always feared that Dylan's famed self-indulgence would result in Dylan's death. Among Dylan's other friends, their extreme reaction was regrettable and mistaken. Dylan would have killed himself anywhere. America provided the opportunity, but that does not mean Dylan would not have sought the opportunity elsewhere. In the end, *Dylan* killed Dylan.

After Dylan's death, the major characters involved with him soon drifted apart. Dylan was the group's unifying core and without that centre to hold them together, there was little reason for them to remain in contact. They lost touch, looking back on their connections with the Welsh poet with a mixture of affection and sadness. Over the years they grew accustomed to retelling their own Dylan tales to anybody who was interested. There had always been plenty of interested listeners, and if those stories became a little embellished over the years, then that was no more than the British experience too. There was that about Dylan on both sides of the Atlantic that encouraged exaggeration. And with the explosion in Dylan's popularity after his death, many of his original American friends found themselves in considerable demand.

The whole original cast of 'Under Milk Wood' rose above their early inexperience to become established actors, and indeed international names. Sadly, Nancy Wickwire and Dion Allen are now both dead, but Roy Poole has become a household name in American film and television, while Sada Thompson (now Stewart) is an established Broadway actress. She became familiar to a British audience when she played opposite Elizabeth Taylor in a London revival of Lillian Hellman's 'The Little Foxes'. When she flew into New York to record her own part in the last days of Dylan, her arrival was heralded by a full-page feature in the variety pages of the New York press. Sada Stewart and Roy Poole are now big news, but both acknowledge that it is their original amateur performances in 'Under Milk Wood', for which they will be remembered. Allen Collins has also gone on to achieve considerable distinction in his profession and it is to Al Collins' enduring credit that he gave the world the only recording of 'Under Milk Wood' in which Dylan himself participated, 'God' indeed 'touched him on the shoulder' that night.

John Malcolm Brinnin continued with his duties at the Poetry Center, but his heart went out of it with the death of Dylan. Within two years Brinnin had settled down to provide his own account of those last days in his book 'Dylan Thomas in America'. While restricted by contemporary mores and the desire not to rake too deeply into some of Dylan's activities, the book had a special impact, speaking volumes for Brinnin's relationship with and love for his poet friend. It stands today as a highly personal and highly emotive account of a vital relationship. If that relationship came to mean more to one protaganist than the other, then that does not lessen its power. Brinnin achieved a certain notoriety with the publication of his book, and has since come to have his life defined by his contact with Dylan. It has not dominated his subsequent life in personal terms but has coloured his existence for the American and British public. The public perception of Brinnin has, however, modified with the passing of years, and a more tolerant society now looks on his account of Dylan's exploits in a different light. Brinnin had intended that his book should close his own personal account with Dylan but that proved impracticable. Rarely has a day gone by without Dylan featuring in the gentle Brinnin's thoughts. He had intended that a memorial service for Dylan in the Poet's Corner of Westminster Abbey would mark the formal end of his association with Dylan's memory, but he then flew from Boston to New York to record his part in that memory for this account. As he said when he disembarked in New York, 'some books are harder to close than others'.

Brinnin has become a successful academic and poet in his own right since Dylan's death, but he knows that it is his association with Dylan that will guarantee him whatever immortality may come his way. He may also suspect that the future judgement will not be as harsh as the past. If a certain inner weakness can be detected in his conduct of Dylan's affairs, then it is the weakness of over-affection. That genuine and sincere affection shines against the background of deceit that has marked other dealings with the unfortunate Welsh poet, and stands today as a rare commodity in any history of Dylan's dealings. Dylan was a man who attracted parasites wherever he travelled, and it is to his credit that Brinnin never descended to any level that would take advantage of Dylan. His only crime, if it can be called such, was that of loving Dylan too deeply. Brinnin is now a dignified elder statesman of international poetry and deserves better than some of the more unbalanced criticism that has wafted his way over the years. He also deserves more status than that of a mere footnote in Dylan's story. But perhaps all those associated with Dylan in those last days are condemned to play minor roles. Dylan had burnt more brightly than most and in so doing had burnt many others out.

Back in Wales Vernon Watkins never quite got over Dylan's death. His widow, Gwen, has recorded his reaction in her thoughtful book 'Portrait of A Friend'. After his death, so Gwen Watkins has written, Vernon 'seemed as though he were actually trying to recreate Dylan in verse, to bring to life again the man he had known'. Her husband, she concluded, 'wanted to bring back again the time when Dylan was alive; the past was almost more to him than the present.'

Gwen Watkins was in two minds about this effect from beyond the grave. She did not welcome it personally but she knew that it was profound, and that it began to affect everything that Watkins was subsequently to write. She also did not agree with Vernon's extreme reaction to John Brinnin's 'Dylan Thomas in America'. She did not share Watkins' somewhat naive view of their mutual friend, and found little surprise in that account of Dylan's indiscretions. She remained more clear-sighted than her husband having witnessed, cooly and dispassionately, Dylan's many betrayals of Vernon's friendship throughout the years. But all this meant little to Vernon. He would labour all the rest of his life in conscious and unconscious tribute to Dylan, working to see 'a true picture restored'. Ironically, when he died, he too did so also in North America.

Dan Jones was also to suffer trials and tribulations in the years following Dylan's death, but in a more immediately practical manner than Vernon Watkins. In addition to his personal grief, Jones also had to cope with the more official duties associated with his new position as one of the executors of Dylan's literary estate.

His immediate concern was with Caitlin and Dylan's family, and to ensure that they did not fall into penury following the death of the family's sporadic breadwinner. To that end there were memorial funds to be arranged and supervised, royalties and contracts to be dealt with to the advantage of Dylan's dependants and a thousand different enquiries and matters pertaining to the future survival of Dylan's work. There were duties to posterity as well as duties to Dylan's loved ones. It was to be an extremely busy time for the energetic and acerbic Jones and after a year of such frantic engagement, even he tireless though he was, felt that he'd had enough. There were by then others who could assume his role, and the strain on his nerves and his time had become intolerable. But Jones was not to escape completely, as he does not escape today. A week rarely passes without some fresh caller at his house in the Mumbles district of Swansea, wanting to know more about 'the real Dylan Thomas'.

For Caitlin, the immediate future turned out better in a financial sense than she could have dared hope. In November

1953, left with three young children and an unspecified and unquantifiable number of debts, Caitlin could have been forgiven a certain despair. But the trust funds that had been established in both America and Britain soon raised substantial sums and began to cover Dylan's many and varied debts. It was reckoned that there would even be a small surplus, over and above the amount owing, to direct to Caitlin and the children.

But the trustees had not been prepared for the sudden and huge increase in Dylan's popularity. Perhaps this was due to the manner of Dylan's passing which had ensured massive publicity and interest in his fortunes. But whatever the reason, the effect was immediate. Just one year after Dylan's death, the income from sales of Dylan books and Dylan records were booming. Caitlin was soon in receipt of over three thousand pounds a year – a very considerable wealth in 1954 – and that figure continued to rise. After Dylan's death, Dylan's family was thus guaranteed a measure of financial security, and to this day the considerable royalties from sales of Dylan's poetry are routed through to Caitlin, who divides half that income between Dylan's three children. The remaining half-share is kept for herself.

Caitlin did not stay in Laugharne after the death of her husband. That was not entirely unexpected. She had never really fitted into Dylan's dark and gloomy village. Caitlin soon left Wales and departed the shores of Britain to settle with her three children in Italy. She has now found new love and contentment in sunnier climes and seems a million miles removed from the tormented wife of the erratic Welsh poet who lived so resentfully in Laugharne. Of Dylan's children, only Aeronwy has kept physically close to Laugharne. Dylan's two sons are both settled thousands of miles away in Australia, but Aeronwy was a major force in the rescue of Dylan's Boat House from almost certain decay and its opening to the public as a tourist shrine.

Dylan's body itself still lies in St Martin's churchyard, about a mile's walk from the Boat House itself. After her husband's funeral, Caitlin applied to the Home Office for permission to re-inter Dylan's remains in the garden of the Boat House as a more fitting final resting place. The Home Office granted approval, but nothing was done about moving the coffin and it is unlikely now that anything ever will. Dylan will rest where he has rested for over thirty years in his simple and unadorned grave, crowded in among his fellow villagers in Laugharne.

For Liz Reitell, the central figure in Dylan's last days, the intervening years have brought ups and downs. Isolated in America and distanced from the immediate events in Laugharne, Liz could do little but mourn her lover in private. Contemporary protocol would allow her no public expression of grief. Her story remained untold for thirty years, until a more relaxed and liberal attitude prevailed and Liz felt that she could at last talk of Dylan and their relationship. History will now allow her a more generous place in the Dylan story than that of the 'lionising American' that has been her lot previously. Liz's involvement with Dylan did not end with his death, however. Liz was script advisor to *Mademoiselle* magazine and worked on their published version of the 'Under Milk Wood' text. She even wrote a television version of the script, which was broadcast by NBC. But such tasks were only matters outstanding and were not enough to satisfy an energetic and anguished woman seeking more substantial fare to quell her sense of loss.

In 1954 Liz left the Poetry Center, feeling, as John Brinnin had felt, that the meaning had gone out of her duties. She embarked on a new career as a freelance artist. During this period she produced work for the Cambodian exhibit at the World Trade Fair in 1957. She also fulfilled dozens of individual art commissions for various New York studios. It was a busy and hectic time and Liz has been the first to admit that she needed it.

Liz's personal life continued in the same eventful vein. She had already been married twice before she met Dylan: in 1941 to Adolph Green, a lyricist and entertainer from New York City; and then to Clement Stabolepszy, an Army engineer, in 1945 in San Francisco. Both marriages failed.

In 1958 Liz married for the third time, and significantly it was to a man who had been intimately involved in the events that surrounded Dylan's last days five years previously: the New York architect and close Dylan friend Herb Hannum. Perhaps Liz needed someone who had known her and known Dylan through those stress-filled times, and would understand something of her now. Herb Hannum certainly filled that bill.

The couple were married in the historic Myre Church in Wysox by the Reitell family minister. Liz returned to regular employment, once again in the service of a famous literary figure; this time Ilka Chase. Her work for Ms Chase included proofreading and research for the author's weekly newspaper column and for her novel 'Three Men on the Left Hand'.

Liz continued in this supportive editorial role until 1959, when she left to join Frank Taylor, the New York film producer as his assistant. In addition to being a film producer of some note and influence, Mr Taylor was also an editorial director of Dell Books. Liz was here intimately involved with the Marilyn Monroe film 'The Misfits', produced by Taylor and written by Monroe's current husband Arthur Miller. In addition to undertaking duties at Dell Books including proofreading and the negotiation of contracts, Liz was placed in charge of the small production company that actually made 'The Misfits'.

The film introduced Liz to Arthur Miller and she became his literary assistant, at the same time undertaking some freelance commissions, editing a book of literary criticism by Howard Moss, another Dylan friend and compatriot, and also editing the book 'The Magic Lantern of Marcel Proust'.

But in 1962 Liz's marriage to Herb Hannum foundered, and she headed back to the place of Dylan's fantasies; Montana. Here the versatile Miss Reitell turned her attention to wildlife, and she joined the University School of Forestry in Montana as a publication specialist. In this capacity Liz became a leading freelance writer, renowned for her articles on environmental issues. In 1967 she met and married her fourth husband, Eldon H. Smith, a biologist with a notable career behind him in wildlife exology and management. But personal happiness continues to elude Miss Reitell, and in 1985 the marriage between herself and Eldon Smith came to an end.

Liz Reitell is now a public information officer for the Columbia Inter-tribal Fish Commission in Portland, Oregon, and works to protect and conserve salmon resources and the Indian treaty fishing rights of the Nez Pierce Tribe of Idaho, the Umtilla and Warm Springs Tribes of Oregon and the Yakima Nation in the State of Washington. Liz has herself summed up her propensity for a multi-relationship and a multi-career life: 'Ms (Reitell's) personal life has been as meaningful as her professional career,' she wrote to the author. 'She has been married fourteen times, always to men named 'Boots', and has raised several large families though never in the house. She is a familiar figure at almost every meeting where drinks are served and has made many friends around the state through her interest in dentistry, her unusual tap-dancing style and her fondness for repeating cowboy homilies in French.'

It should have been the end of the story. But there is one more strand. In retrospect it may become the most important.

After Dylan's death, three men became his literary executors: his agent David Higham; his Swansea solicitor Stuart Thomas; and and his life-long friend, the indefatigable Dan Jones. Of the three, Jones was the dominant figure. He knew Dylan intimately and knew his work from its earliest manifestations. No-one was better qualified to talk about Dylan's work than Dan Jones and it was correct that he should be given the responsibility of protecting that work in the world. The problem was one of scale. Having eagerly embraced the task, Jones soon found himself totally unprepared for the volume of work or its nature. A thousand enquiries seemed to arrive each day, all demanding urgent attention. A hundred issues concerned with publication or gramophone rights bombarded him every moment of the day. At the same time, he was trying to deal with his own private grief. As Jones himself has said, 'All who were closely concerned with Dylan, his work and his family, seemed to be suffering in varying degrees from a kind of hysteria. I myself was not excluded from this.' Most of these enquiries were of a trivial nature, easily resolved. But one may have been in an altogether different class. It came from Liz Reitell. It is her regret to this day that Jones did not respond in the way she wished to her enquiry and to her concern. She would argue further that it is also a loss to the world of literature that he did not.

In the early part of 1954, the long-awaited publication of 'Under Milk Wood' took place. It was an event eagerly anticipated in the literary world, and since Dylan's death, it is a work that has attained the status of a classic. It is something that every student recognises as epitomising Dylan Thomas, and it has been performed all over the world since that first publication. But Liz Reitell found serious fault with the version regarded as standard.

Dylan took a typewritten draft version of 'Under Milk Wood' with him to the US, but on arrival found that there were numerous errors of typography and omission. These required immediate correction even before the first rehearsal. Douglas Cleverdon, who had delivered the offending script to Dylan in England, was well aware that the script was incomplete. There was, he recalls, a whole section in the manuscript entitled 'More Stuff For Actors to Say'. The errors were understandable, and should not be laid at the door of Cleverdon's hard-pressed secretary Elizabeth Fox. There was little time to complete the difficult transition of Dylan's bunched and barely legible writing into a neat typewritten text.

Dylan thus corrected the manuscript in New York, adding a great many new lines and speeches and deleting others. The play when it was first performed was thus noticeably different from the manuscript he had taken out with him from London. The problem was that when the text of the play was published, many of these revisions, new lines, and new speeches were not included, and many of the original typographical errors remained within the body of the published text.

Liz Reitell read the published version of 'Under Milk Wood' in New York. She read with a mounting sense of horror. This was not the play that Dylan had laboured to bring into being. This play differed markedly from the play she knew to be Dylan's final version; the version he had presented to the world at New York's Poetry Center on the evening of 24 October, 1953. She was, as she was to write to Dan Jones on 1 June 1954, 'deeply shocked'. She also believed that something drastic would have to be done.

As Liz wrote to Dan Jones, 'Comparison of the Dent and New Directions edition (the "official" 'Under Milk Wood') with the enclosed corrected manuscript will show ... numerous errors of omission and commission' Among those errors, Liz continued, were 'typographical errors, word, voice and sound-effect changes, minor deletions etc ... two whole sections included which Dylan had struck out ... and another section included by Dylan which has been omitted.' Liz detailed all the problems in a long and painstaking catalogue.

As far as Liz was concerned all this pointed in just one direction. She had sent a copy of the corrected manuscript to the BBC in November 1953 and believed that this would be the actual publication text. Now she realised it had not been used. It seemed clear that it ought to be. 'In all fairness to Dylan,' she wrote, 'I think that the publishers should cease publication and distribution of the version now in print as soon as possible. Both Ruthven (Todd) and I feel very disturbed that the clean and corrected manuscript sent to the BBC ... was not used, for it was the final and accurate manuscript of the play.' Liz felt with a deep sense of what was correct that Dylan's work 'should not come known to the world in a form that did not represent his final and most considered wishes'. She concluded her letter to Dan Jones with a final appeal. 'I am so extremely glad that you are in charge of this, and I know that in justice to Dylan, you will do everything you can to have the matter put right.'

Perhaps the letter caught Dan Jones at a bad time. He was in the middle of all the onerous duties associated with his new and unfamiliar post. As Jones himself has written, 'I was suddenly plunged into an environment unfamiliar to me, the environment of broadcast drama and the theatre.' Jones has continued, 'It would not be too much to say that at one period I quarrelled with all around me on the slightest cause, not realising that they too were suffering from nerves and were really exercising some restraint in dealing with me.' Jones indeed quarrelled with Liz Reitell. And Liz Reitell certainly felt she exercised considerable 'restraint' in dealing with Dan Jones.

Jones' reply to 'Miss Reitell' came in a letter dated 30 June 1954 and postmarked from Rosehill Terrace in Swansea. Jones immediately decried Liz Reitell's last appeal. He mounted his own defence of the published 'Under Milk Wood' text. 'The version used by Dent was prepared from all well-authenticated material available at the time of publication, and the result was an edition for which I see no reason to apologise,' Dan Jones wrote. He continued, 'The opinion of the majority can be wrong but it is noteworthy that the only disapproving voice up to now has been your own', though he did acknowledge that, 'I accept your statement that there is a small supporting chorus of your friends.' Dr Jones concluded his letter by observing that 'it is not appropriate for a work like "Under Milk Wood" be attended by pedantry on its first appearance.'

Liz Reitell received this letter two weeks later and responded almost immediately, on 20 July. She was aware from the tone of Dan Jones' letter that her battle had perhaps been lost before forces were truly engaged but she wasn't going to give up without one last desperate appeal. Her reply made just one last, hurt attempt to set the record straight.

'Don't you think' she asked Jones, 'that the very last playscript, as revised by Dylan's own hand and as presented by him, might be regarded as more representative of Dylan's own judgement and wishes as to what constituted *his* final version than any other?'

Dan Jones never replied. The published version of 'Under Milk Wood' stood. It is one of the most remarkable features of a remarkable story and one with far-reaching implication. It all means that the 'Under Milk Wood' the world has recognised for the last thirty years, the original published version, could just be the wrong one. The real work has somehow become lost in the general turmoil that surrounded the death of its originator. Whether that is tragedy or farce is difficult to decide but one thing is certain: Dylan would have enjoyed the joke.